WEEDS

friend or foe?

"Whatever hour the sun may say, it's always time for weeding;
The dandelion which blooms today, tomorrow will be seeding."

A.A. Milne, writer and poet (1882–1956)

WEEDS

friend or foe?

SALLY ROTH

Reader's Digest

THE READER'S DIGEST ASSOCIATION. INC.
Pleasantville, New York/Montreal

A READER'S DIGEST BOOK

First published in 2002 in the USA by
THE READER'S DIGEST ASSOCIATION, INC.
Reader's Digest Road, Pleasantville, New York 10570-7000, USA

Conceived and produced by
CARROLL & BROWN PUBLISHERS LIMITED
20 Lonsdale Road, Queen's Park, London, NW6 6RD

Editors Becky Alexander, Charlotte Beech, Kelly Thompson
Designer Roland Codd
Photography David Murray, Jules Selmes

Reader's Digest Project Staff
Project Editors Fred DuBose, Kim Ruderman
Development Editor Delilah Smittle
Senior Designer George McKeon
Senior Design Director Elizabeth Tunnicliffe

Contributing Editors Barbara Ellis, Barbara Pleasant

Reader's Digest Books
Editorial Director Christopher Cavanaugh
Executive Editor, Trade Publishing Dolores York
Director, Trade Publishing Christopher T. Reggio

Library of Congress Cataloging in Publication Data

Roth, Sally
    Weeds, friend or foe?: an illustrated guide to identifying, taming, and using weeds / Sally Roth.
    p. cm.
    ISBN 0-7621-0357-4
    1. Weeds. 2. Weeds—Identification. 3. Weeds—Control. 4. Weeds—Utilization. I. Title.
    SB611.R68 2002
    632.5—dc21   2001048810

rd.com
Visit our online store for more
Readers Digest products and information

Reproduced by Emirates in Dubai
Printed by Imago in Singapore

1 3 5 7 9 10 8 6 4 2

CONTENTS

Meet the weeds

"Know your enemy" is the watchword in war, and it works in the battle against weeds, too. Getting educated is the first step in becoming a garden-variety expert on weeds. By knowing their general habits, you'll be able to take a more informed approach to keeping weeds out of your yard—or inviting them in, if you choose. In this chapter you'll learn what defines a weed, and why these plants can be so infuriating. With an understanding of their different styles of reproduction and the many tricks they use for seed dispersal, you'll be able to adapt your gardening methods to keeping weeds at a minimum. You'll also discover that there's a "good guy" side to some of the most despised weeds.

What is a weed?

"Weediness" is in the eye of the beholder. The word "weed" is an epithet of purely human invention; in the botanical world, it simply doesn't exist. Silky red poppies and true blue cornflowers are treasures to cottage gardeners, but to wheat farmers, they're nothing but infuriating invaders that mar the harvest. Dandelions in the lawn have spawned an entire weed-killing industry, but to wild foragers, they are a welcome spring salad green.

A few weeds are so widely scorned that it's hard to argue with their classification. The clinging burrs of burdock, the ubiquitous clumps of chickweed—surely they have no redeeming value? Ask an herbalist, and you'll get a surprising answer. Burdock root has been used in herbal medicine for thousands of years, and chickweed was once depended upon as a cure for the condition delicately called "irregularity."

The simple answer is that a weed is a plant out of place. When a plant interferes with the tidiness of our flower gardens, the sweep of our lawn, the size of the harvest, or even our personal well-being, it's a weed.

PHYSICAL CHARACTERISTICS

We're accustomed to visually attractive form and eye-catching flowers. A few weeds, including the statuesque, flannel-leaved mullein, are pretty enough to catch anyone's eye, but most weeds are easily overlooked. They may be tall and leggy or skinny and spindly, or crawl close to the ground, and most have tiny flowers that go unnoticed by everyone except bees, butterflies, and other nectar seekers.

Weeds become pests because of their adaptability and their abundance. These rugged plants also reproduce themselves so generously that it's a never-ending struggle to stay one step ahead. Most successful weeds have a number of the following characteristics to thank, though luckily, very few have them all:

• *Longevity* Seeds with great longevity that germinate in a range of conditions, welcoming or otherwise.

IN THE EYE OF THE BEHOLDER Whether a plant is a weed depends on individual gardeners. Blue cornflowers are welcome in the cottage garden but are a nuisance in a wheat field.

foreigners, they also frequently lack the natural insect and disease enemies that would otherwise help to maintain the balance of native plant life.

That rugged constitution, combined with a dearth of biological controls, gives weeds a distinct advantage over our more mild-mannered garden friends. Add their super reproductive powers to the equation, and it's a wonder that we have any lawn or garden left.

- *Germination* Discontinuous germination to prevent all seeds from sprouting at once.
- *Seed* Rapid growth and the production of very large amounts of seed.
- *Dispersing* Efficient means of dispersing its seed; strong, hardy growth, competing with the surrounding plants.
- *Chemicals* Poisoning the soil with chemicals that are released from the roots.
- *Resistance* Greater disease resistance.

LIFE CYCLE OF WEEDS

Understanding how weeds grow is key to controlling them—or cultivating them, which as you'll discover, can make them a striking and gratifying addition to your gardening. Start by thinking of weeds as plants: just like the invited guests in your garden, weeds are specialized by season, and sprout and flower in various cycles.

- *Annual weeds* Germinate, grow, flower, and die in a single year. Chickweed, beggarticks, and ragweed are among the many annuals, all of which usually set massive amounts of seed for following generations.
- *Ephemerals* Complete several life cycles in one year, germinating, flowering, setting seed and dying, closely followed by the next generation. Shepherd's purse, chickweed, groundsel, and bittercress are ephemerals.

ADAPTABILITY

Withhold water from your vegetable garden, and within a week or two your plants would be sending out distress calls, then keeling over and giving up. Most of our ornamentals, too, flourish only in certain settings or conditions. We buy perennials and shrubs for clay, sand, seaside gardens, or city lots, following the advice to select plants to suit our site. Our native wild plants are just as persnickety. Walk through a Massachusetts wood in April and you'll nod to trilliums, hepatica, bloodroot, and other Easterners. Take a walk on vacation in Arizona, and you'll meet none of your familiar plant friends.

Except for weeds. Queen Anne's lace decorates summer roadsides from coast to coast. Dandelions are a sign of spring across the continent. Farmers fight thistles in Texas and Pennsylvania simultaneously.

Exactly where weeds get their ability to adapt is open to endless discussion. One big clue that helps us explain why they seem able to rule the world is that nearly all of them actually came from somewhere else. Most weeds did not evolve in this country, slowly developing over eons the preferences for soil and weather patterns that, for example, make the cactus impossible to cultivate in Minnesota. Being

the waiting game

Most of our treasured garden seeds begin to lose viability after a year or two, but weed seeds have a huge dose of patience. Dandelion seed still germinates thickly after 6 years in the soil. Purslane can hold out for 30 years, and some poppies can even lie dormant for over 100 years! All the more reason to keep your weeds from setting seed. They are also masters of knowing when to wake up, monitoring wavelengths of light and degrees of temperature and moisture. One or two varieties can actually plant themselves. For example, the famed wild oats, when moistened, promptly upend themselves and "drill" their way into the ground!

They produce less seed than annuals but have just as many offspring.

- *Biennial weeds* Germinate and grow only leaves their first year, gathered in a cluster called a rosette. The following year, a flowering stem emerges; the plant blooms, sets seed, and dies. Queen Anne's lace and mullein belong to this category. They may produce prolific seed, or a more moderate amount.

- *Perennial weeds* Just like your garden perennials, a dandelion lives on year after year. So do pokeweed, many clovers, and ground ivy. Their first year after sprouting, perennials produce only leaves; bloom follows in the succeeding years.

Seasons of growth

Weeding is a three-season occupation (or four, if you live in a mild-winter area) because weed seeds sprout at various times of the year. Time your weeding to their emergence, and you'll eliminate thousands of future problems with each swipe of the hoe. It's interesting but not essential to know which weeds tailor their growing cycles to which season. Some experts classify weeds into two broad categories: "warm season," for weeds which sprout in spring and summer and flower summer to fall; and "cool season," for weeds which germinate from fall to early spring, then grow and flower quickly in spring.

Other sources save these categories to apply only to annual weeds, calling them "cool-season annuals" or "warm-season annuals," since biennial and perennial weeds are

WARM-SEASON WEEDS

CRABGRASS *page 53*   DODDER *page 46*   FOXTAIL GRASS *page 106*

PURSLANE *page 90*   RAGWEED *page 26*   SPURGE *page 62*

THISTLE *page 42*   YELLOW WOOD SORREL *page 82*

COOL-SEASON WEEDS

CHICKWEED *page 112*   CLOVER *page 118*   DANDELION *page 116*

DEAD NETTLE *page 73*   GROUND IVY *page 68*   PLANTAIN *page 84*

SPEEDWELL *page 126*   WILD GARLIC *page 22*

voilà — velcro!

Pants studded with burrs are just an annoyance to most, but to George de Mestral, a Swiss hiker, they inspired a million-dollar idea. After a run-in with burdock, he took a closer look at the burrs under a magnifying lens. When he saw the way the tiny hooks on the seed fastened into the fabric of his pants, he went to work. After experimenting with less-than-perfect prototypes, de Mestral presented his patented Velcro to the world in the 1950s.

usually evident at least three seasons of the year. The terminology isn't nearly as important as a basic awareness that there are two main seasons when weeds appear: fall to early spring and spring to summer. As always, the most important antiweed rule is to get them out before they set seed or spread rampant roots.

The flush of green seedlings that arise in fall through late winter are the start of the cool-season weeds, which sprout when the soil is chillier than 60°F. When the air warms up, cool-season annual weeds like henbit, purple dead nettle, and chickweed take off like a rocket, hurrying to bloom and set seed before heat does them in. Dandelions, clover, and other perennials whose bloom peaks in spring may also be considered cool-season weeds, of the perennial persuasion. In fall, remove annual weeds when you see them sprouting and evict established perennial weeds, and you'll have a head start on the following season (see pages 152–159).

In late spring through summer, the warm-season weeds come into their own. Now the soil is filled with seedlings of crabgrass, foxtail grass, and purslane, which germinate when the soil warms to above 60°F. Because garden plants are sprouting or growing at the same time, these weeds are best discouraged by mulch or hand weeding. Pre-emergent herbicides also can discourage the summer flush of warm-season lawn weeds (see pages 160–163).

PROPAGATION HABITS

One of the most distinguished characteristics of weeds is their willingness to "go forth and multiply." Their highly successful techniques are generally variations upon one of two basic methods—seed or spreading roots—although some weeds may use a two-pronged attack. Understanding how weeds propagate themselves can be key to controlling them.

In the weed directory (see pages 18-129), a fact file is provided for each weed, detailing its propagation technique.

Self-sowers

Annual weeds are the chief offenders when it comes to producing more seed than any gardener could want. But perennials believe you can't get enough of a good thing, too. Just one dandelion plant holds the power in its innocent yellow flowers to generate more than 15,000 seeds each year. A single plant of purslane takes it to an even greater extreme, ripening as many as 50,000 seeds in a single summer.

Not all these seeds fall on fertile ground, thank goodness. Birds, mice, and other seed eaters take a big share, and other seeds may land on concrete or other inhospitable sites. Still, with all that potential piling up year after year, it's not surprising to hear that every handful of soil holds thousands of weed seeds, just waiting for their chance to sprout.

Spreading roots

If seeds are a means of propagating in the future, roots are a method for the present. Vegetative spread occurs in one of four ways—through stolons, runners, rhizomes, or roots. *Stolons* and *runners* are both creeping stems that sprout above the ground and then send down roots. Stolons are often in branch form, and may root before they even hit the earth, as in the case of the blackberry bush. *Rhizomes* are underground stems of the type produced by couch grass, nettles, ground elder, and hedge bindweed. They usually grow close to the surface and have small buds along their length that leap into life should the growing point be snapped off. Some thistles and field bindweed send out *horizontal roots* to multiply, which can produce new buds at any position along their length. Finally, plants with deep *taproots*, such as dandelion and dock, despite relying principally on seed dispersal, will also regenerate themselves if their roots are cut up.

Seedling weeds may look like an advancing army, but they are easy to dispense with. You can hoe them off or bury them alive in just minutes. Weeds that increase their territory by spreading roots, however, include some of our most insidious garden pests. In most cases, only the painstaking removal of each creeping underground stem or root does the trick. Even chemical controls find Bermudagrass and other spreaders a tough battle (see pages 160-163). The best approach is to monitor your yard and garden. Should a notorious spreader show up or leap to another part of the yard, remove it completely (see pages 158-159) as soon as you see it, and dispose of all pieces in the trash. After weeding out a spreader, watch closely for any signs of regrowth and have another go at it. Often the only solution is to remove the

TAKING ROOT Complex and vigorous root systems mean that weeds can propagate even when hoed or deprived of light. From left to right: blackberry (stolon roots), wild strawberry (runner roots), dandelion (taproots), and nettle (rhizome).

desirable plants from a bed and dig deep to evict all traces of the invader before replacing those plants you want.

SEED DISPERSAL

Most seed-producing weeds have evolved masterful methods of dispersing their produce, many of which are opportunistic in character. All kinds of helpers spread the growth of weeds—most of them unintentionally, and others by design. Herbalists, gardeners, and even the U.S. Department of Agriculture have all been responsible for weedy plagues, although the plants were dispersed with the best of intentions. But in most cases, weeds depend on innocent helpers to get their seeds to a bit of welcoming ground.

Wind

Seeds with fuzz, silky hairs, or wings on the seed coat are all designed to go with the wind. Many weeds go one step further and actively shoot their seeds out once they are ripe. For example, oxalis, hairy bittercress, and ground elder all give their seeds a little carefully-timed boost. There's no way to ward off wind-blown seeds, but you can get rid of the plants before they release their seed (see pages 152-163).

Water

Aquatic weeds (see page 171) depend on water to carry along the next generation, snug in their waterborne seeds or through bits of plants ready to root. But land weeds, too, can spread by waterways. Purple loosestrife is the cautionary tale

quick fix for stick-tights

Two low-tech tools—a fine-toothed comb and an old credit card—hasten the removal of burrs and other weed "stickers" from clothes. Hold the fabric as taut as possible. Use the comb to lift stick-tights from fuzzy sweaters, corduroy pants, and other fabrics with a thick nap. Scrape cotton jersey T-shirts, khakis, linen skirts, and other low-nap fabrics with a stiff credit card.

here; its seeds ripened in gardens and then were carried by wind and (rivulets of) rain to streams and lakes. Since a single purple loosestrife plant produces millions of seeds, it's no surprise that many waterways are splashed with purple. Water also transports the largest seed in the world, the coconut, since it can float on water to sow coconut palms on distant shores.

Birds

Our feathered friends are responsible for many of the weeds in our yards. Weeds offer nourishing seeds and berries, and at least some of those pass through the avian digestive system unscathed. Deposited with a dab of "fertilizer," the seeds of mulberry trees, poison ivy, ragweed, pokeweed, and many others suddenly spring up in our lawns or gardens, even though the parent plants may be far away.

responsible water gardening

Even an isolated small garden pool can hold the beginnings of a weed problem in the wild. In cities as well as in the country, raccoons, birds, and other wildlife are likely to visit your pool for a sip or a splash. When they leave, they may carry seeds or bits of greenery between their toes or in their fur or feathers. Should the hitchhikers drop off at another watery home, they may take root and spread whatever plants you're growing. Many gardeners are less knowledgeable about water plants than other garden residents, and unwittingly bring home plants that may be pests in other areas. The hardiness of aquatic plants is also less well known. Water hyacinth, for example, a weed that infests many southern waterways, was once thought incapable of surviving northern winters, but the plants have been found thriving along a river in zone 6 after a winter outdoors. If you're unsure of the habits of water garden plants, stick to natives or ask your USDA extension agent about the potential risk.

THE POWER OF FLIGHT Birds snack on the berries and seeds of weeds that are then transported in the bird's digestive system, to be deposited wherever the bird may land.

surreptitious. The seeds of Queen Anne's lace, for instance, can cling to a careless sleeve by the dozens. Weed seeds can also come home in the tread of your boots or glued to the grill of your car. Just use a little common sense when you clean up after an outdoor adventure, and avoid dropping weed seeds where they could cause you labor later.

Woodpeckers, jays, nuthatches, and other birds cache seeds for eating later. Not all of these seeds go down the hatch, and those that make their way to soil can crop up as weeds. If you keep a bird feeder, you already know about the delights of unexpected sunflowers, which spring up wherever a bird drops a seed.

Animals
Diet and fur or feathers are the two ways animals spread weed seeds. Like birds, your backyard mice, raccoons, deer, and other animals may gift you with deposits that contain the start of weeds. Squirrels plant "weed" gardens in the fall, burying acorns and nuts that pop up into seedling trees that are usually unwelcome in our gardens. Far more frequently, weed seeds travel in the fur of wild animals, farm animals, and our beloved pets.

"Hitchhiking" is one of the most ingenious devices for seed dispersal, and many weeds make the most of it. Comb the burrs from your dog's ears, and those that fall to the ground during the grooming operation can easily start a plantation of burdock or beggarticks. Guard against an invasion of weeds by grooming pets indoors, where you can sweep up and dispose of the weed seeds you comb out.

People
The hooks and barbs that give weed seeds a grip in animal fur or feathers can also latch on to our clothes on an outdoor jaunt. Burdock is easy to steer around because its wayfaring seeds are big and noticeable, but other weeds are much more

WEEDS THAT SPREAD BY WIND

DANDELION *page 116*   FLEABANE *page 61*   KNAPWEED *page 39*

THISTLE *page 42*   WILD LETTUCE *page 72*

WEEDS THAT SPREAD BY WATER

KNOTWEED *page 88*   YELLOW NUTSEDGE *page 50*

DUCKWEED *page 74*   PONDWEED *page 92*

WEEDS THAT SPREAD BY BIRDS

BEGGARTICK *page 33*   DOCK *page 102*

JAPANESE HONEYSUCKLE *page 74*   MULTIFLORA ROSE *page 99*

PIGWEED *page 24*   POISON IVY *page 98*   POKEWEED *page 83*

RAGWEED *page 26*   SMARTWEED *page 89*   THISTLE *page 42*

WEEDS THAT SPREAD BY "HITCHHIKING"

BEGGARTICK *page 32*   BURDOCK *page 28*

COCKLEBUR *page 128*   DOCK *page 102*   PIGWEED *page 24*

QUEEN ANNE'S LACE *page 52*

Where do weeds come from?

Nearly all our most problematic plants hail from foreign shores. Only a handful of common invaders call North America home. Of the rest, about one-third originated in Central and South America; another third in Europe; and the remainder mainly in Asia and Africa. Some are so widespread worldwide that it's almost impossible to discern their origins.

Tracing the history of weeds gives us a brief lesson in the basic stages of American settlement and immigration. Most of the early invaders came from Europe, imported by colonists on purpose or by accident. Teasel was imported for combing the tangles out of sheep fleece, for example, but thistles were probably an accidental import, hidden perhaps in contaminated grain. With the notorious era of slavery came a few African weeds, and more recently, an influx of Japanese weeds put down roots in their new homeland. As our globe has grown smaller with easier world travel, weeds moved right along—and continue to do so.

Potential problem causers

It's harder than you might think to gauge whether a plant will be a territorial thug. The U.S. Department of Agriculture (USDA) certainly didn't anticipate any problems when it set loose Japanese honeysuckle upon North America. Similarly, the American nursery trade had no reason to suspect that purple loosestrife would within a few decades paint almost a quarter of the country with purple in summer. Scientists are constantly watching for signs of potential weed problems. Warm-winter areas get particularly close scrutiny because

the best-laid plans

Some of our biggest troubles have arrived courtesy of the U.S. Department of Agriculture, which distributed plants like those below to farmers and conservation organizations with the best of motives: to prevent erosion, supply fast-growing forage, or feed and shelter wildlife. Although they also deserve credit for their many excellent plant introductions, the department can also be blamed for unleashing the following weeds on an unsuspecting public:

Autumn olive, Japanese honeysuckle, Johnsongrass, kudzu, multiflora rose, reed canary grass, Tartarian honeysuckle the climate is so favorable that things can quickly get out of hand. California's list of "noxious weeds"—those designated as official pests by state or federal agencies—runs much longer than the lists for many regions with cold winters. Florida and Hawaii are also under close watch, because of immense problems with Australian and other lush tropical and semi-tropical plants that can quickly overwhelm native flora. Keep abreast of your local situation by contacting local agencies or an official of the USDA.

GARDEN STRAYS

Gardeners have been to blame for some weed scourges, as overenthusiastic plants leaped the garden gate to colonize wild areas. In the Pacific Northwest, honesty, or money plant (*Lunaria*), now infiltrates native woodlands; in the Northeast, dame's rocket splashes woods' edges; in California, fountain grass and pampas grass rise along the roadsides. Usually, flowering plants don't stray too far from the garden, however.

The weedy habits of some garden plants may not contaminate wild areas, but they can cause definite added work in your own yard. If you seek to minimize weeding, avoid garden plants that:

weeds native to...

NORTH AMERICA	Cocklebur, common milkweed, poison ivy, ragweed, wild onion, witchgrass
CENTRAL AND SOUTH AMERICA	Hydrilla, pigweed, water hyacinth
EUROPE	Curly dock, foxtail grass, lamb's quarters plantain, purslane, quackgrass, thistles, wild garlic
ASIA OR AFRICA	Johnsongrass, kudzu, Queen Anne's lace, velvetleaf

- *Self-sow abundantly* (annual poppies, bachelor's buttons, California poppies, cosmos, cleome, dill, feverfew, larkspur, tansy);
- *Spread fast by creeping roots* (mints, pink evening primrose, sundrops, tansy, and most perennial sunflowers, especially Jerusalem artichoke).

NATIVE WEEDS

Plants that evolved to flourish in a particular area usually live in balance with the rest of the environment, so that they rarely reach weed status in their homeland. A few all-American native plants are notorious troublemakers, however. Most of us could do quite well without poison ivy, poison oak, and pokeweed, but keep in mind that these American weeds serve an important purpose: their berries are an important food source for songbirds and other wildlife.

Some gardeners consider native wildflowers as weeds, although the same plants might be prized in gardens a thousand miles away. Brilliant orange California poppies are much more appreciated in say, New England, than they are in the West where they grow "like weeds."

EVER-SPREADING MINT Popular with many gardeners for its culinary uses, mint can spread out of control if left unmanaged. Grow mint in a pot or in plastic container placed in the soil to contain its creeping root system.

Pros and cons of weeds

Weeds at their worst can disrupt natural ecosystems, reduce the garden harvest, and mess up the beauty of a well-tended lawn. But even the darkest plague of dandelions has its silver lining. Weeds can also improve soil fertility and its crumbly texture or tilth, attract butterflies and birds, ease our health problems, and decorate our living rooms. Some weeds are also mighty tasty!

HOME USES FOR WEEDS

Putting your weeds to practical use in the home will make you feel resourceful. It also will connect you to a long line of herbalists and country cooks, who made do with the weeds that grew nearby.

- *Edible weeds* If you can't beat them, you may as well eat them. The very same sorrel that disrupts your flower bed with its rosette of long, curling leaves has been valued for years by the French as well as international gardeners, who know that its acid-rich leaves add a piquant touch to cream soups and sauces. Varieties of dandelion developed for milder flavor and larger leaves fill rows in the plots of specialty growers, for sale to restaurants and gourmet greengrocers. For a more exotic flavor, how about some homemade candy based on kudzu? For more on edible weeds, see pages 145-148.
- *Herbal remedies* Plants we now call weeds were favored for centuries for their healthful effects. Modern research has crossed several weeds off the remedies list, due to the dangers of possible toxins, but many others are still ready to serve as a homegrown medicine chest. For more information, see pages 140-144.
- *Home decor* Hang pressed and framed weeds on the wall, and visitors will admire your botanical specimens. Only you need to know they're the trophies of your yard-and-garden weeding expeditions. For details and further decorative ideas, see page 149.

WEEDS IN THE GARDEN

Less-than-perfect weeders, take heart. A few weeds in your garden are not going to negatively affect your prized plants. Conventional gardening advice teaches us that weeds

USES FOR YARROW The leaves of yarrow (*Achillea millefolium*) are said to help tackle oily skin and hair, and may also heal skin abrasions. The flowers can also be used: They are pretty in dried arrangements and potpourri.

compete with garden plants, and that's true—weeds do use nutrients and moisture from the soil. But desirable plants also compete with each other.

Our garden plants have a much easier life than those in the wild, which is why weeds usually don't affect their vigor. When rains are scarce, we turn on the drip hoses or sprinkler. An occasional serving of fertilizer provides a generous diet.

In an established garden, your standard for weeds doesn't have to be zero tolerance. The exception to this comforting advice occurs with weeds that spread by aggressive roots. Just as mint can overwhelm an herb garden, so can root-spreading weeds infiltrate in and among our prized plants, squeezing out even those that seem well settled in.

When weeds invade the garden, the competition for sunlight is a more important factor for other plants than weeds' use of nutrients and water. Seedling garden plants need your help against weeds of any kind. Annual weeds grow so quickly that they can overshadow the bed even before your treasured seeds break through the soil.

WEEDS IN THE WILD

Evicting alien plants from wild lands is a hot issue in some environmentalist circles, because such weeds disrupt the harmony of natural ecosystems. Rarely, however, do weeds make deep inroads upon undisturbed wild lands (purple loosestrife and Japanese honeysuckle are two notorious exceptions). Weeds usually grow best where we humans have already disrupted the natural order of things: along roads, in pastures and rangeland, and in vacant lots. Our gardens and grassy yards are highly unnatural, too, which is why they're so inviting to weeds.

Even the worst weedy plagues may eventually achieve a better balance. Hand weeding and herbicides keep many in check, but more promising are biologic controls that were formerly lacking, which is one reason the plants spread unchecked. Small beetles that munch hungrily on purple loosestrife leaves were released in 1995 and are busily doing their job. A tiny wasp that infests the seeds of multiflora roses was discovered a few years ago in wild multiflora roses, and is likewise the object of hopeful scrutiny.

WILDLIFE AND WEEDS

Weeds may not always be as showy as cultivated flowers, but as far as songbirds, rabbits, and other wildlife are concerned, they provide many benefits:

- *Insects* They harbor zillions of insects, some of the most important links in the food chain, meaning that the number of beneficial predator insects is also higher— more spiders, praying mantises, and assassin bugs.
- *Parasites* Weeds also attract parasitic braconid wasps and other beneficial insects as their many small flowers are well suited to the nectaring habits of these tiny insects.
- *Food* Weeds' leaves, flowers, seeds, and berries are vital items on the everyday menu of nearly all wild creatures, their very abundance being more tempting than a single isolated plant or three of ornamentals.
- *Hosts* Some weeds are sought by egg-laying butterflies, serving as host plants for the caterpillars to come.
- *Nectar* Their flowers supply nectar to thousands of insect species, including butterflies, and to hummingbirds. Their many small blossoms, held in clusters, are in the arrangement preferred by many insects.
- *Shelter* Their leaves offer a variety of shelter and homes.
- *Materials* Weeds supply soft fibers, bark, and other building materials to construct nests.
- *Safety* Colonies of weeds provide a corridor for wildlife to move safely from one place to another.

ATTRACTING WILDLIFE Joe Pye weed (*Eupatorium purpureum*) grows very well in the wild, and the nectar contained within its tiny florets is delicious to butterflies.

weeding triage

Keep beds of seedlings and young vegetables, flowers, and herbs as free of weeds as possible.

Monitor frequently for invasions of weeds that spread by roots, and remove immediately.

Pay particular attention to highly visible plantings: the flowers around the mailbox, the front lawn, foundation plantings.

Weed around expensive, rare or favorite plants.

Keep nonaggressive garden plants well weeded. Your Siberian irises may keep blooming no matter what weed tries to force its way in, but the blue Himalayan poppy you're coddling may not recover from a weed attack.

Weed directory

The color photos and detailed descriptions of the more than 70 weeds in this illustrated directory will not only give you the confidence to recognize weeds that pop up in your yard but also to make informed decisions as to the fate of your bold intruders. You'll learn where each weed is most likely to show up, its identifying characteristics at various stages of growth, and its general habits and alternative names. The information provided will equip you with everything you need to defend your yard from unwanted, invading weeds, and will show you how to get rid of these unwelcome guests if they do manage to raise their ugly heads. You will also discover how to make the most of the more desirable weeds in your yard—whether as a garden feature, as part of a meal, or as alternative medicine! Good-bye weedy foes, hello friends!

Friend?

The very profuseness of yarrow makes it perfect for an informal or cottage-type garden, where it can sow itself with abandon. You can correct its lax posture with stakes, but allow a few plants to be leaners as they will weave among more upright plants to give the garden a more relaxed attitude.

Short varieties are lovely with roses, especially if you front them with lavender to disguise the usually bare lower stems of the yarrow. Herbally speaking, yarrow was honored with its species name *Achillea,* because it reputedly was used by Achilles to stop bleeding and heal the dreadful wounds of soldiers in the battle of Troy.

- **HARVEST** Snip fresh foliage anytime, for drying on screens or in loose bunches. Cut flowers soon after the blossoms open.

- **MEDICINAL USE** Make a wash for minor cuts and abrasions by boiling two tablespoons of dried foliage in a cup of water, or brew a bitter tea for occasional use in treating stomach difficulties.

- **DECORATIVE USE** Use flowers in bouquets or dried arrangements. Press them for notecards, or use sprigs of dried blossoms for gift decorations.

Foe?

Knowing one's place, and keeping to it, is an important asset for a garden plant. Although a beauty in the perennial border with its feathery foliage and abundant flowers, yarrow can quickly get out of hand. It spreads fast by both expanding roots and prolific seeds. Luckily, it is easy to control in the garden.

Established plants develop a thick mass of densely interwoven roots and send out exploratory creeping roots that aggressively crowd out neighbors. The small seeds are pale gray or tan wafers, light enough to be borne on the wind, but also frequently dropped at the foot of the parent plant.

- **MULCH** Learn to recognize the seedlings by their signature feathery foliage, then bury in mulch.

- **HOE** Use a sharp hoe to slice the tops off.

- **SPADE** Keep clumps in bounds by slicing off extra growth with a sharpened spade.

Achillea millefolium

Yarrow

"Millefolium" means "thousand leaves," and indeed, yarrow has millions of lacy leaflets arranged on its branching stems. The foliage and flowers add delicacy to a garden, softening nearby plants. Many gardeners let yarrow plants stand all winter because of the contribution of their dark brown seedheads, especially beautiful when crowned with snow.

Yarrow can be recognized easily by its distinctive bitter, medicinal, and chrysanthemum-like smell and by its appearance. It is a relaxed plant that often sprawls when it reaches full height. Each stem is topped by a flat to slightly domed, branching cluster of many tiny flowers, which may be white, rose red, pale pink, or tawny orange to russet shades. Colored flowers are rich in hue when they open but soon pale with age, presenting a gentle multihued effect.

 **fact file**

LIFE CYCLE	perennial
SITE, SOIL & SEASON	sun to part shade; highly adaptable; well-drained; blooms from early summer through fall
DISPERSAL	seed and spreading underground roots
ULTIMATE HEIGHT	about 2 feet
OTHER NAMES	achillea, milfoil, sanguinary, woundwort

As a groundcover, goutweed wins the race, blanketing a 3-foot-diameter area in just one season of growth. Creeping roots spread fastest in cooler climates in a shaded site; in hot areas and full sun, goutweed is less aggressive but still hard to keep under control.

■ **GARDEN USE** If you have a patch that is surrounded on all sides by wide areas of solid, deep paving or buildings—such as the strip between garage and driveway—you may want to use goutweed as a fast, dense groundcover. Buy young plants and space them 18 inches apart. Mulch with long-lasting bark chips (see page 157).

Aegopodium podagraria

Goutweed

Goutweed spreads to form dense colonies. The variegated variety, with its leaves edged in and splashed with creamy white, is much more common than the solid-green species.

"Leaves of three, let it be" is the watchword for poison ivy, but also can apply to goutweed. In early spring, each stem develops a pair of three-leaved stems, ending with another group of three at the tip. This similarity to the leaf of the ash tree gives the plant its common name of "ground ash."

Leaves hug the ground at first; then the toothed, pointed leaflets enlarge as the smooth stem elongates throughout the season. Lacy clusters of tiny, creamy-white blossoms appear in summer; smaller clusters form at leaf axils along the stem. Plants tend to go dormant in cold winters.

Unfortunately, this plant doesn't know the meaning of the word "stop." One of those nursery-bought or passed-along plants that many gardeners wish they'd never invited into the garden, goutweed spreads like wildfire and is extremely difficult to eradicate. It leaps out of gardens to colonize other areas of the yard, as well as nearby woods and wild sites. If you don't want your garden swallowed in a sea of goutweed, learn to recognize the plant so you don't make the mistake of bringing it home by intention or accident.

Although its name suggests an honored history as a treatment for gout (a disease marked by the buildup of uric acid and inflamed joints), the name is actually a corruption of "goatweed," a nickname given to this favored fodder.

■ **HAND PULL** Get comfortable and settle in for a long session. Remove as many roots as possible, then fork the soil and rake to expose any overlooked bits. If new plants spring up in a few weeks from overlooked roots, lift them with a trowel. Dispose of all parts in the trash. Do not compost.

■ **SPOT HERBICIDE** Apply to foliage in spring to summer, following directions on container. Repeated applications may be needed. (See advice on using herbicides, pages 160-163.)

 fact file

LIFE CYCLE	perennial
SITE, SOIL & SEASON	near gardens or where garden debris has been dumped; sun to shade; spreads fastest in part to full shade, in fertile soil, but is highly adaptable; blooms in late spring to summer
DISPERSAL	creeping roots
ULTIMATE HEIGHT	about 6 inches
OTHER NAMES	bishop's weed, ground elder, herb Gerard, ground ash

Allium spp.

Wild garlic, wild onion

Distinguished by their signature scents, wild garlics and onions were once prized for eating and home medicines but today are mostly scorned as lawn weeds. Most common are field garlic (*Allium vineale*), found in clumps of tall, skinny, dark green leaves, and wild garlic (*A. canadense*), similar with flat instead of round leaves. Because their fast and early growth outpaces lawn grass, they can make lawns look untidy.

The weedy members of this group may be visible in your lawn year-round. Narrow leaves arise from a white-bottomed stem that springs from a bulb underground, and may grow in a thick clump or singly. Although members of the lily family, all of the wild onions and garlic share their familiar odors, which are immediately noticeable when a leaf is pinched. Several species look very much alike, but all these plants are edible, and control measures are the same.

- Long, skinny, erect leaves may be round and hollow, or flat and grassy. Some species, including wild leek, have broad leaves, but are usually not pesty in gardens.
- Leaves are usually much darker green than grass.
- Pink, white, or lavender flowers are borne in a cluster atop the single stem, depending on the species.
- Flowers often smell sweet.
- Wild garlics form tiny bulblets that drop to the ground to start new plants.
- Like a scallion, the stem is pale to white at the base.

 fact file

LIFE CYCLE	perennial; grows from bulbs
SITE, SOIL & SEASON	most species grow in sunny lawns, a few in shade; will sprout in poor to fertile, well-drained soil; most species bloom in late spring to summer
DISPERSAL	bulbs
ULTIMATE HEIGHT	6 to 12 inches, depending on species
OTHER NAMES	field garlic, crow garlic, prairie wild onion, wild leek, meadow leek, ramp, colicroot, stargrass, meadow shallot

Friend?

Garlic flavor is intense in the wild species, which were commonly gathered by rustic country folk a few centuries ago. "Civilized" opinions, however, were much different. In the 1699 volume, *Acetaria: A Discourse on Sallets,* John Evelyn noted that "we absolutely forbid it entrance into our salleting, by reason of its rankness... and that the eating of it was part of the punishment for such as had committed the horrid'st crimes." On a more practical note, he warned "to be sure, 'tis not for ladies palates, nor those who court them." If you enjoy the flavor of cultivated garlic, try the weeds.

Like other onions, these weeds are exciting to modern medicine for their potential to lower blood pressure, reduce cholesterol, fight infection, and ward off the common cold.

■ **HARVEST** Snip leaves anytime, slicing off as much as desired. Dig bulbs from fall through early spring, when they are plumpest.

■ **CULINARY USE** A little goes a very long way, so begin with just a few small bulbs in your pastas and casseroles. The skinny tops, washed and sliced finely with scissors, add bold flavor to scrambled eggs, soups, and tomato sauces. Flowers and bulblets that form after the flowers also are edible; separate for green salads, potato salad, or soups.

■ **MEDICINAL USE** The scent of garlic comes from allacin, an antibiotic-like substance that inhibits the growth of bacteria and fungi. You can try its effectiveness for sore throat with a simple gargle, made by pouring a cup of boiling water over two or three chopped bulbs. Steep for several hours, then strain and gargle.

Foe?

If the uniform appearance of your lawn is important to you, wild garlic and onions will be near the top of the enemies list. They spring into growth in late winter, before many turf grasses start growing, and quickly dot the lawn with shaggy clumps of eye-catching dark green leaf blades. Mowing isn't a good solution, because the weeds will quickly regrow to tower over the grass.

■ **TRANSPLANTING (OR POACHER'S) SPADE** A narrow but deep-bladed transplanting or rootball spade is the best weapon against wild garlic or onions. Its blade is deep enough to reach under the bulbs, and its handle is strong enough to lever out the clump. It removes a smaller amount of soil than a full-sized shovel, so it will cause less damage to the lawn. Dig close to the clump, with the blade at a very slight angle, then lift. With your hands, pick out every bulb from the soil, even the tiny ones. Dispose of them in the trash, not on the compost pile. Replace the cleaned soil in the hole, then tamp, smooth, and scatter grass seed to patch the lawn.

■ **SHOVEL** A pointed shovel or spade is as effective as a transplanting spade, but removes a bigger bite of your lawn. Use as described above.

■ **TROWEL** For a few small clumps of wild garlic or onions in an established lawn, you can use a sturdy trowel. Choose one with blade and shaft forged from one piece of strong metal, because you'll be using it like a crowbar to lever out the clump of bulbs.

Amaranthus retroflexus

Pigweed

A weedy relative of the ornamental cockscomb and celosias, grown for their colorful plumy flowers, pigweed is a coarse plant that springs up in newly sown gardens and established plantings. In fact, it grows anywhere it can find a hospitable bit of open space. It is most noticeable in fall, when the foliage and stem take on a reddish tinge. Despite the plant's large size, it is easy to hand pull at any stage. The seeds are extraordinarily long-lived, remaining viable for at least 40 years. Pigweed was once revered as a grain crop, dating back to the Aztecs, because of its abundant, protein-packed seeds.

Gardeners often overlook young pigweed plants when weeding the garden, because they lack the typical lax posture or sprawling form that say "weed." Their medium-sized, pointed leaves are borne alternately on the stout, usually branching stem. In late summer, dense, spiky clusters of tightly packed tiny green flowers hide an estimated 100,000 seeds per plant! No wonder pigweed is one of the most common pesky plants in gardens and farm fields.

- Slightly wavy-edged leaves are attached alternately to the stem, each leaf slightly drooping from a long leaf stalk.
- Leaves enlarge as the plant grows, and may eventually reach 6 inches in length.
- Roots have a distinctive red color and grow downward.
- Usually grows singly, but may occur in thicker stands.
- Most easily identifiable in late summer to fall, when the flower spikes and seedheads are apparent.
- Stems and seedheads persist through winter, but leaves drop off after cold weather.

 fact file

LIFE CYCLE	annual
SITE, SOIL & SEASON	sunny, open places, including vegetable and flower gardens, cracks in sidewalks, and gravel driveways; thrives in almost any well-drained soil; blooms in late summer through fall
DISPERSAL	seeds
ULTIMATE HEIGHT	can reach 9 feet, but usually 3 to 4 feet tall
OTHER NAMES	redroot pigweed, green amaranth, careless weed, Chinaman's greens, lighthouses

The Zuni people of the American Southwest believed that the rain gods brought the seeds of amaranth, as pigweed is also known, from the underworld and scattered them over the earth. The Zuni ground the seeds with black corn meal, added water, and shaped the mixture into patties for steaming and eating. Amaranth meal was so culturally vital to the Aztecs that the conquering Cortez made cultivation of the grain punishable by death. Today an improved version of pigweed is used in commercial cereals and other grain products.

Pigweed greens are high in vitamins and are mild-tasting when eaten raw or cooked like spinach. If you're a birdwatcher, you'll enjoy the many finches, sparrows, siskins, and other seed-eaters that flock to the standing plants in fall and winter.

- **HARVEST** Gather young leaves and more mature foliage anytime it's available. The tiny seeds are impractical to gather in large quantities, but you can rub ripe seedheads into a paper bag in fall or winter to collect seeds for use. To remove the chaff, pour out the seeds onto a tray and blow with a hairdryer turned to low power.

- **CULINARY USE** Young leaves are most tender, and best for fresh salads. Steam or boil older leaves as you would spinach. Leaves are high in vitamin C, beta carotene, calcium, and iron. Sprinkle ripe black seeds on muffins or breads before baking for a nutty crunch; they are rich in lysine, an amino acid that combines with others to form complete proteins, as well as vitamins E and B complex.

- **WILDLIFE** Let pigweed grow in meadow gardens, casual flower gardens, or under the bird feeder. The plants will attract lots of entertaining songbirds, which perch on the plants to eat the seeds. Game birds and small animals will glean seeds that drop to the ground.

Pigweed got its nickname "careless weed" from the belief that only a careless farmer or gardener allowed the plants to grow. Pigweed's presence may be an insult to your housekeeping abilities, but in the home garden it is simple to control, and even a number of overlooked plants won't be detrimental to your garden. Despite the size of the mature plant, the roots easily give up their grip. Pulling pigweed is one of the more gratifying weeding chores, because your pile of results looks impressive compared to the effort you expended. Compost all plants that haven't yet gone to seed.

If pigweed is left to grow wild, it can crowd out other plants, and deprive them of light and nutrients in the process. It can also irritate the skin if you touch the tiny hairs on the stems or touch the prickly seedheads.

- **HAND PULL** Pigweed can be itchy to work around, so wear long sleeves to pull the plants. Wait until the soil is moist, after a rain, for easier removal.

- **HOE** Chop and lift the roots of the plant. Shake off soil and compost plants that haven't yet set seed.

- **HAND HOE** Use a sharp-bladed hand hoe in tight quarters to lift out young pigweed plants. Chop sharply downward near the roots and flip the plant out of the soil.

- **SPOT HERBICIDE** To avoid dislodging bricks or other pavers, spray young pigweed plants that pop up in paving cracks with the appropriate herbicide, following label directions.

Ambrosia artemisiifolia, A. trifida
Common and giant ragweeds

These two plants look nothing alike except for their flowers, which are upright candelabras of greenish spikes, coated with yellowish pollen at flowering time. Both species branch from a single stem, which may be smooth, downy, or hairy. At peak season, the windborne, allergy-causing pollen can form a visible haze over infested areas.

It's worth learning to spot the ragweeds from seedling stage so that you can yank them out before the allergy season. Like other leafy weeds that bloom late in the year, these plants are easy to overlook among the lush greenery of the summer garden. Common ragweed has thin, lacy leaves, up to 4 inches long, while giant ragweed lives up to its name, with huge, stout 3- or 5-lobed leaves (lobeless near the top of the plant) that can stretch to over a foot across. Giant ragweed is huge from the time it sprouts; the stem is thick and stout and perfectly vertical. Common ragweed is shorter, has a bushier look, and may sprawl.

Male, or staminate, flowers of both species are held on noticeable clustered spikes, sometimes drooping in common ragweed, at the tips of the branches, and also in leaf axils in giant ragweed. Female, or pistillate, flowers are hidden in leaf axils of upper leaves. In winter, the plants remain standing, with some dead leaves clinging to the stems. Ragweeds may appear singly in the garden but often grow in thick stands where seeds have fallen from the previous year's plants.

Friend?

If hayfever is not a problem for you, ragweed is worth growing in a wild garden to attract wildlife.

- **WILDLIFE** Many birds are fond of ragweed seeds, although only those with strong beaks can crack the hard seeds of the giant species. Birds and small animals often seek shelter from bad weather or predators among the plants of giant ragweed.

Foe?

Ragweed pollen is so irritating to the nasal passages that it can even cause sneezing fits if carried indoors by a pet or clothes dried outside. Though a generous self-sower, it is fairly easy to keep under control.

- **HAND PULL** Identify these plants when young, and weed them out as soon as you spot them.

- **MULCH** Use a 2- to 3-inch layer of grass clippings or other mulch to smother seedlings.

- **HOE** Chop with a hoe to uproot common ragweed at any stage of growth and to remove medium-sized giant ragweed plants (larger plants are too big).

- **STRING TRIMMER** Cut down thick patches or scattered plants of giant ragweed with a trimmer, slicing off the plants near ground level.

- **SPOT HERBICIDE** To avoid repeated cutting back, dab spot herbicide on the cut stem of lopped-off giant ragweed plants.

 **fact file**

LIFE CYCLE	annual
SITE, SOIL & SEASON	will grow in any sunny, open ground, including cracks in sidewalks and gravel driveways; dry to wet soil; blooms in late summer
DISPERSAL	seed
ULTIMATE HEIGHT	common: to 6 feet; giant, to 18 feet
OTHER NAMES	common: bitterweed, hayfeverweed; great: bitterweed, hayfeverweed, wild hemp, horsecane, richweed, buffaloweed

Anagallis arvensis

Scarlet pimpernel

This weed is a dainty low grower with bright flowers that open only in sunshine. Usually not plentiful enough to reach pest status, it is easy to remove with simple hand measures. In England, where it is more common, it is often called "poor man's weatherglass" because of the flowers' propensity for folding themselves up to protect pollen during bad weather.

The tiny, starry blossoms are deep red-orange, not blood red. Plants may also have bright blue flowers. Pairs of diminutive, pointed leaves are joined to the elongated stems at separated intervals, with a single blossom arising from the axil of each pair of leaves. As the lax stem lengthens, new buds and blooms are produced for a long period. Seedpods mature into a little round ball at the end of each stalk.

fact file

LIFE CYCLE	annual
SITE, SOIL & SEASON	grows in any bit of open ground where the plant has enough room to spread its stems; any soil, thrives in dry spots as well as moister ones; blooms mid- to late summer
DISPERSAL	seed
ULTIMATE HEIGHT	4 inches
OTHER NAMES	bird's eye, eyebright, shepherd's clock, poor man's weatherglass, wink-a-peep

Pimpernel is a fun plant because it's a weather prognosticator and pocketwatch all rolled into one. Show your kids how to check for the open blossoms that predict a good day for a picnic, or the tightly closed buds that say, "stay inside." Blossoms allegedly open wide at 8:00 A.M. on the dot, and close up at 3:00 P.M., although you may find your pimpernel follows its own schedule depending on your latitude and time zone. In areas where pimpernel is not a widespread pest, it makes a pleasing plant in a garden, even though you have to stoop to see it best. Its genus name, *Anagallis,* comes from a word meaning "to laugh aloud." Although the weed is no longer used in herbal medicine, the Roman historian Pliny recommended it for removing intestinal obstructions—another way of saying it was once used as a laxative.

■ **ORNAMENTAL USE** The blue form, available through seed catalogs, makes an appealing wash of color in rock gardens or in cracks in paving. The orange variety can be a tricky color to work into a garden plan, but still worth tolerating for its cheerful, small but welcome flowers in late season.

In areas where it flourishes, scarlet pimpernel may increase to such numbers that it becomes too much of a good thing. Control it with mulch or hand weeding.

■ **MULCH** Bury young plants or established clumps with a 2-inch layer of grass clippings, shredded bark, or other fine-textured mulch.

■ **HAND PULL** Grasp the stems where they emerge and pull steadily to uproot plants that pop up in cracks of paving or among gravel. The fine roots easily lift from soil.

■ **HOE** Use a sharp-bladed hand hoe to scrape or chop off plants in flower beds. Turn roots up and let them wither away in the sun, or add to the compost pile if not yet gone to seed. A long-handled hoe is a quick way to evict pimpernel from vegetable gardens.

Friend?

urdock is so vigorous and its foliage so bold that it deserves at least a little consideration as a garden plant. Leaves and stems are edible, but bitter; the root is more commonly used as a vegetable, especially in Japan. Burdock also was used medicinally, and shows promise in modern trials because of its natural anti-microbial effect; concoctions made from the root also act as a diuretic.

- **HARVEST** Collect fresh leaves anytime available. Dig the root before flowering; first-year roots are much easier to dig than those in their second season. Wash your hands after handling burdock leaves as the juice is very bitter.

- **MEDICINAL USE** Crumpled in the hand to release the juice, the leaves soothe insect stings or mosquito bites. To ease skin sores, eczema, or acne, place one tablespoon of chopped leaf in a cup of water for about 4 hours, then splash on the affected area.

- **CULINARY USE** Burdock root has a mild taste, something like potato. Scrub with a brush, slice thinly, and add to sautés or curries.

- **ORNAMENTAL USE** If burdock crops up, why not let it grow to add some wild drama? Cut off and dispose of the burrs in the trash before they mature.

Foe?

urdock is rarely an abundant pest unless a plant has sown itself year after year. Eradicate it when the plant is young for easier removal, or do nothing beyond removing its seeds and wait for it to die a natural death at the end of its second year.

- **DO NOTHING** Allow burdock to flower, and the plant is fooled into thinking its mission is accomplished; this biennial will usually not make a return appearance the year after it flowers. Be sure, however, to remove all burrs before they mature.

- **SHOVEL** You'll need to dig extra deep to remove the entire taproot, which may be anchored as far as 3 to 4 feet underground. But there's usually no need to go to such lengths: Dig out as much as you can, and repeat if the plant tries to regrow.

- **SPOT HERBICIDE** Spray leaves with a systemic herbicide that will be taken into the root. Repeated applications may be needed. (See pages 160-163 for advice on the safe use of herbicides.)

Arctium lappa

Burdock

With its big, coarse leaves, there's no overlooking burdock should it show up in your garden. In its first year, burdock forms a gound-hugging rosette of ruffled leaves, but in its second year, burdock undergoes a transformation. Each wedge-shaped leaf frequently lengthens and broadens to more than a foot long and a foot across, and the thick stems of the leaves also grow to a foot or more in height, lifting the leaves above the ground in a huge clump. Leaves are deep green and slightly hairy on top and wooly-white beneath. In mid- to late summer, clusters of unremarkable purple flowers appear on a stout stem that rises from the center of the plant. They are soon followed by the trademark green burrs that mature to familiar brown. These make burdock one of the most easily recognized weeds. The burrs linger all winter, until a careless animal or pant leg brushes against them and carries them to new ground.

 fact file

LIFE CYCLE	biennial
SITE, SOIL & SEASON	almost any open niche in sun to part shade; usually a weed found along undisturbed edges by buildings rather than in the garden or lawn; blooms summer to early fall
DISPERSAL	seed
ULTIMATE HEIGHT	usually 3 feet
OTHER NAMES	badweed, beggar's-buttons, buzzies, cocklebur, great burr, horse burr

Atropa bella-donna

Deadly nightshade

All plants known as "deadly nightshade" belong to the large nightshade family, Solanaceae, which also includes eggplants, peppers, and potatoes. The unique *Atropa bella-donna* stretches to head-height, and its large flowers resemble the chalices of Canterbury bells, an unrelated garden favorite. In North America, its range is limited almost entirely to a few isolated areas of the eastern United States, but in Europe and Asia, it's a much more common sight. It usually shows up in gardens by invitation, rather than by accident. Its pretty posies can pack a deadly punch to careless users.

Deadly nightshade is a big plant, growing to 6 feet tall. It stands erect, with many branches in the upper part of the plant. Flowers bloom for a long period, with new blossoms opening singly at leaf axils until late summer.

- Flowers are deep, wide tubes, fluted at the top into a five-pointed "star" when viewed from above.
- Flowers may be purple to maroon in color.
- Each blossom matures into a shining black berry, backed by a green star of sepals. Crush a berry beneath your shoe and purple juice and many seeds will spurt out.
- Gleaming black fruit are about ½ inch across, and are often two-lobed in appearance.
- Leaves are long, pointed ovals, up to 6 inches in length, smaller toward stem tips.
- All parts are poisonous when ingested.
- The thick, fleshy root bleeds red sap when broken.

fact file

LIFE CYCLE	perennial
SITE, SOIL & SEASON	sun to part shade; moist soil; blooms early to late summer; shining black fruit in early fall
DISPERSAL	seed; creeping rootstock
ULTIMATE HEIGHT	to 6 feet
OTHER NAMES	belladonna

Deadly nightshade is a special plant to include in an herb garden—not for use, but as a conversation piece and a cautionary tale of the lengths to which vanity will take us (see "Foe" below). The height of the plant also makes it useful in perennial and mixed borders, as long as you have no small children visiting who might be tempted by the shiny berries. Valued by gardeners for its stature, its simple foliage, and its long-blooming purple flowers, it is a plant to handle with respect.

- **GARDEN USE** Keep this plant well away from edible or medicinal herbs. Use as a centerpiece in an isolated bed or in herb gardens. In flower beds, combine with cosmos, fountain grass (*Pennisetum* spp.), and other summer-blooming plants of fine texture. Corral roots with buried barricades to control the spread.

The species names of this plant translates to "beautiful woman," but "beautiful dead woman" is more like it. Big, languid eyes were the benefit of using this plant, which causes widening of the pupils—but a little too much, and those bedroom eyes quickly glazed over into coma and death. Hyoscoamine is the substance that gave the desired limpid gaze; this alkaloid and others contained in the plant also make it useful—in the hands of experienced doctors only— for stimulating the heart and treating neuralgia. In the garden, the determined roots may become invasive. The plant may spread to wild areas and seed itself into other parts of the yard.

- **SHOVEL** Don gloves to work around this plant to avoid possible irritation or ill effects. Cut back top growth for easier handling. Dig deeply to pry out the thick, creeping roots; dispose of them in the trash.

- **HERBICIDE** Apply an appropriate product, following label instructions. Repeated application may be necessary to get rid of the weed completely.

Bellis perennis

English daisy

Bellis means "the pretty one," and these low-growing little white daisies with their pink-tipped petals scatter instant charm across a swath of green grass. Still, some lawn enthusiasts bemoan their presence because they mar the velvet perfection of smooth turf. In the cooler, moister areas where English daisies feel most at home, they show up in large numbers, blooming early enough to set seed for next year before the lawn mower beheads them. It's inevitable that you'll have to mow through these flowers if they occur in your yard; since their bloom period is so long, your grass would be quite shaggy if you waited until they were completely finished.

Once invited into a garden bed, English daisy quickly hops out, sowing itself into the lawn. From a distance, these small daisies look white, but the little nosegay of flowers opens from deep pinkish buds, and upon close inspection, you'll see that their petals remain touched with rosy pink.

- The flowers are usually crowded with petals, often with an almost fluffy appearance that hides the central disk of the daisy, rather than a single row of petals around a yellow center. Flowers close at night and on dreary days.
- Flowers arise on bare stems from the center of the plant.
- The bracts beneath the flower are purplish pink.
- Leaves grow in a compact, flat rosette; may take over a small patch of lawn but usually intermingle with grass.
- Leaves have smooth margins and widen toward the far end. They are downy to the touch.
- Fibrous root system, which is surprisingly large for such small plants.

fact file

LIFE CYCLE	biennial or perennial
SITE, SOIL & SEASON	flourishes in cooler areas, infiltrating the lawn; blooms from late winter through spring
DISPERSAL	seed
ULTIMATE HEIGHT	6 inches
OTHER NAMES	lawn daisy, bairnwort, childing daisy, European daisy, herb Margaret, bonewort, May gowan

English daisy lifts the spirits even better than the first dandelion of the season, which no matter how despised is often looked at fondly when it tells us winter is on the wane. Because this weed is nowhere near as pervasive nor aggressive as dandelion, we can enjoy its appearance as a cheerful harbinger of spring. Cultivated varieties with flowers in rich shades of pink to crimson also are available. All colors are delightful with early blooming spring bulbs. In oldtime herbal lore, English daisy was esteemed as an aid to mending broken bones; hence, "bonewort." Its flowers were used as a gentle aid to digestion and intestinal distress, and an infusion of flowers was brewed to soothe coughs and colds as well as aching joints. Today, the flowers are more likely to be pressed for crafts than added to the medicine chest.

■ **HARVEST** Snip flowers with scissors soon after opening for use in crafts or herbal remedies.

■ **MEDICINAL USE** Steep a tablespoon of flowers, minus their stems, in one cup of boiling water for 10 minutes; strain and cool. Sip one to two tablespoons, several times daily, to help relieve joint pain or coughs.

■ **GARDEN USE** Sow seeds in pots until big enough to transplant into the lawn, or buy started plants. Gives a fresh look to plantings of mini-daffodils, blue scilla or chionodoxa, and also softens the look of tulip beds. Grows well in containers and windowboxes, for a spirit-lifting spring show.

Fans of perfect green lawns aren't charmed at all by the rustic beauty of daisies marring the greensward. Hand control measures are the way to go if infestation is minimal; chemical control is the fastest way to get rid of a large number of these weeds without disturbing the turf.

■ **HAND TROWEL** Use a sturdy trowel to lift out individual plants. Shake off soil, fill in the hole, and scatter grass seed on the bare place.

■ **BROADLEAF HERBICIDE** Use a chemical formulated for broadleaf weeds and apply with a lawn spreader or spray attachment, depending on the product used and its recommended method of application. Pre-emergent herbicide, applied before the leafy clumps appear, may prevent the daisies from ruining the look of the lawn. (See pages 160-163 for advice on safe use of herbicides.)

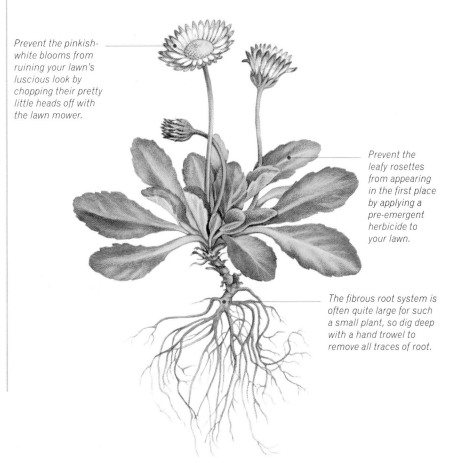

Prevent the pinkish-white blooms from ruining your lawn's luscious look by chopping their pretty little heads off with the lawn mower.

Prevent the leafy rosettes from appearing in the first place by applying a pre-emergent herbicide to your lawn.

The fibrous root system is often quite large for such a small plant, so dig deep with a hand trowel to remove all traces of root.

Bidens spp.

Beggarticks

This sneaky weed is easy to overlook accidentally. Except for a couple of beautiful, showy species of *Bidens*, these weeds bear blossoms that are practically invisible from a short distance. Birds, mice, and other small furry creatures, however, are quick to note the location of beggarticks for their nutritious seeds.

Since the plant lacks the sprawling habit of many weeds and has almost delicately cut leaves, it sidles in among ornamentals without getting a second glance from the gardener. Beggartick plants bear a resemblance to some desirable garden plants—they look like a more open version of a tall marigold, for instance, making the matter of identity even trickier.

- A single stem emerges from the soil, usually bare for its first several inches, then branching, to ultimately about 5 feet in height.
- Foliage is usually sparse, except in *Bidens aristosa* and *B. pilosa*, the most floriferous and garden-worthy members of the genus.
- Leaves are held on opposite sides of the stem and are divided into 3 to 5 leaflets, with the center leaflet usually noticeably longer than the others. Leaflets may themselves be further divided, creating a ferny look.
- Blooms midsummer through fall, with yellow petals when present.
- Seeds ripen to deep brown to black in fall, with barbed prongs at the end. Devil's bootjack (*B. frondosa*) seeds are two-pronged, shaped like old-fashioned "bootjacks," U-shaped devices for removing boots without bending.

 fact file

LIFE CYCLE	annual
SITE, SOIL & SEASON	usually in sun but also in shade; moist to wet soil, but may also occur in dry or sandy soil; blooms late summer to fall
DISPERSAL	seed
ULTIMATE HEIGHT	3 to 5 feet, depending on species
OTHER NAMES	devil's bootjack, tickseed, stickers, pitchforks, Spanish needles, burr marigold, sticktights

Two species—*Bidens pilosa* and *B. aristosa*—make an eye-popping show in the late-blooming garden, but sow themselves fast and furiously for an ever-larger display. Appreciators of these two almost identical plants, usually called tickseed sunflower, would agree with Thoreau, who wrote: "It is a splendid yellow… Full of the sun. It needs a name." All species are eagerly sought by seed-eating finches.

- **GARDEN USE** In a wild garden, birdseed garden, or meadow, the two tickseed sunflower species sow themselves into great billows of golden yellow, silky-textured flowers. Both these species lack the barbs that make beggarticks such a nuisance. Let them spread at will in a meadow or wild garden for an unbeatable late summer to fall display.

- **WILDLIFE** The fragrant blooms of tickseed sunflowers are attractive to butterflies, while seeds of all species attract songbirds.

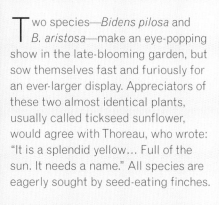

Too generous with their irritating seeds to be desirable in the backyard, beggarticks are best pulled upon sight unless you have a discreet corner where they can grow without grabbing the clothes or fur of passersby. Painstaking hand-picking or combing is the only way to remove the seeds of beggarticks once they latch on to fibers or fur. Be careful where you put the combings: Seeds dropped onto the ground will sprout next year's plague. Most species occur as isolated plants, and are easy to hand pull when they reach moderate size. Although most do best in wet soil, improving drainage may not get rid of a beggarticks problem, since they adapt to dry soil as well.

- **HAND PULL** Grasp the plant as near the bottom of the stem as possible and give a firm yank; the shallow taproot and fibrous side roots are satisfyingly easy to remove from the soil.

- **MULCH** The multitude of seedlings of *Bidens pilosa* and *B. aristosa* are easily disinvited by smothering with a 2-inch layer of grass clippings, newspaper topped with bark mulch, or other mulch that blocks the light and assures their demise.

Brassica spp.
Wild mustards

Mustard-seed necklaces, in which a single seed floated in a glass locket, were all the rage in the fifties, harking to the Christian scripture that began "If ye have faith as a grain of mustard." Although that fad has passed, the flavor of mustard is a perennial favorite, used to add a spicy bite to everything from hot dogs to Chinese egg rolls. The jars of mustard that can be found in just about every refrigerator owe their beginnings to these weeds, which sweep the winter and spring landscape with wide splashes of yellow. Pretty enough for a garden, the plants make a good "filler" in early spring, dabbing pale to lemon yellow about the garden or meadow.

The mustard family, or Cruciferae, is a huge one, boasting more than 3,000 species. But all have one thing in common: Flowers with four petals arranged in a cross shape ("crucifer"). *Brassica nigra*, black mustard, is most common, and highly variable in height. The plant's tall, branching, thin-stemmed habit soon becomes familiar, no matter which species you're looking at. Seedpods also are distinctive.

- Four-petaled yellow flowers begin blooming in late winter and peak in early spring.
- Occur in numbers, from several plants to a field full.
- Leaves are very variable, but usually notched into rounded lobes.
- Seedpods and leaves have a sharp, peppery flavor.
- Flowers borne in long clusters at the tips of branches, opening from the bottom first. They mature into long, skinny seedpods that lengthen and swell, showing the shape of the row of round seeds inside.
- Seeds are very dark brown outside, but yellow inside.

 fact file

LIFE CYCLE	annual
SITE, SOIL & SEASON	highly adaptable to soil; found in full sun; may be found in bloom all year round
DISPERSAL	seed
ULTIMATE HEIGHT	usually 2 to 4 feet, depending on species
OTHER NAMES	black mustard, brown mustard, rocket, poor man's cabbage, yellow cress

A hot dog just wouldn't be the same without a squiggle of mustard, but thank goodness the old folk remedy of "mustard plaster" has become passé: This poultice supposedly drew out sickness, but the volatile oil in the seeds produced such a searing heat that it was capable of blistering the skin. In a meadow garden or cottage-style informal planting, black mustard (*B. nigra*) adds color and airiness, with its thin branches tipped with flowers that make a show for weeks. Enjoy the sprightly flavor of wild mustard leaves in green salads or in cooked dishes.

- **HARVEST** Collect fresh leaves anytime. Snip ripe seedpods before they split open and release the seeds. Dry in an open tray, and then rub between rubber-gloved hands to extract the seeds.

- **CULINARY USE** Mustard greens are definitely hot—spicy hot. Taste-test before adding them to soups, sauces, salads, and other dishes. Prepare large amounts of gathered greens as you would spinach, by simmering until softened. Crush ripe seeds in a mortar and add a bit of vinegar to make your own version of Mr. Gulden's famous condiment.

- **GARDEN USE** Sprinkle mustard seeds among bachelor buttons, oxeye or Shasta daisies, or around daffodils and tulips, where the fast-growing mustards will camouflage dying bulb foliage. Mustard is excellent for early color in a meadow or natural garden, too. To prevent a crowd of seedlings, clip off seedheads before they mature.

Mustard rarely colonizes an established garden, but it may crop up in a newly prepared bed or in a bare veggie garden over winter. Despite its usual abundance, mustard is easy to discourage.

- **MULCH** Depend on a 2-inch layer of grass clippings to stop young mustard seedlings from zooming into adulthood.

- **HOE** A few swipes with a hoe will quickly evict young mustard plants. A well-aimed chop with the hoe will uproot bigger plants, before the flowering stage.

- **HAND PULL** Yank out occasional mustard plants that have the temerity to infiltrate your garden. Even when they are at blooming size, they are not too difficult to uproot with a strong pull.

Capsella bursa-pastoris

Shepherd's purse

A common weed of vegetable gardens and annual beds, shepherd's purse usually appears individually or in scattered outbreaks. It has the typical form of a member of the giant mustard family, or Cruciferae, beginning with a rosette of leaves held tight to the ground. Slender flowering stems emerge from the center of the plant. The blooms, openly spaced along the stem, with few leaves between, are fleeting, quickly changing to the easily identifiable seedpods. These are tricornered and look exactly like the leather bags toted by country sheepherders tending their flocks, hence the name "shepherd's purse." You can almost imagine a loaf of crusty peasant bread and a strong-flavored chunk of cheese inside.

The plant's long, skinny taproot gives it the ability to penetrate cracks in paving and even hard-packed soils, but this same long root allows for easy hand weeding.

- Leaves are slim, from 2 to 4 inches long, and divided into several sets of lobes, each with rounded, toothed edges.
- Leaf form is highly variable. Those on flowering stems usually lack lobes and may have smooth edges.
- Flowers are four-petaled; usually white, but may also be yellow or pinkish.
- Buds at the bottom of the stem open first, and lower flowers mature into seedpods before those at the top even begin to bloom.
- Dead seed stems persist into winter.

 fact file

LIFE CYCLE	annual
SITE, SOIL & SEASON	can be found among lawn grass, but is usually in garden beds; sunny, well-drained soil; leafy rosettes may be seen any time of year, even in winter; bloom season is any time from late winter through fall.
DISPERSAL	seed
ULTIMATE HEIGHT	flowering stems, up to 2 feet
OTHER NAMES	shepherd's bag, pepperplant, caseweed, pick-purse

Although it may be small, the plant can help prevent erosion in unused soils. The determined root of shepherd's purse helps aerate compacted soils, allowing water to penetrate instead of running off, opening the soil, and giving easier access to the roots of other plants. It is often an early arrival on mistreated ground, such as along pathways or on empty lots where heavy machines have been at work.

Like other mustard-family plants, this weed has a peppery bite to its leaves. It's tasty in salads as an unusual fresh green. Smaller songbirds appreciate the plentiful seeds—as many as 2,000 on a single plant—and rabbits and other animals nibble the greens, especially in winter when fresh foliage is scarce. Shepherd's purse was formerly used to stanch internal bleeding, but modern medicine has supplanted its use with better choices.

■ **HARVEST** Collect fresh leaves any time before flowering; they lose their flavor and become tough once in bloom.

■ **CULINARY USE** Wash leaves, chop into bite-sized pieces, and add to green salads for a spicy tang. Alternatively, stir chopped leaves into mild cream soups or chicken broth to pep up the flavor.

■ **DECORATIVE USE** Collect dried stems of seedpods for everlasting arrangements. They add intriguing contrast to a soft-textured winter bouquet of foxtail grass.

Only its occasional abundance makes this weed a pest. Its life cycle is abbreviated in individual plants, but because seeds may sprout any time, the plants are often a constant presence. Seeds are superabundant and long-lived in the soil—a double whammy for gardeners. Still, the plants are easy to lift from the soil with a few minutes of hand labor.

■ **HOE** A long-handled hoe makes quick work of this weed. Sever the rosette from its taproot with a chopping motion, and the problem is finished.

■ **HAND HOE** Slice off or lever out individual plants between established garden citizens. Toss them onto the compost pile.

■ **MULCH** Bury young plants with a 2-inch layer of grass clippings or several layers of newspaper topped with shredded bark, before the flowering stalks emerge.

■ **HAND PULL** This is fast and easy. Grasp the leaves in one hand, as close to the base as you can, and give them a twist to free the taproot in one quick yank. This works best after a rainfall when the soil is moist.

Cardamine hirsuta

Bittercress

Bittercress is a common weed in gardens. This species is especially widespread and abundant in Europe, but it also occurs in North America—as do several relatives, including sand bittercress (*C. arenicola*), small-flowered bittercress (*C. parviflora*), and mountain bittercress (*C. clematitis*), a shade-loving species.

A member of the vast mustard family, this weed has a rosette of basal leaves that looks very much like that of many other mustards, and very similar to a sprig of watercress. If you rub a leaf gently between your fingers, you will feel the soft hairs that distinguish this species, and that make it less useful and appealing to humans. Bittercress has the pleasantly peppery flavor of most of its relatives, but it also has a distinct bitter note that is to few people's tastes.

The small white flowers are borne on a bare, slender, branching stem that grows from the center of the plant. Each blossom has four petals, one of the hallmarks of the mustard family. Flowers are replaced by long, skinny seedpods that burst open at the slightest touch when ripe, scattering their tiny seeds. The seedpods are held very erect, reaching upward from each stem tip where a blossom grew. Roots are thin and fibrous and are relatively easy to hand pull from the soil.

fact file

LIFE CYCLE	annual or biennial
SITE, SOIL & SEASON	sun to part shade; moist to dry soils; blooms early to late spring
DISPERSAL	seed
ULTIMATE HEIGHT	a few inches to nearly a foot tall
OTHER NAMES	hairy bittercress, land cress, lamb's cress, touch-me-not

Foe?

Bittercress infests flower gardens, herb gardens, vacant lots, and anywhere else its seeds can find a hospitable spot of open soil. Remove any plants before seedpods begin to form, to stop them from spreading.

Although rock cress (*Arabis* spp.) and some other mustards have showy flowers worth enjoying in the garden, bittercress has only sparse, small blossoms to offer.

■ **HAND PULL** Learn to recognize the basal rosette of bittercress leaves and yank before it has a chance to flower. As with all weeds, the task is easiest when the soil is moist.

■ **HAND HOE** A sharp-edged weeding hoe makes quick work of evicting bittercress from flower gardens.

■ **HOE** Use a long-handled hoe to lift the weed from vegetable gardens, working in between the plants. Hoe once a week to keep it away.

Centaurea spp.

Knapweeds, centaurea

Pretty flowers, and lots of them, are the reason the Centaurea tribe has outgrown its welcome. Invited first to gardens, bachelor's buttons (*Centaurea cyanus*), spotted knapweed (*C. maculosa*), and a few other troublesome species quickly made a leap for freedom. They now bring their soft pastels or brilliant blue color to roadsides, wheatfields, and rangeland, crowding out valued native grasses and flowering forbs, and quickly creating swatches of nearly pure centaurea.

Fluffy flowers, usually only an inch across, that resemble thistles are the first clue to spotting a centaurea or knapweed. Bachelor's buttons are usually bright blue, but may also be deep purple, white, rose, or pink; the weedy *C. maculosa*, *C. diffusa*, and *C. repens* are frequently a pretty, soft rose-pink or pale purple, but may also be white. Yellow starthistle (*C. solstitialis*) has yellow blossoms. All begin life as basal rosettes of long, narrow, usually deeply lobed or toothed leaves, usually with a grayish cast or silvery undersides. Flowers are held in branching bouquets on the thin, often bare stems that arise from the plant at bloom time; *C. diffusa* and *C. solstitialis* bear sharp spines on the urn-shaped chalice that holds their blossoms. The seedheads are marked with a basketweave design created by their overlapping scales.

fact file

LIFE CYCLE	annual, biennial, or perennial, depending on species
SITE, SOIL & SEASON	any well-drained soil in full sun; bloom season, late spring to fall
DISPERSAL	seed
ULTIMATE HEIGHT	up to 3 feet, depending on species
OTHER NAMES	*C. cyanus:* bachelor's buttons, cornflower, corn centaury, ragged robin; *C. maculosa:* spotted knapweed, purple starthistle; *C. repens (Acroptilon repens):* Russian knapweed; *C. solstitialis:* yellow starthistle

Farmers' wrath aside, we'll let bachelor's buttons remain a beloved old-fashioned garden favorite. But the other knapweeds mentioned above deserve their place on the noxious weeds list. Although they may create a pretty pastel effect in large meadow gardens, they're too pushy to stay put. Keeping ahead of seedlings is a daunting task, so better to not invite these plants in to begin with. Besides their aggressive self-sowing nature, knapweeds are on the official noxious weeds lists of many states, making it illegal to harbor them on your home grounds. Be wary of the spread of other *Centaurea* species: They also may hold the potential to become serious pests. Twenty years ago, knapweeds had hardly begun to gain a foothold in the American West; nowadays, they are so ubiquitous that permanent signs have been erected along roadways and at tourist areas, with pictures of the weed so that it can be eradicated wherever it crops up.

- **HAND PULL** Exert strong, steady pressure to remove the taproot of young plants.

- **HOE** Chop with the blade of a hoe to sever the plant from its root or lever it from the soil. Compost the remains, unless they have already begun to set seed.

- **SPOT HERBICIDE** Spray plants that infiltrate gravel driveways or other areas in large numbers.

Foe?

Chenopodium album

Lamb's quarters

This all-too-common weed sprouts in abundance in the bare soil of vegetable gardens and among flowers. Look first at the pale green leaf to pinpoint this plant: It is diamond-shaped, or, with a little imagination, you can picture the wedge-shaped footprint of a waddling goose. Turn a leaf over and you'll see the pale underside that gives the weed the name "white spinach." This is a super-speedy plant, rising to great heights just a few weeks after the sprouting seed breaks ground; and it frequently occurs in large colonies.

Still, lamb's quarters is easy to overlook because it doesn't shout "weed!" from a distance. The flowers are tiny, but they form in long, tightly packed clusters that are diagnostic even when dried to brown in winter.

- At first glance, the plant often looks powdery.
- Leaves are smooth or shallowly lobed around the edges.
- The leaves grow to as long as 4 inches and are held away from the stem on long leaf stalks.
- The bottom of the stem is bare, with branching form beginning about 6 to 12 inches above the soil surface.
- In crowded beds, plants show little branching; in open areas, they look more like an openly branched shrub.
- Clusters of nubbly, greenish flowerheads form at the tips of branches and in leaf axils in summer through fall.
- The plant is killed by frosts, but the leafless branches stay standing over winter and seedheads become feathery.

 fact file

LIFE CYCLE	annual
SITE, SOIL & SEASON	sun to part shade; highly adaptable to most well-drained soils; blooms in late summer through fall.
DISPERSAL	self-sown seed and seed dispersal by birds
ULTIMATE HEIGHT	up to 6 feet
OTHER NAMES	pigweed, goosefoot, fat-hen, mutton tops, white spinach, white pigweed, baconweed, blackweed

Friend?

After a bout of ridding the garden of lamb's quarters, it may be hard to muster charitable feelings toward this plant. Perhaps it's time for a refreshing lunch break, complete with lamb's quarters salad. As you toss the leaves with a light vinaigrette, consider how the nutritious seeds and greens of lamb's quarters have graced the tables of country folk and the feeding troughs of their animals for centuries. Think also of the dozens of songbird species that depend on its myriad seeds to sustain them through a long, hard winter. If you enjoy watching birds, it's well worth tolerating a small crop of lamb's quarters for their benefit; their visits will keep the winter scene lively.

- **HARVEST** Snip leaves before they reach 2 inches long for best flavor. Leaves shrink fast when steamed or sautéed, so pick about twice as much as you intend to serve.

- **CULINARY USE** Pick young leaves to add variety and a mild spinach flavor to green salads. Use in place of spinach in casseroles, on pizza, or on pasta shells, dressed with light oil and garlic and feta cheese. These leaves are more nutritious than spinach, having a higher content of beta carotene, iron, calcium, and potassium than Popeye's fabled greens.

- **WILDLIFE** Embrace the presence of lamb's quarters in meadow gardens and bird-attracting plantings. The seeds are a magnet for finches and other songbirds, which will forsake the best-stocked feeder to forage for the tiny, oil-rich black seeds.

Foe?

A single plant can produce an amazing 75,000 seeds, many of which will be cleaned off by birds even before they drop. It is the millions of seeds which have dropped, and lay in wait in the soil, that make this weed one of the most common garden troublemakers. Learn to recognize lamb's quarters seedlings and you'll save yourself more strenuous weeding duties later, when the taproot lengthens and the stem toughens, making it very hard to hand pull. Like other tap-rooted weeds, it's best to pull this one when the soil is thoroughly moist; it will give up its grip much more easily than in dry soil.

- **HAND PULL** Yank out isolated specimens as soon as you see them. Smother large infestations of newly sprouted seedlings under a 2-inch blanket of grass clippings or newspaper.

- **HOE** As this weed often springs up in abundance, once-a-week cultivation really helps to keep it in check. Slice the seedlings off below the surface, or chop the soil to uproot them.

- **HAND HOE** Use a sharp-bladed weeding tool to behead lamb's quarter seedlings mercilessly in established beds.

- **PRUNE** For the inevitable overlooked plants that you notice only when they're shoulder-high, use a pair of pruners to cut off the plant at soil level.

- **SPOT HERBICIDE** If lamb's quarters comes up with a vengeance in gravel driveways, douse the plants with an appropriate herbicide, following label instructions.

Cirsium spp.
Thistles

Ouch! There's no mistaking a thistle. Armed with sharp spines on leaves, stem, and flowerheads, these plants are definitely an unwanted presence in the garden. Aesthetically speaking, however, thistles are interesting and beautiful plants. Their stout, barbed foliage and bold flowerheads are architectural artifacts, and perhaps we would welcome them for dramatic foliage if they weren't so darned prolific and painfully pointy.

Thistles come in all shapes and sizes, from the almost dainty Canada thistle (*Cirsium arvense*) that throws a smoky purple haze across roadsides and meadows, to the immense artichoke (*Cynara scolymus*), whose flower buds make a delicious meal when steamed and drizzled with lemon butter. The genus *Cirsium* includes most of the weedy species that interrupt the garden. Most grow from a basal rosette of spiny leaves, from which rises the flowering stem topped by purple puffs of bloom. Bull thistle (*Cirsium vulgare*) and Canada thistle are the most common backyard weeds among the thistles. Thistle-like plants called sow thistles may also show up. (see *Sonchus* spp., page 110).

- Leaves are strongly toothed, with sharp, visible spines at the tips of the lobes.
- Flowering stem is usually sparsely leafed.
- Flowers are powderpuffs of soft purple to rosy pink that mature to white puffs of thistledown and break into parachutes, sending seeds airborne once ripe.
- Florets are held in a cup-shaped receptacle that may also be armed with spines.

 fact file

LIFE CYCLE	annual, biennial, or perennial, depending on species
SITE, SOIL & SEASON	open soil in full sun; bloom season from early summer through fall
DISPERSAL	windborne seed; *C. arvense:* Canada thistle also by spreading roots
ULTIMATE HEIGHT	3 to 5 feet, depending on species
OTHER NAMES	*C. vulgare:* bull thistle; *C. arvense:* Canada thistle; wild canary thistle

Thistles are much better friends to animals than to us humans. Birds help keep them a constant part of the scene by inadvertently spreading (undigested) seeds. Goldfinches and other songbirds that are acrobatic enough to maneuver around the spines are so strongly attracted to thistle seeds that a patch of the plants is practically guaranteed to be a good bird-watching site. (By the way, there's no need to look askance at the thistle seed feeder hanging at your bird station; the skinny black "thistle" seeds sold as birdseed are actually the seeds of a golden daisy flower, *Guaroztica,* not a thistle at all.) Even the fluff that parachutes those pesky seeds to faraway sites is made use of by wildlife: Our feathered friends line their nests with the silky white thistledown. Fluffy thistle flowers are rich with nectar, so they're popular with butterflies and other insects, too.

■ **WILDLIFE** Admire birds and butterflies on thistles away from your home. Bats also visit the plants to pick off night-flying insects attracted to the nectar-rich blossoms.

Tolerating thistles is not only a painfully silly thing to do, it's also illegal. Thistles are number one on many official lists of noxious weeds, and lots of towns and cities have ordinances requiring their removal. Still, thistles keep showing up where they're not wanted, which requires us gardeners to deal with their removal. Dress yourself for battle: These opponents mean business. Wear leather gloves that extend up your wrists, a long-sleeved shirt, and sturdy shoes that won't get pierced by thistle spines. Bag the remains of the plants; even a single overlooked leaf can be a painful experience weeks later when you accidentally stumble upon it.

■ **SHOVEL OR TRANSPLANTING SPADE** Dig deep to pry out the strong taproot. Once the plant is uprooted, carefully place it in a paper grocery sack, holding it by the root. Put the paper bags of thistle plants into a plastic trash bag for disposal. Do not compost. If you are digging Canada thistle, make sure to pull out all running roots from the soil.

■ **SPOT HERBICIDE** Turn to chemical warfare to wither a few scattered thistle plants. Apply an appropriate spot herbicide according to label directions. Dispose of the dried remains after the plant dies, as described above, to prevent mishaps later.

Convolvulus spp.

Bindweed

Both hedge bindweed (*Convolvulus sepium*) and field bindweed (*C. arvensis*) are twining, green vines decorated with morning-glory-like trumpet flowers. It is useful to note that *Convolvulus sepium* may nowadays be listed as *Calystegia sepium*, depending on your reference source. Field bindweed is the smaller of the two species, with leaves about half the size of those of hedge bindweed, and flowers about an inch across, as opposed to those on hedge bindweed which can reach about 3 inches wide on some plants. Look for them sidling up to a fence where they escape the lawn mower long enough to begin climbing, winding their way up taller ornamental neighbors, or traveling along the ground if left unattended. They also twist around each other as they grow.

Field bindweed, otherwise called small bindweed, looks very like its larger relative, hedge or great bindweed, at first glance. A closer look shows a difference in leaf shape, as well as the size of leaves and flowers: Field bindweed has shield-shaped leaves, while hedge bindweed has heart-shaped ones. Both have leaves placed alternately along the stem, and white blossoms that tend to be tinged with pink. Bindweeds seldom appear in home landscapes, but are real pests in farm fields.

- Usually a few vining stems emerge from the same point.
- White flowers open from pointed pink buds and are in full bloom in the morning, withering by midday. New blossoms open each day during the bloom season.
- Seedpods are plump and round.
- The spreading roots of field bindweed (*C. arvensis*) may reach 20 feet deep underground, making it the harder of the two species to control. The roots of hedge bindweed (*C. sepium*) are fleshy and spreading, but much shallower.

 **fact file**

LIFE CYCLE	perennial
SITE, SOIL & SEASON	full sun; almost any soil; bloom season summer through fall
DISPERSAL	seed and creeping roots
ULTIMATE HEIGHT	vines grow up to about 9 feet long
OTHER NAMES	hellweed, lily-vine, lady's nightcap, wild morning glory, bellbind, cornbind

Bindweeds would be ideal for covering a fence, except for those spreading roots. It's nearly impossible to keep the smaller field bindweed (*Convolvulus arvensis*) in its place, because it will outrun almost any barrier; hedge bindweed (*C. sepium*) is worth a try as a fence cover, however, because any errant vines that spring up away from the parent can be uprooted without resorting to deep-soil dynamite. The white flowers are pretty against their background of thick green foliage.

■ **GARDEN USE** Bindweeds are suitable for wild gardens and large meadows, where their rampant spread is not a problem and their white flowers look cheerful both close up and from a distance. You probably won't want to extend the welcome mat to field bindweed, but the larger-flowered, less Napoleonic hedge bindweed makes a fast-growing beautifier for a chainlink fence, whose open weave provides a fine trellis for the twining stems.

Tenacious as just about any weed alive, bindweeds are difficult to eradicate from garden beds and any nearby lawn areas they may creep into, due to their spreading roots. Those of the smaller field bindweed (*Convolvulus arvensis*) can grow incredibly deep, while those of the hedge bindweed (*C. sepium*) are much shallower (see facing page). Regular monitoring and religious uprooting or other control measures will help you stay one step ahead of these fast-moving vines. However, hand pulling is not practical because of the extensive root systems.

■ **SHOVEL OR TRANSPLANTING SPADE** For shallower-rooted hedge bindweed and new plants of field bindweed, dig deep to get the main plant, and then carefully pull out as many of the spreading roots as you can extract. Should new vines emerge from roots left behind, repeat the treatment as often as necessary.

■ **MULCH** To smother the vining growth and reduce the food supply (provided to the roots by the leaves through photosynthesis), cover bindweeds with several thick sections of newspaper topped with some shredded bark—or use

corrugated cardboard. Watch for escapees beyond the mulched area, and either dispatch these with a shovel or cover them, too.

■ **SPOT HERBICIDE** Apply an appropriate product, following directions on the label. Repeated applications may be needed, especially for field bindweed.

Cuscuta spp.

Dodder

Dodders are the weirdest weeds you will ever encounter. These leafless plants are a pale, sickly whitish color; they grow in swarming tangles of twisting vines around other plants' stems; and they are not rooted in the soil. Plants from Mars? No, just parasitic plants that suck their nourishment from the life-giving sap of their green, leafy hosts. Their appearance in home gardens is erratic and usually not a yearly occurrence, thank goodness. Control is a simple matter once you spot these unusual weeds.

Three species of dodder may appear in the garden, and all of them share the same general look. Immediately recognizable because of their odd color, these twining weeds give many gardeners a sense of unease because they seem to appear out of nowhere. Actually, dodders do grow from seeds, which sprout in the soil and give rise to a young vine that immediately clambers onto the nearest green host. Suckers along the stem attach to the stem of the host plant, and the attachment to the soil breaks off, leaving the dodder to finish its life as a complete parasite. You'll need to stoop to get a good look at the pretty, whitish, star-like flowers of dodders; an inexpensive magnifying glass will provide an expanded view of the suckers and flower structure.

- White, yellow, or orange-tinged tangle of vines, looking like a tangled clump of thin string tossed into the garden.
- Amazingly fast growth.
- Tight clusters or single flowers at the ends of short stems, depending on species.
- Suckers leave a dotted line of marks on the host when a piece of dodder is pulled away.

 **fact file**

LIFE CYCLE	annual
SITE, SOIL & SEASON	wet to dry soils, depending on species; usually most prevalent summer through fall
DISPERSAL	seed, parasitic stems
ULTIMATE HEIGHT	limited to size of host plant and its neighbors
OTHER NAMES	devil's guts, angel's hair, strangleweed, lovevine, hellbind

Foe?

This one really is a foe. Get dodder out of your garden as soon as you spot its sickly tangle of matted vines. It literally sucks the lifeblood from your favored plants, as well as making an unsightly mess of the garden. It weakens the host plant and costs you extra time waiting for your ornamentals to recover after the dodder is removed.

- **HAND PULL** Remove dodder whenever you see it. Peel off every tiny bit of vine you see; because this weed needs no roots, it can quickly regrow from just a short overlooked section of stem still attached to the host. Place a ground cloth beneath the host plant before you take off the dodder, to catch any stray bits. Do not compost this plant; dispose of it in the trash. Be careful not to drop pieces of the vine elsewhere.

- **PRUNE** Hand removal is a tedious job, so if you notice the dodder before it gets out of hand, you can clip off the host plant and ditch the whole thing, dodder and all, in the trash. For severe infestation, you'll soon be able to judge which method is the most efficient: cutting back infected host plants or hand removal of the vines.

- **MULCH** Follow up dodder removal by applying several layers of newspaper (top it with some shredded bark) over the soil beneath the former host plants. This will prevent any seeds that may have been shaken out by the weeding operation from getting a start next season.

- **CULTIVATION** Hoe weekly beneath formerly infested plants for the next two to three growing seasons. To prevent dodder seeds from getting a leg up, use a handheld or long-handled hoe to scrape the soil surface beneath a former host plant.

- **MONITOR** Many gardeners are never troubled by dodder. Nevertheless, because of its sporadic nature, it's a good idea to keep alert for dodder's appearance so that you can nip it in the bud. Monitoring is vital for two or three growing seasons after a dodder infestation, so that you can remove young dodder plants long before they weave their tangled web.

Cynodon dactylon

Bermudagrass

As a lawn grass, this plant is welcomed for its thick turf and ability to stay lush and green in drought and heat. As a weed, this infernal grass is one of the worst. That's because once it moves in, it's nearly impossible to get rid of. Problems usually begin when it leaves the lawn to colonize flower beds.

At first, it looks a lot like crabgrass (*Digitaria*); but bermudagrass stems are stronger, more wiry, and form mats that are much harder to get rid of. If you pull up a clump of grass and find it has many tentacles of white roots growing in all directions, you are the unlucky host of bermudagrass.

- Very long, creeping stems hug the ground.
- Branches arise from joints along the creeping stem and grow erect, eventually blooming with clusters of skinny four- to five-fingered spikes, each up to 2 inches long.
- The upright stems are leafy, while the creeping, flat stems have sparse leaf blades between upright branches.
- Foliage is dark gray-green and may be hairy or smooth.
- Narrow, pointed leaf blades held at an angle of about 45 degrees to the stem, with a long, distinctive sheaf where the base of the leaf hugs the stem.
- Tufts of fibrous roots at base of parent plant and at joints in aboveground stems.
- Running roots, which are hard, scaly, and whitish with a sharply pointed tip, may travel 10 feet or more from the parent plant and burrow as deep as 2 feet.
- Dies back in cold weather; roots may persist and sprout new growth in spring.

 fact file

LIFE CYCLE	perennial south of Virginia; grows as annual in colder climates
SITE, SOIL & SEASON	sun; adapts to many soil types but prefers average to dry soil; also thrives in wet places, where it withstands flooding
DISPERSAL	superfast, spreading via aboveground stolons and belowground running roots; rarely by seed
ULTIMATE HEIGHT	prostrate creeper with many long stems; at flowering, stems may rise to about 12 inches
OTHER NAMES	devil grass, scutch grass, wire grass

Foe?

Learn how to recognize bermudagrass so that you can eradicate it before it gets a serious roothold. It infiltrates quickly, entwining its roots around and through those of desirable plants. Control is difficult because the white running roots are brittle and new plants will spring up from any bit of broken root left in the soil. The only long-term solution is complete eradication. Otherwise, you will be fighting bermudagrass battles year after year.

- **HAND PULL** If you are careful and determined, you may be able to eradicate a minor infestation of bermudagrass, or at least keep it to a moderate level, by uprooting every bit of the weed you see during the growing season. When soil is moist, pull up each piece of leafy grass and unravel the underground roots from wherever they have traveled. Dispose of all weedlings in the trash; do not compost. Unless you are able to spend hours doing painstaking weeding throughout the growing season for years to come, other methods, like herbicides, offer a better approach to the problem (see "Herbicide," right).

- **BARRICADE** If your lawn—or your neighbor's lawn—includes bermudagrass, install plastic or metal strips around every ornamental bed to help keep bermudagrass in its place.

- **BEWARE PASSED-ALONG PLANTS** Examine the roots of plants you get as gifts to be sure you are not importing this dreaded pest to your gardens. The strong, sneaky roots can hide effectively among the thick roots of daylilies, Siberian iris, and other plants often shared over the garden fence.

- **ROTARY TILLER AND COVER CROP** For organic gardeners, bermudagrass is a tough enemy to outwit. In fall, remove all desirable plants from the affected bed and transplant them elsewhere. Turn the soil with a rotary tiller. Sift the soil to remove as many pieces of the weed's root as possible, then plant a thick stand of rye, millet, or other smother crop, whose quick, thick growth will crowd out the weed. Repeat the treatment in late spring to early summer, then allow the cover crop to stand until fall. It may take two years of repeated sowings before the bed is free of bermudagrass.

- **HERBICIDE** Apply systemic weedkillers specifically targeted to bermudagrass, following the label directions. Monitor for new growth and repeat application as recommended. If the weed is a perennial problem in your beds, you may want to consider the drastic but effective measure of removing all ornamentals, completely weed-killing your garden beds and lawn area, and replanting the lawn with another, less-aggressive grass species.

Friend?

Yellow nutsedge adds eye-catching architecture and is very pretty with fall asters. On large properties, where wildlife is appreciated and there is room for weeds to run wild, this plant is a fine one to encourage.

- **WILD GARDEN USE** Transplant misplaced yellow nutsedge from the lawn or flower bed to naturalistic meadow gardens, in company with late bloomers such as blue mist flower (*Eupatorium coelestinum*) and rich purple ironweed (*Vernonia* spp.).

Foe?

Yellow nutsedge interrupts the uniformity of a lawn and can proliferate at a frustrating rate in fertile, moist soil. Control measures take patience because of the tubers, each of which will happily sprout a new plant. Hand pulling won't work because the tubers will strip off the fibrous roots as they are drawn up through the soil.

- **SHOVEL OR TRANSPLANTING SPADE** Dig deep and wide—at least 6 inches from all sides of the stem— to remove roots. Sift soil through your fingers or sieve to ensure that you extricate all tubers. This approach is best for garden beds and for scattered plants in lawns.

- **SPOT WEEDKILLER** Apply a product specific to yellow nutsedge control, per label directions. Repeated applications are often necessary.

Cyperus esculentus
Yellow nutsedge

As ornamental as high-priced bog garden plants, this common weed is widespread on three continents. Its only fault is its prolific reproduction: Unlike other sedges and rushes, which tend to stay in nicely behaved clumps near water, this plant knows no bounds. It sidles out of its homelands along rivers and ditches to infest lawns, gardens, and farm fields. In bloom, it's an attractive plant, with showy clusters of golden brown seeds. Out of bloom, it looks like a nitrogen-starved grass, with yellowish leaves. Ducks depend on the tubers for food; the tubers are sold commercially for planting in hunting areas and nature sanctuaries.

The "nut" in its name refers to the small tubers formed on the roots, and the "sedge" to its membership of the grasslike sedge family, with leaves that feel distinctly triangular (three-cornered). Recognize this plant by its propensity to spring up in lawns and garden beds, where other sedges rarely occur, and by its distinctive color, flowers, and unmistakable tubers.

- A single-stemmed plant, with smooth, grassy leaves.
- Leaves are pale green to greenish yellow, with long sheaths that overlap where they are attached to the stem.
- Easily evident in summer, when it quickly outgrows newly mown grass around it.
- A cluster of bottlebrush-flower stems radiates from the top of the main stem, with several leaves held below.
- Flowers are tiny and have a yellowish cast.
- Seedheads turn from yellow to golden brown or chestnut brown as they mature.
- A cluster of fibrous roots bears several to many little, hard tubers, like tiny potatoes, near the end of roots.

fact file

LIFE CYCLE	perennial
SITE, SOIL & SEASON	sun to shade; prolific in wet soil, but also grows in lawns and flowerbeds; flowers midsummer to early fall
DISPERSAL	tubers sprout new plants; also by seed
ULTIMATE HEIGHT	to 3 feet; more often, about 1 to 2 feet
OTHER NAMES	chufa, earth almond, ground almond, nut grass, rush-nut

Datura stramonium

Jimsonweed

An attractive plant, jimsonweed looks like a small, stout tropical tree. Leaves are big and toothy, lending the plant an assertiveness that draws attention. But be warned: The plant carries enough poison literally to kill a horse or any other animal unlucky enough to try a nibble. This weed is too toxic to experiment with, even for its once-reputed narcotic and aphrodisiac effects.

In just a few weeks of growth, jimsonweed outpaces any neighboring plants to spread its stout branches and big leaves, which can reach 8 inches long. At first glance, the plant looks something like an oversized eggplant plant, and it often appears singly in either vegetable or flower gardens. The trumpet-shaped, summer-blooming flowers are so beautiful that they (or their close relatives) have starred in paintings by Georgia O'Keeffe.

- Leaf edges are deeply and irregularly toothed.
- Bruised foliage has an unmistakably rank, fetid odor.
- Each upward-facing flower may be 6 inches in length.
- Although blossoms differ in hue from one plant to the next, they are usually white, tinged with cool lavender (deepest in color at the center and paling at the flared edges of the trumpet).
- Blooms are followed by the trademark, ultra-spiny, egg-shaped fruits, which hold dozens of seeds waiting to start the next crop.

fact file

LIFE CYCLE	annual
SITE, SOIL & SEASON	open space in full sun; any well-drained to dry soil; sprouts in late spring to summer, flowers summer through fall, and dead stems stand through winter
DISPERSAL	seed
ULTIMATE HEIGHT	to 5 feet
OTHER NAMES	devil's apple, devil's trumpet, fireweed, Jamestown weed, mad apple, stinkweed, thorn apple

Although the pretty flowers have their attractions, jimsonweed's poisonous alkaloids make it a plant to avoid. Concentrated in the leaves, fruits, roots, and seeds, they can cause nausea and headache at the least, and loss of sight, mania, coma, and death at the worst. "Jimson" is a corruption of Jamestown, the early Virginia village where some settlers went mad after eating the weed. Even if you never make the mistake of sampling it by mouth, you're likely to brush against it, at which point it's too late to realize you are one of the unlucky souls who are susceptible to the dermatitis it can induce. Admire it in the wild, where you can watch the sphinx moths that gather when the flowers gleam at dusk, but, for safety's sake, evict it from the garden when you spot it.

- **SHOVEL** Uproot larger plants with a long-handled shovel. Wear long sleeves, long-legged pants, and gloves when handling the plant. Do not compost—there is no sense taking the risk of spreading any possible lingering toxins around vegetable plants.

- **TRANSPLANTING (OR POACHER'S) SPADE** In tight quarters, where favored ornamentals are near the weed, use a narrow-bladed transplanting shovel to lever out jimsonweed. Wear protective clothing and dispose of the plant in the trash.

- **HAND PULL** Wear gloves to pull up young plants whose taproots yield without extraordinary effort when the soil is moist after rain. Dispose of young jimsonweed plants in the trash.

Foe?

Daucus carota

Queen Anne's lace

This very common weed sneaks into vegetable patches, snuggles up in flowerbeds, and quickly infiltrates wilder meadow and cottage gardens. The thick growth of lawn grass usually keeps it out, but the ferny plants are likely to pop up in gravel areas or even in patio cracks, wherever they can find some sunny open space. The lacy, white flowers are undeniably pretty, and the tall, branching plants have an airiness that lends them to garden use—if only they weren't so maddeningly prolific!

If you've ever grown carrots, you already know what Queen Anne's lace foliage looks like in its first year of growth—ferny and deep green, held in a nosegay near the ground. This "weed" is really a carrot in disguise: Botanically it is the same species, the only difference being that it hasn't been selected by plant breeders to have a thicker, oranger, tastier root. In its second year, the stem elongates and the 3- to 4-inch-wide flower clusters appear. They are flat or slightly domed, sometimes dished, a dense cup of delicate lace often centered by a small deep purple dot. In winter, the brown, leafless stems hold cupped and curled seedheads that make a perfect receptacle for fluffy new snow. Several other weeds have flowers that are similar to the white umbels of Queen Anne's lace; when in doubt, sniff the root: although skinny and pale, it smells like the carrot that it is.

fact file

LIFE CYCLE	biennial
SITE, SOIL & SEASON	sun to part shade; any soil except wet; leaf rosettes apparent year-round; flowers summer through fall; dead plants stand through winter
DISPERSAL	seed; fuzzy seeds stick to animals and clothes
ULTIMATE HEIGHT	can grow to 3 feet
OTHER NAMES	bird's-nest plant, wild carrot

Friend?

Enjoy Queen Anne's lace as a reliable, long-blooming flower, and for the lively and lovely creatures it will bring to your garden.

- **ORNAMENTAL USE** Allow a few plants to grow among cosmos, tall zinnias, cleome, and other easy annuals, or introduce it to the perennial beds: It makes a beautiful partner for taller blue salvias (such as *Salvia guaranitica* and *S. azurea*) and Russian sage (*Perovskia atriplicifolia*). Also, shake seedheads around the feet of trellised clematis or climbing roses to add a wonderful softness.

- **WILDLIFE** Nectar-rich flowers are a draw for butterflies, bees, wasps, moths, colorful beetles, and many other insects. Songbirds and small animals nibble the seeds.

- **MEDICINAL USE** Simmer about a tablespoon of ripe seeds in one cup of water for 10 minutes; strain and sip to relieve flatulence.

- **CULINARY USE** Slice the washed root to add a mild carrot flavor to salads and soups; be sure of identification before using (poisonous wild hemlock is similar in appearance but does not smell like carrot).

- **DECORATIVE USE** Press flowers and paste on dark notecards.

Digitaria spp.

Crabgrass

This sneaky weed sprouts quickly and spreads like lightning, each plant covering several square feet of open ground whenever the soil and season are warm. The lawn care industry no doubt loves this weed, which accounts for a large part of their business. Crabgrass isn't entirely nefarious, though: Its silver lining is the fact that it stands up to drought without losing any of its lush green look.

Crabgrass makes its first appearance in late spring as a small clump of grassy leaves, but you'll usually notice it first in summer, by which time it has become a sprawler. The long stems spread out in every direction, growing roots at the joints to continue the takeover. Leaves are a bright, rich green, and usually softly hairy on close inspection. The flowerheads, which appear in midsummer to fall at the tips of stems, resemble fingers (or digits, hence *Digitaria*).

fact file

LIFE CYCLE	annual
SITE, SOIL & SEASON	leaf blades apparent in any sunny, open soil from late spring through fall; flowers summer to fall
DISPERSAL	seed; broken sections of stem will reroot at joints
ULTIMATE HEIGHT	usually low-growing, but flowering stems can reach 2 to 3 feet tall among other plants
OTHER NAMES	finger grass

Friend?

Should your premium turf grasses falter in summer heat, you may be thankful for the presence of this highly territorial weed. It keeps lawns vivid green without supplemental water. Because it dies after setting seed, it will leave a brown lawn behind for winter, however. Crabgrass is a weed for wildlife lovers to welcome. Its seedheads will bring flocks of native sparrows, finches, buntings, and other seed-eaters to your backyard.

- **LAWN ALTERNATIVE** No need to import crabgrass; it'll find your lawn on its own, especially if your turf is less than perfect. Let the plants grow at will and you can enjoy a lush lawn even at the height of summer.

- **WILDLIFE** Practice passivity and let crabgrass find a home in meadow gardens, where it will wend its way among flowering plants to provide a banquet for birds in fall and winter. Its seeds are especially popular with ground-feeding birds, including juncos, doves, and towhees as well as sparrows. Rabbits also enjoy grazing on crabgrass, which may distract them from nibbling on your marigolds or other desirable plants.

Foe?

Crabgrass seems to grow almost faster than the eye can follow. In the lawn, your easiest recourse is herbicide because it's hard to extricate the weed from the thick lawn grasses. But in vegetable and flower gardens, rock gardens, and ground cover plantings, crabgrass is gratifyingly pleasurable to uproot because the entire clump usually comes up with one easy pull.

- **HAND PULL** Gather the plant at the base, holding as many of the spreading stems in your hand as you can. Exert constant, slow pressure to pull out the central group of fibrous roots. Then uproot any stems that didn't relent when you pulled their parent. Compost the weeds, but bury them as soon as possible with other plant material so they don't reroot in the pile.

- **PRE-EMERGENT HERBICIDE** Choose a commercial product, organic or synthetic, and treat your lawn areas in early spring, before crabgrass seeds sprout. Read labels to find an appropriate product and follow all label directions.

- **SPOT HERBICIDE** Spray crabgrass with spot weedkiller or your own soapy mix should it sprout between cracks in paved areas, to avoid disturbing bricks or other pavers by pulling the roots.

*Dipsacus fullonum
(synonym, D. sylvestris)*

Teasel

Teasel never fails to garner attention when it's in bloom, due to its great height, rigidly erect posture, and big, dramatically spined flowerheads. Teasel is a weed that was initially spread by humans, who took it along wherever they made woolen cloth, so that the soft nap on the finished wool could be "teased" up at the end of the process. Spread by civilization, teasel went wild and is now an uninvited guest in gardens.

This weed is easy to identify from the get-go, when the big, coarse leaves form a stout rosette. Should you somehow miss this, you'll notice the tall, strong stem, armed with spines, that emerges to hold a pronged candelabrum of oval flowerheads at nearly head height. Even in winter, teasel is unmistakable as its dead brown stems stay stiff and straight, while still holding the remnants of last year's flowers.

- In the first year, its rosette leaves are pointed oval in shape, and sometimes with scalloped or wavy edges.
- A stiff, prickly stem elongates in year two, clasped by pairs of leaves that have no stems themselves.
- Second-year leaves form a cup at the stem, which collects rainwater—hence the name "Venus's bath."
- Many tiny, purple, occasionally white, flowers bloom on the flowerheads, which can look a little like thistles.
- At the bottom of each flowerhead, a group of skinny, spiny, green bracts curve upward around the bloom.
- Flowers occur in a three-pronged form: A bigger central blossom and two others on outward-angled branches.

 fact file

LIFE CYCLE	biennial
SITE, SOIL & SEASON	dry soils of almost any type; leaf rosette seen year-round; blooms in summer; dead plants persist all winter
DISPERSAL	seed
ULTIMATE HEIGHT	5 feet or more
OTHER NAMES	card weed, clothier's brush, fuller's teasel, fuller's thistle, gipsy combs, Venus's bath

Few fullers (or cloth-makers) are still in the trade of boiling and combing woolen cloth, but you may still find the stiff, dried seedheads of teasel useful for fluffing up articles of clothing. As a garden plant, teasel is worth tolerating because of its outstanding architecture. Its erect posture adds backbone to more delicately textured plantings. In dried arrangements, teasel adds an emphatic vertical line that looks best in a tall vase with modern décor.

- **HOUSEHOLD USE** Teasel seedheads do a decent job of raising the nap on suede shoes and felt hats and can even smooth a badly pilled sweater. Cut in fall when they are naturally dry, with a bit of stem for a handle. Snip off the thorny bracts at the base of the flowerheads with pruners, and use leather gloves to handle the prickly stems while you work. Teasel seedheads are also favorites with those who enjoy making simple craft projects.

- **GARDEN USE** Generally you will host only a few plants, which you may decide to let grow if they're serendipitously placed, for their contribution of unusual form in the garden. Sprinkle a few seeds among billows of loose-limbed cosmos or ornamental grasses to add a visual exclamation point.

Teasel rarely occurs in enough abundance to be a real pest, except along roadsides and in fallow fields, where it can sow itself into fairly dense colonies. Remove the occasional plant that may appear in your garden with the method that works best for you. You'll need a deep-bladed garden tool to get out the determined taproot.

- **SHOVEL** One swift lift, and your teasel is nothing but a memory. Dig deep to pry out the strong, deep taproot, and shake off any clinging soil. Toss plants that haven't yet set seed on the compost pile; even the prickles will decay to nourish a future garden.

- **TRANSPLANTING (OR POACHER'S) SPADE** In the tight quarters of an established bed, it is best to use a narrow-bladed shovel to remove teasel plants without disturbing the roots of neighboring ornamentals. Compost the remains.

Elymus repens

Quackgrass

Like most grasses, quackgrass is most easily recognized in flower, but you won't want to wait before evicting the fast-spreading weed from your patch. Like other pest grasses, this species has long, jointed running roots that travel below the ground, throwing up new plants anywhere and everywhere. A relative of wheat, quackgrass is often infected with ergot, a fungal disease of grain crops that can cause madness in those who ingest it (and is sometimes blamed for the mental instability that caused van Gogh to sever his own ear). Ergot-infected quackgrass was sometimes used by herbalists to stimulate the circulatory system; unfortunately, the results were unpredictable and often fatal.

Distinguishing one grass from another is enough to drive even experienced botanists to distraction, so the best course of action is to eliminate any grass plants you see sprouting in your gardens unless you know for sure they are invited plants. The flowering heads of quackgrass are fairly diagnostic, though, being narrow and closely packed spikes.

- Thin, flat leaf blades are smooth to the touch on their undersides but rough above.
- Stems curve upward from the rootstocks; look for the curve at the base before the stem becomes erect.
- Long, trailing, ground-hugging stems root at their joints.
- Flowering spike, to 6 inches long, is narrow, flat, and dense, with bristly spikelets that are angled upward and closely packed along the stem.
- Long, creeping, yellowish underground rootstocks, which can grow quickly in any direction.

 fact file

LIFE CYCLE	perennial
SITE, SOIL & SEASON	sun; poor to average, well-drained soil; thrives in gravel and sand; flowers summer to fall
DISPERSAL	seed; spreading roots
ULTIMATE HEIGHT	to 3 feet
OTHER NAMES	couchgrass, bluejoint, false wheat, quitchgrass, squitch, twitchgrass, wickens, witchgrass

No pal to gardeners, quackgrass is a tough, almost indestructible grass for pastures or for areas where grass is hard to grow. It thrives in sand and other difficult conditions, and forms a thick turf that looks presentable when mowed with the blade set fairly high. In days gone by, the weed's rhizomes were used to treat urinary incontinence.

- **EROSION CONTROL** Encourage quackgrass on steep slopes or sandy soils, where its network of roots will hold the soil in drenching rains.

- **GARDEN USE** Although flowering plants have a difficult time competing with it, quackgrass makes a pleasing backdrop for shrubs and young trees. For a unique naturalistic planting, plant a group of three young pines, partnered with shining sumac (*Rhus copallina*) and three to five clumps of switchgrass (*Panicum virgatum*), in the midst of a quackgrass "meadow" area. In fall, the sumac foliage will flame against the deep pine green, bolstered by the bleached tones of the grasses.

- **HERBAL USE** Medicinal use of quackgrass is no longer recommended.

Quackgrass is quick to send its roots snaking among desirable plants and hard to eradicate. That makes it a good agent for erosion control, but a troublemaker in the yard and garden. Attack it quickly and with persistence. Once it has settled in, your problems have multiplied because slicing through the roots increases the problem as new plants spring up from each severed section. Quackgrass can just as easily become a pest in lawns as it can in garden beds, especially if your desirable grass is less than uniformly dense. Quackgrass is also a big troublemaker in meadow gardens and naturalistic plantings. Even though its casual look really suits the style of these gardens, its determined roots will soon crowd out more desirable garden citizens.

- **ROTARY TILLER** Chopping quackgrass roots into many pieces could be the start of a gardening nightmare, but regular tilling will keep the plants from getting established. If quackgrass invades your vegetable garden or annual beds, try this method at the end of the growing season (and between rows during the growing season). Repeat weekly. Do another thorough tilling or two before replanting the bed in spring. Any sprouts that do show up unexpectedly will be easy to hand pull as long as you pull them out as soon as you spot them.

- **SHOVEL AND HAND PULL** Combine the two techniques to remove trailing underground stems from garden beds. Be sure to dig up all branches of the running roots, and be alert for strays that regenerate a few weeks after the operation. Dispose of all pieces in the trash; do not compost.

- **HERBICIDE** Spray or brush with contact herbicide specifically recommended for the plant or for grassy weeds. Repeated application is usually necessary.

Epilobium angustifolium, E. hirsutum

Willowherbs

Very few American gardeners will nod in recognition at the name "willowherb," a weed more common on the other side of the Atlantic. But say the name "fireweed," and every gardener in the Pacific Northwest as well as some other regions of America will know the plant. Willowherbs are graceful plants with glossy leaves, and abundant, small flowers, invasive in the regions where they have gained a foothold but rarely a serious garden problem. In fact, they are usually invited into American gardens rather than voted out.

Although the many species of willowherbs vary in size and flower, they all share the shape of their leaves, which are long, narrow, and pointed, like those of "willows." In general, the plant's form is branching, with flowers held in long clusters interspersed with small leaves. Look close and you'll see another identifying characteristic, even if the blossoms are solitary instead of in the usual many-flowered spike:

- The stamens of each flower extend beyond the petals.
- Flowers of *Epilobium angustifolium* are bright rosy purple, but may veer toward pink or be pure white. They open first at the bottom of the spike, then continue upward.

- Flowers of *E. hirsutum* have the same rosy petals but white stigmas, like drops of thick cream on the blossom.
- Willowherbs are rarely found singly and grow into colonies by means of spreading underground stems, or stolons, which root as they go. Stolons are white.
- Flowers mature into long, thin seedpods.
- Mature seedpods split to release tufts of silky, white-haired parachutes to send the seeds on the wind.

 fact file

LIFE CYCLE	perennial
SITE, SOIL & SEASON	grows best in cooler regions; sun to shade, adaptable to various soils; blooms summer to fall
DISPERSAL	seed, spreading stoloniferous roots
ULTIMATE HEIGHT	*E. angustifolium:* to 3 feet; *E. hirsutum:* 6 feet
OTHER NAMES	*E. angustifolium:* fireweed, rosebay willowherb; *E. hirsutum:* apple pie, cherry pie, codlins and cream, great hairy willowherb

In 1944, a New York newspaper reporter wrote: "London, paradoxically, is the gayest where she has been the most blitzed." He said that rosebay willowherb, also known as fireweed, was the cause: "It sweeps across this pockmarked city and turns what might have been scars into flaming beauty." In the American Rockies, Pacific Northwest, and other areas where wildfires are common, fireweed is just as warmly embraced— in the wild—thanks to its ability to cloak fire-ravaged wildlands with rosy purple bloom. In the garden, however, willowherbs can be a little too invasive for anything other than casually planted areas. Yet they are not too difficult to keep confined to the desired area, despite their takeover tendencies.

Frequent monitoring and regular hand pulling will keep their spreading stolons in check. Improved cultivars of willowherbs of several species are sold at nurseries, offering a variety of flower color and plant form. If invasiveness doesn't scare you off, they're well worth planting for their bright color and late-season bloom.

■ **GARDEN USE** Best for regions where summers are moderate and not scorching or humid, willowherbs are perfect for adding a big splash of summer color to the garden. Let them spread in wilder gardens, use them to blanket a slope, or partner them with *Miscanthus* spp. and other swishy ornamental grasses.

Too much of a good thing is a possible problem with willowherbs. In western North America, they often achieve weed status because seeds spread far and wide on the wind. If wild areas provide the seeds, your soil may soon hold the makings of a pesty population. Monitor and use simple methods to keep them in control.

■ **MULCH** Bury very young seedlings with a 2-inch layer of fine-textured mulch, or with several sheets of newspaper or cardboard covered with a more decorative camouflage such as shredded bark. Keep an eye on them to make sure stolons haven't sneaked out the edges to sprout into new plants.

■ **HAND PULL** Pull out willowherbs with a slow, steady force when soil is moist. Be sure to remove all the connected white stolons springing from the parent plant.

■ **GARDEN FORK** If a bed is heavily infested, turn the soil with a fork to expose all bits of root. Remove and dispose of in the trash.

Remove willowherbs before their lovely flowers have a chance to turn into long, skinny seedpods that burst to send their seeds out on the wind.

All species of willowherb have long, narrow leaves. Identify young plants, and bury them with a layer of mulch before they get the opportunity to grow any further.

The underground stems root as they spread so remove all pieces of root when weeding to reduce the risk of colonization.

Friend?

The larger brother of *Equisetum arvense, E. hyemale* has become the darling of the decorating set in the twenty-first century, adding panache to oriental-style interiors and filling planter boxes outside modern office buildings with its tall, bare, green stems. The smaller *E. arvense* isn't as eye-catching because of its "ferny" look, but it is just as valuable in gardening situations. Highly drought tolerant, it's also a great soil holder on erosion-prone slopes. It makes a fine impromptu scrubber for birdbaths and rocky pools, too. If you notice the plant and decide you don't want it, uproot all underground stems to eradicate it.

- **GARDEN USE** Start horsetail on difficult, stony, or dry slopes, where it can spread at will to prevent the soil from sliding. Don't be fooled by its growth habits the first year or two: This plant is slow to get established, but once it's happy, it sprints.

- **HOUSEHOLD USE** Grow horsetail at the base of the birdbath, where it's in easy reach for a quick swab of algae-covered water basins. It's also handy for cleaning the grill of the outdoor barbecue.

Foe?

Horsetails have fooled many a gardener because they are often slow to settle in. Give them a year or two in loose, rich garden soil, however, and they can run rampant, sending out underground roots to support an ever-thickening, ever-expanding colony of plants. New plants may pop up many feet away from the original parents, and can even cross beneath brick or other paving. If you aren't planning to corral the plants in a pot or give them free rein in a natural part of the yard, think long and hard before you invite these potential nuisances into your favored beds. Once they get a roothold, you'll need to exert patient, persistent methods to evict them.

- **HAND HOE** When soil is moist, insert a hand hoe or claw tool beneath the base of a horsetail plant. Lift to expose the roots, being careful not to snap them off. Carefully unearth and remove as many of the connected roots as possible, using a hand tool when needed. Monitor for any new growth and repeat as often as necessary. Dispose of roots in the trash; do not compost.

- **SPOT HERBICIDE** Apply an all-purpose weedkiller as directed on the container, shielding any desirable plants. Repeated applications may be necessary.

Equisetum arvense

Horsetail

This peculiar plant, which grows in dense colonies that look like a miniature forest of pine trees from a distance, is among the oldest plants on earth. Rub a piece of stem between your fingers, and you'll notice the distinctive grit of fine sandpaper; the plants contain tiny grains of silica. In early stages of growth, look for the pale, jointed, reproductive shoots, tipped by spore cases. In summer, the wiry-feeling foliage of horsetail is equally distinctive.

- "Fertile" stems emerge in early spring. They are pale tan, unbranched, and vertical, tipped with an oval, cone-like feature that holds the spores.
- "Sterile" stems have several whorls of slender, green branches around the green stem. Arranged in overlapping tiers, these branches create the appearance of a bunched horsetail.

 **fact file**

LIFE CYCLE	perennial
SITE, SOIL & SEASON	sun to shade; dry, loose soils to wet, rich soils near water; new shoots appear in early spring, "leafy" growth late spring to fall
DISPERSAL	spores; spreading underground stems that root along the way
ULTIMATE HEIGHT	up to 2 feet
OTHER NAMES	common horsetail, scouring rush

Erigeron spp.

Fleabane

Fleabane is a lot more successful a weed than it ever was a flea repellent. The *Erigeron* genus is a big one, with many cultivated ornamentals belonging to it, as well as some highly prolific weeds. Among them are daisy fleabane (*E. annuus*) and common fleabane (*E. philadelphicus*), both likely to be familiar to every gardener who's ever pulled a weed. Fleabanes afflict nearly every garden. You'll want to keep them out of the vegetable patch, but you may enjoy them in flower gardens, where their bloom season often fills the gaps between peaks of perennial seasons.

One glance at the flowers is enough to recognize fleabanes: They are small daisies with zillions of thread-thin petals. However, as easy as they are to identify as a group, they are tricky to separate by species. Luckily, you don't need to know which is which to give them the heave-ho.

Although they come as uninvited guests, fleabanes do have some good qualities—a bounty of flowers on easygoing plants. If you can think of them as a quaint filler in the flower garden, you may find their constant presence less of a nuisance. Besides, you can always try brewing up an anti-pest potion from those you do decide to yank (see "Herbal Use," below).

- **GARDEN USE** Tend a few fleabanes among self-sowing annual flowers, including Shirley poppies, larkspur, and bachelor's buttons. The tall, branching stems of tiny, fresh, white daisies look pretty in meadow gardens, too.

- **HERBAL USE** Botanist John Bartram recommended fleabane as a snakebite antidote, but you'll want to limit its use to less than life-and-death occasions. And to combat fleas? Dry the foliage and flowers and sew into muslin bags to put in your pets' bedding. Success is dubious.

fact file

LIFE CYCLE	annual and perennial
SITE, SOIL & SEASON	sun or shade; adapted to most soils; various species bloom spring through fall
DISPERSAL	seed
ULTIMATE HEIGHT	most species to about 2 feet
OTHER NAMES	daisy fleabane, frostroot, little buttons, mourning bride, old man, Philadelphia fleabane

Fleabane just doesn't know when to stop. Each small daisy begets dozens of progeny, and, when that feat is multiplied by hundreds of flowers per plant, the results are horrifying to any gardener. It is useful to be able to recognize this plant in its seedling stage so you can smother the multitudes when you see them.

- **MULCH** Spread a 2-inch layer of fine-textured mulch, such as grass clippings, over young seedlings. Bury older rosettes beneath several layers of newspaper or overlapping cardboard and top these materials with more decorative mulch, such as shredded bark.

- **HAND PULL** Uproot fleabane plants at any stage of growth with a determined pull-and-twist motion. Compost those that haven't yet gone to seed.

- **HOE** Slice through the soil to kill off young fleabane plants or seedlings. Use a chop and lift motion to uproot more entrenched plants.

- **HAND HOE** In tight quarters, behead your fleabane invaders with a handheld hoe. Chop downward sharply at the base of the leafy rosette, then twist your wrist to uproot.

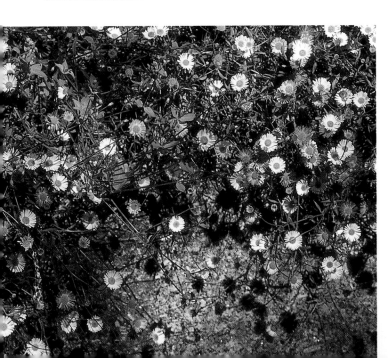

Euphorbia spp.

Spurge

Not all spurges are weeds. Many are beloved garden plants, valuable for adding unusual foliage and form to perennial gardens. The poinsettia, too, is a spurge. But spurges also hold notorious status in the weeds hall of fame. Cypress spurge (*Euphorbia cyparissias*) is aggressively invasive, both in gardens and where it has made the leap into the wild. Spotted spurge (*E. maculata*) has an even worse reputation: This annual now exists in most of the world. Even ornamental spurges may become invasive to the point of weediness in gardens, a good reason to keep an eye on any plant named *Euphorbia*.

They differ a lot in form and color, so the fastest way to narrow down your identification is to break the stem. All spurges exude a white, sticky sap. But avoid skin contact—it can be toxic. Once you see the telltale sap, take a look at the flowers. Although they vary in form, many species have clusters of flowers, with a leaf-like bract held beneath them.

- Colored bracts make the flowers look much bigger than they actually are. Bracts may be chartreuse, red, white, or other colors.
- Actual flowers are very small, but attractive to nectar-seeking insects.
- Root structure varies according to species. Many have taproots; others have spreading roots that root along the way to establish dense colonies.
- Look for spurges in vegetable and flower gardens, or in low-maintenance meadows.

 fact file

LIFE CYCLE	annual and perennial
SITE, SOIL & SEASON	sun to partial shade; adaptable to most soils; most species bloom spring to summer
DISPERSAL	spreading roots or seed
ULTIMATE HEIGHT	depends on species; many about 2 feet tall
OTHER NAMES	various spurges are nicknamed garden spurge, graveyard weed, kiss-me-dick, kiss-me-quick, milkweed, snake milk, wartweed, and a variety of other names; in Massachusetts, *E. cyparissias* was once known as "welcome-to-our-home"

Foe?

Once you have identified a weed as a spurge, handle with care. Wear impenetrable gloves and long sleeves when you're working around these weeds, no matter how innocuous they seem. Try not to get the juice on bare skin, avoid touching your eyes, and certainly don't lick your fingers! The sap contains powerful toxins that can cause drastic health effects; just brushing against the foliage can cause serious skin irritation that lasts for days. Many spurges spread rapidly by means of underground stems or roots, and broken pieces quickly sprout anew. Roots are tenacious and do not yield easily to hand pulling. Even herbicides have a hard time killing spurges. Mechanical means of removal are your best bet.

■ **SHOVEL** Get to the root of your spurge problems by giving the infested area a thorough going over to uproot every plant and every piece of root. Do not compost; dispose of remains in the outdoor trash.

■ **HOE** Sprawling but low-growing spotted spurge (*Euphorbia maculata*) has amazingly tough roots for its small size, so it's very difficult to hand pull. Hoe it out with a sharp blade and some elbow grease. Do not compost. The presence of this weed is a sign that your soil is poor: In fertile ground, other weeds quickly crowd it out of existence.

Fallopia japonica

Japanese knotweed

This is one of the newer weeds on the American scene. In some areas of the Northeast and the Atlantic coast, it's one of the most despised pests, but, in many other regions, gardeners are still blissfully ignorant of its massive takeover abilities. Japanese knotweed is pretty, which is where the problem began. Cultivated in gardens for its lacy sprays of greenish white flowers, it quickly escaped beyond the garden gate. The vigorous plant spreads into huge, dense jungles of greenery, suffocating any other plants in its path.

This gigantic weed has a stem that looks like bamboo at first glance and new shoots that resemble asparagus, but in its growth habits it's more like kudzu.

- Stems are woody, even though the plant dies back to the roots each winter.
- New spring shoots are magenta and chartreuse in color. They're erect and pointed, with distinct joints visible on the stem. In an established plant of Japanese knotweed, they will be hidden among the old stems.
- The 4-inch-long leaves are alternately spaced on the stem. Held on longish stems, they are triangular in shape, with a pointed tip, straight top, and rounded sides.
- Sprays of tiny, greenish white flowers emerge where leaves join the stem; leaf edges are wavy.
- Flowers are followed by clusters of fruits. Inside the whitish "wings" of each seed are small, dark brown seeds.

fact file

LIFE CYCLE	perennial
SITE, SOIL & SEASON	sun or shade, almost any soil; dies back to ground in winter
DISPERSAL	seed, spreading roots
ULTIMATE HEIGHT	a sprawler; each stem can reach 10 feet or more
OTHER NAMES	none

Foe?

Get rid of this invader whenever you spot it. Although it's a good-looking plant, it quickly gets out of control in the garden, and it may hold the potential to be a pest. It already covers hundreds of acres of wild lands, and has infiltrated city parks and other public spaces. Like other highly invasive perennial weeds, it's difficult to kill with herbicides, so evict with a sturdy shovel. However, should you be plagued with this pest, the spring shoots are tasty (but tart!) when

combined with apples or pears in fruit pies or puddings.

- **SHOVEL** Dig deep to remove the spreading rhizomes. Continue the operation until you are sure the soil is free of any leftover pieces of root. Lay the roots on a patio or other solidly paved area to wither and die in the sun. Then dispose of them in the trash. Only stems that have not yet gone to seed can be composted.

Moss gardens are revered in Japan and by some dedicated Western gardeners. In sites where other plants (including grass) have a hard time growing, moss creates a sweep of green that looks good all year.

- **LAWN ALTERNATIVE** Unlike lawn grass, moss can flourish even in shade as dense as that beneath maple trees. Nurture it, and eventually you can develop a garden of subdued attitude. Keep the moss free of twigs and leaves with a soft broom. Install paths or stepping stones through the mossy area; foot traffic will quickly make moss look shabby.

Funaria hygrometica

Moss

This gets a roothold only when conditions are weighted against the growth of competing plants. It usually shows up under shade trees or on bricks and other paving in shady gardens—anywhere where sunlight rarely reaches and the air is heavy with moisture. Lawn lovers despise moss because it interferes with the look of their lush turf.

Various mosses cause problems, but hygrometic moss is one of the most common mosses of lawns and gardens. The minuscule "evergreen" plants have thin, threadlike leaves of shining green crowded on the stem. But when moisture is scarce, the moss dries out to a yellowish cast, which is quickly reinvigorated to lush green when rain comes again.

- Forms a solid patch of growth.
- Individual stems look like very tiny conifers or ferns.
- From a few feet away, the spore-bearing parts look like a layer of sparse hairs rising above the greenery.

fact file

LIFE CYCLE	perennial
SITE, SOIL & SEASON	wet to moist areas; full shade; acidic soil; visible year-round
DISPERSAL	spores
ULTIMATE HEIGHT	forms very low, solid mats
OTHER NAMES	hygrometic moss

Moss makes pathways super-slippery, especially when it's wet. It also holds water against any masonry or against your roof, hastening deterioration of the material beneath. Combat moss by enlisting its enemy—sunlight—or with chemical or mechanical treatments.

- **HAND PULL** Moss lifts off in satisfyingly big pieces, making it quick work to remove even very large colonies. If your infestation is more insidious, with thin strands of moss snaking through the lawn, chemical treatments or a stiff raking may be more effective. Dispose of moss on the compost pile.

- **RAKE** Before reseeding a patch of weak lawn with a more appropriate grass cultivar, remove moss by raking it off with a metal-tined leaf rake. Also use a rake to remove moss from existing lawn, unless the grass is weak and will be damaged by the operation.

- **IMPROVE DRAINAGE** Wet soil is hospitable to the growth of moss, at the expense of lawn grass. Improve growing conditions by encouraging water to drain away from the area, and amend soil by digging in copious amounts of compost.

- **INCREASE LIGHT** Remove lower limbs of trees to allow more light to fall on the ground beneath them. Grass will have an easier time competing with moss.

- **GROUNDCOVER** Install liriope, vinca, or other shade-tolerant groundcovers instead of lawn grasses. These will eventually crowd out the moss.

- **HERBICIDE** Apply a product specifically labeled for moss control, following directions on the package. This is good when moss has colonized paving, but be sure to protect desirable plants nearby.

Friend?

Cleavers was touted as a cure-all in the golden days of herbal medicine. It even was employed as a weight-loss aid according to John Gerard in his sixteenth-century *Herball*. Many of those remedies have failed to hold up to modern scrutiny, but the plant can still be employed to soothe skin irritations and to help speed up the healing of minor cuts and scrapes.

- ■ **MEDICINAL USE** Collect fresh leaves, crush with your hands, and lay against skin to soothe irritation and perhaps help heal cuts and scrapes.

Foe?

Unless you enjoy the tedious work of picking stick-tight seeds off your socks or your dog, you'll want to remove this weed as soon as you spot it—or at least before its seeds begin to form. The stem hooks can definitely be painful should you rub them the wrong way.

- ■ **MULCH** Bury young cleavers plants beneath a 2-inch-deep layer of wood chips, or other mulch.

- ■ **HAND PULL** Wear gloves. Grasp the stem where it emerges from the soil and pull. You're unlikely to get the root, but the plant will not regrow. Remove any branches that break off during the operation. Toss on the compost pile if it hasn't yet set seed.

- ■ **HAND HOE** Scrape cleavers off with a sharp-bladed hand tool. It won't regrow from roots left in the soil.

- ■ **HOE** Chop off at root. If it hasn't yet set seed, use a hoe blade, not your hands, to place on compost pile.

Galium aparine

Cleavers

With leaves that grow in whorls like green petticoats around the stems, this weed looks appealing, especially when it crops up in shade gardens to cover bare spaces with its long, lanky stems. Reach to pull it, though, and you'll sing a different tune: Its stems are armed with sharp prickles. After its tiny blossoms ripen to seeds, it will cause you even more aggravation because the seeds are covered with tiny barbs that allow them to stick like glue to anything that brushes by. Luckily, it usually shows up singly in beds and shrub gardens, rather than in mass invasions.

Cleavers is a pesky plant, quickly recognized as a member of the *Galium* genus by its trademark leaf arrangement, with six to eight leaves making a circle around the stem. Fine-tune identification with a careful touch of the stem, which will reveal a full armor of tiny, downward-pointing barbs. The vegetative growth, which covers a lot of ground through the branching stems, is more likely to catch your attention than the unremarkable tiny greenish blossoms.

- ■ Long, slender, pointed leaves arranged in whorls, with six to eight leaves joining the stem at the same point, and bare stretches of stem between whorls.
- ■ Stem barbs may be only at joints or along the entire stem; run thumb and forefinger down the stem and you won't get pricked, but rub it up and you'll feel it for sure.
- ■ Blossoms form anytime from late spring to early fall, and are borne in branching clusters at the stem tips.
- ■ Seeds are grayish brown, about ¼ inch across, and covered with fine, hooked bristles.

fact file

LIFE CYCLE	annual
SITE, SOIL & SEASON	shade to sun; any moist soil; blooms in summer
DISPERSAL	seed that spreads on passing animals
ULTIMATE HEIGHT	a weak-stemmed sprawler; may lean against soil or relax against neighboring plants, with stems reaching to about 2 feet
OTHER NAMES	English goosegrass, bedstraw, catch weed, gripgrass, scratch weed, bur head, beggar lice, stick-a-back, sticky willy, cling rascal

Geranium robertianum

Herb Robert

This smaller relative of popular perennial garden geraniums is not a weed to get too worked up about—unless you are one of those who love a perfect lawn, which herb Robert can ruin by wiggling into any bare spot. Similar weedy species include dove's foot cranesbill (*Geranium molle*), whose seeds often contaminate lawn grass seed mixes, and alfilaria (*Erodium cicutarium*), which has densely ferny leaves.

Look closely at herb Robert, however, and you will see that its dainty, pink flowers and small, ferny leaves possess a diminutive charm.

- Reddish seedlings sprout in multitudes in earliest spring, maturing into early-blooming plants.
- Stems are relaxed and sprawling, with many branches.
- Leaves are finely cut, much divided, and turn red in fall.
- Reddish purple, five-petaled flowers are ½ inch across.
- Seedpods are long and slender—like a crane's beak.
- When ripe, the seedpods split and curl backward.
- Roots are fibrous and do not spread.

fact file

LIFE CYCLE	annual
SITE, SOIL & SEASON	full sun; any moist to dry soil; blooms spring to fall
DISPERSAL	seed
ULTIMATE HEIGHT	to 18 inches
OTHER NAMES	dragon's blood, storkbill, cranesbill

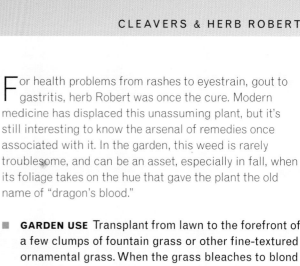

For health problems from rashes to eyestrain, gout to gastritis, herb Robert was once the cure. Modern medicine has displaced this unassuming plant, but it's still interesting to know the arsenal of remedies once associated with it. In the garden, this weed is rarely troublesome, and can be an asset, especially in fall, when its foliage takes on the hue that gave the plant the old name of "dragon's blood."

- **GARDEN USE** Transplant from lawn to the forefront of a few clumps of fountain grass or other fine-textured ornamental grass. When the grass bleaches to blond in fall, the weed will add a ferny foreground of contrasting red. For those who appreciate the details, herb Robert is also fun to snuggle among larger perennials, where its stems can lean at will. It is also a good plant for crevices in stone walls: The roots can get by with very little soil and they aren't aggressive enough to disturb stones.

- **HERBAL USE** Crush fresh leaves and apply to insect bites or other skin inflammations. Hold in place with a wrap of cheesecloth for 10 minutes.

- **DECORATIVE USE** Press the flowers and foliage for use in notecards, papermaking, or other crafts.

Foe?

It's hard to get too worked up about such a modest adversary, but if herb Robert mars the perfection of your greensward, you can apply chemicals to eradicate it. In garden beds, hand pulling or other swift and easy methods are the answer.

- **MULCH** Bury seedlings beneath 2 inches of fine-textured mulch, such as grass clippings.

- **HAND PULL** Uproot occasional plants at any stage of growth by pulling them out by hand. The fibrous roots easily leave the soil with one short tug. Compost if they haven't yet gone to seed.

- **HOE** Use a long-handled hoe or a hand-held hoe to scrape off seedlings and older plants, then compost the plants.

- **PRE-EMERGENT HERBICIDE** Apply according to label directions to prevent the seeds that are in the soil from sprouting.

Glechoma hederacea

Ground ivy

Ground ivy is one of those frustrating, invasive weeds that make many a committed organic gardener wish they could reach for an herbicide. Its slim stems grow at quite some rate, rooting wherever they get the chance. There is an alternative to endless hours of nit-picking, though: Unlike other aggressive spreaders (bermudagrass, for instance), ground ivy is a weed you can learn to live with. It will not crowd out established plants, and it has ornamental value due to its bright blue flowers. It even has an herbal history as a headache remedy, something to keep in mind when you're ready to pull your hair out over this weed.

A slender, square stem and pairs of rounded, scalloped-edge leaves are the giveaway to ground ivy's identity, along with its hallmark habit of galloping over the ground so fast you'll swear it's grown 6 inches every time you turn your back. The stems hug the ground to travel, with stems rising erect to hold up the deep blue flowers to bees and other nectar sippers. The plant often hitchhikes into gardens by way of contaminated, passed-along plants, so examine each garden gift with a sharp eye before you plant.

- The leaf surface looks quite pebbly due to the pattern of the veins.
- Flowers are rich blue to purple blue and are held in the axils where leaves join the stems. They are small and tubular, shaped like those of salvias and other plants in the mint family.
- Leaves have a strong odor that some find unpleasant.
- Fibrous roots sprout from stem joints that touch soil.
- Stems may also travel underground, rooting on the way.

fact file

LIFE CYCLE	perennial
SITE, SOIL & SEASON	sun to shade; almost any moist soil; blooms in spring and dies back to roots in winter
DISPERSAL	creeping stems root along the soil; plants propagate from broken bits of stem
ULTIMATE HEIGHT	flowering stems may grow to about 6 inches tall, but plant is typically a ground-hugger
OTHER NAMES	cat's foot, creeping Charlie, gill-over-the-ground, hedge-maids, robin runaway

With a weed as speedy as this one, it's easier to change your view of it than to eradicate it from your yard. On the plus side, ground ivy is not a competitor of most garden plants. It won't starve them or shade them out of existence, and its creeping stems aren't powerful enough to shoulder them aside. So if you are the proud owner of a ground ivy plantation, enjoy it as a not-bad groundcover among ornamentals or shrubs.

- **GARDEN USE** You may not choose to invite ground ivy into your garden voluntarily, but if you already have it, let it spread as a deciduous groundcover among tulips and other spring bulbs, or with hostas and ferns in shady areas. Consider it a living mulch in sunnier gardens, where its foliage will help shield the soil from the heat of the sun—and block out other, less pleasant weeds. You will need to keep it under firm control: Use a plastic or metal edging strip to keep the ground ivy from spreading into lawn areas.

Like many of its minty relatives, ground ivy will take over your garden given half a chance. If the outbreak is a small one, eradication is possible with organic methods. For major infestations, your only choice is chemical herbicides. Its slender stems move at an unbelievable rate, rooting wherever they touch ground; and any bit of brittle stem overlooked when weeding quickly continues the infestation. When ground ivy infiltrates lawn grass, it may crowd out your prized turf, and it smells peculiar when you mow it.

- **HAND PULL** Weeding out ground ivy is a character-building exercise in patience. It's actually a great way to calm down after a trying day. Use your sensitive, dexterous fingers to lift each strand of stem and pile it onto a ground cloth for disposal in the trash. Be careful not to drop any sprigs, or you'll spread the problem. Combine hand pulling with a pronged hand tool, to expose and help lift out any underground rooting stems. Work with care, because the stems break easily.

- **HERBICIDE** Chemical warfare is often unsuccessful the first time with ground ivy, because the plant is likely to keep growing past a farther rooted point, requiring repeated applications. Be sure to protect ornamentals from the chemical. Follow label directions to ensure safety.

Ipomoea spp.

Morning glories

Morning glories prove the adage that a weed is a plant in the wrong place. A trellis of 'Heavenly Blue' (*Ipomoea tricolor*) may indeed be ethereal, but when self-sown vines are devouring your garden, it's hard to hear the sound of angel trumpets. Luckily, they are simple to control with just a little hand work and preventive maintenance. The quickest recourse is to mount strings on a bean tower for them to climb, so you can pretend they're a happy accident.

Big, silken flowers are the glory of these climbing vines, but the beauty is fleeting: New flowers open each dawn and fade with the noonday sun. Most species have heart-shaped leaves, pointed at the tip, although ivy-leaved morning glory (*I. hederacea*) lives up to its name. The plants climb by twisting their stems around each other and any support they can reach, ever higher until they run out of things to climb. The vines die as soon as they are touched by a hard frost.

- Blossoms are wide, flared trumpets, in beautiful, clear colors that vary depending on species and parentage. They may be blue, pink, rose, deep purple, or white.
- Flowers have a faintly visible "star" outlined within the flaring end of the trumpet.
- Slender, sharply pointed buds of varying maturity are held in clusters or singly at leaf axils.
- Seedlings are distinctive, with a deeply notched pair of first leaves.
- Seedpods are round, inflated capsules, which open to release hard, brown seeds.
- Roots are usually taproots, but in some species large, potato-like tubers form on the roots.

fact file

LIFE CYCLE	annual (*I. pandurata* is perennial but rarely shows up in gardens)
SITE, SOIL & SEASON	full sun; any well-drained soil; blooms summer to frost
DISPERSAL	seeds
ULTIMATE HEIGHT	climbs to about 15 feet
OTHER NAMES	trumpets, wild jalap; *I. pandurata*: man-of-the-earth

Most gardeners are delighted when their morning glories self-sow, guaranteeing a new crop of cheerful flowers for the next season. They're also often taken by surprise when the progeny blooms in a color totally unlike that of the parent plant. That's because some selected varieties, including ever-popular 'Heavenly Blue', revert to their species heritage in following generations, giving rise to purple, pink, or white flowers. Because of their taproots, morning glories are hard to transplant successfully. If you can't enjoy them where they happened to sprout, it's better to plant a new pack of seeds than to attempt relocation. To prevent self-sowing, remove the vines before the seedpods mature and open.

- **GARDEN USE** Supply volunteer morning glories with a trellis, a tepee of twigs, or another support to add height to your garden. Rather than attempting to transplant to a more favourable site, give young plants a few pieces of string to cling to, which guides them to a more suitably situated trellis. Tie one end of the string to a rock, set at the base of the seedlings, and tie the other end to the desired support. As long as the string is angled even slightly upward, the vines will obediently wind themselves along.

Individual morning glory volunteers are quick to hand pull, but a platoon calls for a slightly different strategy. Dispatch a quantity of unwanted morning glories by hoeing them off or burying them alive with a shovelful of mulch. If they sprout on open soil between perennials that are not yet in full growth, your chances are good that the morning glories will quickly be shaded into oblivion once the perennials kick into gear, requiring you to do absolutely nothing.

- **MULCH** Cover seedlings with 2 inches of fine-textured mulch, newspaper topped with shredded bark, or a piece of cardboard cut to cover the space. They'll quickly succumb.

- **HAND PULL** One fast yank and isolated specimens are history.

- **PRUNE** Snip off vines at the soil surface and they are likely to give up the ghost and never regrow.

- **HOE** Slice off young or older plants with a fast swipe at or just below soil level. Then compost the unwanted plants.

Lactuca spp.

Wild lettuce

Little parachutes of wild lettuce can come in on the wind to any small space of open soil. You'll find the prickly leaves sprouting in flower and vegetable beds, in gravel driveways, cracks in sidewalks, and in other unexpected places, although they rarely manage to get a start in lawns. Some species are at home in shade and show up in manicured beds of hostas and impatiens. The plants are definitely weedy-looking, with spiny leaves and tiny flowers that even a mother would be hard pressed to call pretty, but they're highly popular with songbirds, who relish the plentiful seeds.

Wild lettuce looks nothing like those specialty breeds in your refrigerator bin or vegetable garden, but it does share a few characteristics. Like garden lettuce, the sap in wild lettuce is white and milky, bitter with the lactucarium that made the plant popular with old-time herbalists. Leaves are long and slim, usually pointed at the tip and finely toothed at the edges. Most species are extraordinarily tall, perhaps so that their seeds can take to the wind without interference.

- Leaves may be smooth, hairy, or spiny underneath, depending on the species.
- Flowering stem is tall and scraggly, with smaller leaves staggered along its length.
- Flowers are tiny daisies, yellow except for blue lettuce (*L. pulchella*), which is named for the color of its flowers.
- Flowers are held sparsely in open, branching clusters at the top of the very tall stems.
- Flowering stems may be multiple or single.
- Roots are fibrous, unlike the taproot of garden lettuce.
- Seeds are topped by a tuft of short, white hairs, which serve as a parachute to disperse them with the breeze.

Wild foragers seek out wild lettuce early in the spring, to collect the greens for salads and soups. There are much tastier wild weeds available for the picking; wild lettuce leaves quickly become so bitter that they require several changes of water during cooking to make them palatable. The blue flowers of *Lactuca pulchella* add an interesting change of pace in shade gardens, but wild lettuces are usually worthless as ornamental plants. They say "weed" just a bit too loudly. For attracting finches, however, the plants are superb, so you may want to tolerate a few plants in a wild meadow garden to bring birds to your backyard. Medicinally, lettuce is complicated to prepare for internal remedies; you can try daubing the sap on warts for a homemade solution to skin problems.

Only a few plants of wild lettuce are apt to intrude in your garden, and they are easy to remove before they set seed for following generations. The early growth looks something like that of thistles, but isn't nearly so spiny; still, you'll want to wear gloves when working on removal.

- **HAND PULL** A simple, strong, twisting pull will dislodge younger plants, as well as some older plants in deep, loose soil. Compost the remains.

- **HOE** Use a strong, chopping motion to uproot older plants. Toss them on the compost pile if they haven't yet flowered.

fact file

LIFE CYCLE	annual
SITE, SOIL & SEASON	open, dry soil in sun to shade; blooms summer to fall
DISPERSAL	windborne seed
ULTIMATE HEIGHT	up to 7 feet
OTHER NAMES	blue lettuce, fall lettuce, milkweed, tall lettuce, wild opium

Lamium album, L. purpureum

Dead nettle

Qualifiers like deaf, dumb, and dead mean just one thing when it comes to nettles: Unlike stinging nettles (*Urtica dioica*, page 122), they do not sting, as they lack the hairs that inject irritating venom into passersby. They are part of the big and varied mint family and show their heritage with square stems. White dead nettle (*Lamium album*) is a garden plant that occasionally goes bad when it escapes the intended planting bed, while purple dead nettle (*L. purpureum*) is one of the most attention-getting weeds of North America.

- The leaves have scalloped edges, with pointed tips in *L. album* and more roundly pointed tips in *L. purpureum*.
- Tubular, lipped flowers of the typical mint-family shape.
- *L. purpureum* has many bright rose-purple flowers; while *L. album* has less showy, white flowers.
- *L. purpureum* sprouts in fall, grows throughout winter, and blooms as soon as warmer weather sets in.

fact file

LIFE CYCLE	annual
SITE, SOIL & SEASON	sun to partial shade; any well-drained soil; both species bloom in spring
DISPERSAL	*L. album:* underground stems; *L. purpureum:* seed
ULTIMATE HEIGHT	*L. album:* to 2 feet; *L. purpureum:* to 12 inches
OTHER NAMES	*L. album:* deaf nettle or dumb nettle; *L. purpureum:* purple deaf nettle

White dead nettle is usually an invited garden guest. But even if some purple dead nettle creeps in, you've got to look on the bright side while trying to get rid of it: Although a garden full of it may seem to scream "bad housekeeping!" the plants do prevent erosion, and act as a living mulch during freezes and thaws, helping to moderate soil temperatures for the roots of neighboring plants. The flood of rich reddish purple flowers also adds some color to the garden. All are good reasons not to get overly upset by the presence of this ever-present weed.

- **GARDEN USE** Dead nettle flowers are a welcome bright touch in early spring and look good enough to invite in among the white daffodils.

White dead nettle only shows up in unwanted areas if brought in with contaminated, hand-me-down plants, so the enemy designation applies only to its purple-flowered relative, which is a fact of life across most of the United States. One of the most common backyard weeds, purple dead nettle moves into winter beds with a vengeance, covering every inch of bare soil that isn't blanketed by chickweed or dandelions. Because of its abundant seeds, there's no hope of getting rid of it forever. But you can minimize its aggravation with a few simple steps.

- **MULCH** The fastest way to discourage purple dead nettle at any stage of growth—just bury all parts of the plant with a load of fine-textured mulch, so that light can't reach the leaves.

- **HOE** A few fast swipes, and purple dead nettle seedlings are history. Older plants may regrow from the roots, so lift them out with a chop of the hoe blade. Collect and add to the compost pile.

- **HAND HOE** Use this tool in established beds where there's no room to work with a full-size hoe. Chop or cut through the plants below the soil surface, so they don't regrow.

Lemna spp., Wolffia spp.

Duckweed

Duckweed reproduces faster than most plants on Earth, a record that makes other weeds green with envy. Good thing it's so small. However, this aquatic plant multiplies at such a rate that it soon covers almost every available inch of open water. It is a favorite food of ducks and other water dwellers.

From a distance, you may mistake this weed for a green film of algae on the surface. But up close, duckweed is intriguing. The itty-bitty, flat, green leaves support a tiny, fleeting flower, which only those with a magnifying glass or microscope can appreciate. Seeds aren't necessary for reproduction, because duckweed does fine by creating new divisions all by itself. As reproduction is vegetative, the film of green on even the largest pond may be made up of identical clones, all starting from one small but mighty duckweed plant.

- Appears first as small, green dots on the water surface.
- These are the smallest aquatic plants, with a leaf of the largest species checking in at only ⅓ inch long. Others are only a small fraction of that size—truly minuscule.
- Quickly multiplies to cover more and more of the water in a solid sheet of green that is easily broken apart when stirred by a hand or by the breeze.
- May be marked by trails of ducks or other animals that have swum through the mat of floating weeds.
- Threadlike roots trail from underside of leaves, dangling into the water. The tiniest *Wolffia* species are rootless.
- Flowers usually sunken at the edge of the leaf.
- Leaves may be round or elongated and branching, depending on species.

Friend?

Duckweed is a staple for wildlife, which consume vast numbers of the tiny plant in just one gulp. It is also eagerly eaten by pheasants and other land birds that dine at the water's edge. In home gardens, duckweed is fascinating to watch because of its superfast spread. It has a practical use, too: It slows the growth of algae by keeping the water shielded from sun.

- **CONVERSATION PIECE** For a close-up look at the wonders of nature, float a few duckweed plants in a shallow bowl of garden-pool water on the patio table, where you can keep an eye on them as they multiply. By the time you get from first course to after-dinner coffee, the plants will have noticeably increased, amazing one and all.

Foe?

In a small garden pool, duckweed can reach pest proportions in a matter of days. Once it arrives in your water feature, whether on contaminated plant material or on the feet of wild birds or animals, frequent removal is necessary unless you like the look of green rather than clear water.

- **NETS** Use a fine mesh net with a long handle to scoop out the duckweed from your water garden. No matter how thorough you think you are, you're bound to overlook one or two plants—which is all duckweed needs to start a whole new colony. Make the netting operation a once-a-week routine, and you'll be able to keep it under control with very little time and effort. Compost the plants you scoop out.

fact file

LIFE CYCLE	perennial
SITE, SOIL & SEASON	aquatic; any still, fresh water; dies back in cold winters but otherwise visible all year
DISPERSAL	tiny plants cling to bodies of animals and birds and are transferred to new locations; floods also disperse the plants
ULTIMATE HEIGHT	minute; floats flat on surface of water
OTHER NAMES	frogbit, frog's buttons, watermeal

Lonicera japonica

Japanese honeysuckle

The sublime but reviled Japanese honeysuckle earns its weed status because it doesn't know when to stop. In bloom, this vine is unmistakable because of its colorful, tubular blooms and legendary honey-sweet scent. The dense tangle of vines is evergreen in all but the worst cold.

- Stems are bare and woody at the base. Leafy growth begins several feet above ground level.
- Clusters of outward-facing flowers with flared lips grow from leaf axils and at branch tips.
- Flowers are white after opening, soon turning to yellow.
- Rounded, smooth-edged leaves are paired on the stems.
- Smooth, roundish, blue-black fruits in summer to fall.

 fact file

LIFE CYCLE	perennial
SITE, SOIL & SEASON	sun to shade; almost any soil; blooms in late spring to early summer, with occasional flowers into fall
DISPERSAL	seeds dropped by birds and animals; also sends up new plants from spreading roots
ULTIMATE HEIGHT	climbs to 20 feet, sometimes more
OTHER NAMES	gold-and-silver flower, honeysuckle, wild honeysuckle

Friend?

In the garden, the plant is better behaved than in the woods, where there are no pruners or hoes to keep it in check. If you have it, enjoy it. If you don't, weigh the effects on nearby wild lands before you consider planting Japanese honeysuckle in your garden.

- **GARDEN USE** The fragrance of honeysuckle can bring the romantic out in anyone, making it an old-fashioned favorite for planting around porches and sitting areas. Oddly enough, many old honeysuckle vines in gardens never throw up shoots from the roots; well-mannered, they stay in one place. The vine is heavy and needs a sturdy support.

- **WILDLIFE** Hummingbirds are attracted to the nectar-rich blossoms. The dense, tangled stems and thick foliage shelter the nests of catbirds, cardinals, Carolina wrens, and other songbirds. Fruits nourish generations of birds and other wildlife.

- **CRAFT USE** Saplings that have been hugged for a few years by a honeysuckle vine acquire a spiral shape as the unfortunate tree tries to expand within the strong coils of the vine. These young trees are often cut by country folk and craftspeople for making walking sticks.

Foe?

To native plant-lovers and some environmentalists, honeysuckle is anathema. Because it crowds out other plants, the vine is one of the worst scourges of wild areas and is often the object of seek-and-destroy missions by concerned conservation groups. Although rarely problematic in the garden, it may be pesky if your land was recently cleared and still holds the roots of honeysuckle vines. It may even trail along the ground if the plant has no vertical support.

- **SHOVEL** Young plants may be possible to eradicate with a shovel, but, because the roots travel so far, the youngsters may in fact be connected to a massive root system that also holds their parents. Dig all the roots you can, using your hands to pull up the side roots carefully, then monitor for new growth. Dispose of them in the trash.

- **SPOT HERBICIDE** Apply an appropriate herbicide to honeysuckle plants, following label directions. Repeated applications are likely to be necessary.

Malva neglecta, other *Malva* spp.

Mallows

Even prized garden mallows such as the pretty purple-striped *Malva sylvestris* 'Zebrina', occasionally known as high mallow, can be a little too enthusiastic in their self-sowing tendencies. However, the weediest of the mallow clan is the little troublemaker known as low mallow, common mallow, or cheeses (*M. neglecta*).

Five petals with the look of satin are the hallmark of mallows, which usually occur in shades of pink or white. Garden varieties, including the eager self-sower *M. sylvestris,* have medium to large flowers and a bushy, upright habit of growth, but the weedy common mallow (*M. neglecta*) is a smaller-flowered, sprawling plant. Multiply its size by 50 percent and you'd have another interesting ornamental for the garden, but, with flowers too small and too few to notice from a distance, it's relegated to weed status.

- Except in cultivated varieties, mallows usually have a much larger amount of foliage than they do of flowers. Blossoms tend to get lost among the leaves.
- Petals may overlap, but usually show separation at the base. They are usually notched at the tip.
- Leaves are glossy, rich or bright green, and vary in shape by species. Although smaller, they generally resemble the basal leaves of hollyhocks in shape—wide and rounded, with scalloped edges.
- Seeds are arranged as wedges in a circle, like a sliced wheel of cheddar, which is where the weed gets its nickname of "cheeses."
- Root is a slender taproot.

 fact file

LIFE CYCLE	*M. neglecta:* annual or biennial; other species: annual, biennial, or perennial
SITE, SOIL & SEASON	generally full sun; well-drained to dry soil; blooms spring and summer, often into fall
DISPERSAL	seed
ULTIMATE HEIGHT	varies by species; most about 2 feet tall; *M. neglecta:* to about 6 inches from ground
OTHER NAMES	*M. neglecta:* cheese flower, cheeses, common mallow, country mallow, low mallow; *M. sylvestris:* high mallow

Mallows may be overly prolific, but they also add an old-fashioned quality to modern gardens. When your beds are filled with 'Purple Wave' petunias and other particularly floriferous hybrids on the market, it can be a relief to let the eyes rest on a plant with plenty of soothing foliage. The simply shaped flowers also have their own country-garden charm. Mallows have been employed by herbalists for years upon years. The related American globe mallow, *Sphaeralcea angustifolia,* had one of the most unusual uses among medicinal herbs: Its root was used to prevent injury by blade or flame. Traditionally, the tea was drunk before ceremonies by the Sword Swallowers of the Great Fire fraternity of the Zuni tribe in the American West. Hence mallows offer modern herbalists opportunity to appreciate medical history. You could do some medicinal experimentation of your own with high and low mallow—but definitely for decongestion purposes rather than for sword-swallowing performances!

■ **GARDEN USE** Combine taller mallows with daylilies, roses, and other early summer bloomers. Most species have an extended period of bloom that will keep your garden colorful until the next wave of perennial bloom. Lower-growing common mallow is a decent plant to enjoy along stone walls or among the cracks where it likes to settle; it also looks good with the fine lace of white sweet alyssum.

■ **HERBAL USE** Try an infusion of high mallow (*M. sylvestris*) or low mallow (*M. neglecta*) to quiet the cough and relieve the congestion of a summer cold. Crumble about a teaspoon of dried foliage into half a cup of cold water, and let it stand for eight hours. Strain and swallow just one teaspoonful of liquid. Repeat three hours later if needed.

Way back in 1900, in her classic *How to Know the Wild Flowers,* Mrs. William Dana Starr was already complaining about high mallow (*Malva neglecta*): It "overruns the country dooryards and village waysides," she wrote. That's still the case today, except that the weed has increased its territory to include cracks in city streets and suburbia. Although it usually isn't abundant, it is quite common. For those not inclined to harvest the plants for medicinal use, the solution is simple:

■ **HAND PULL** Grasp the plant at its base, gathering all stems in your hand, and use a steady twisting motion to uproot *M. neglecta.* Taller mallows also are fairly easy to yank, even at flowering stage.

Employ a dandelion fork to give some extra leverage if needed. Compost the plants.

■ **TROWEL** Dig up mallows with a sturdy hand tool. Insert the blade beside the root, bend the handle backward, and pry the root out, while simultaneously pulling on the plant.

■ **TRANSPLANTING (OR POACHER'S) SPADE** If your hand strength is limited, use a narrow-bladed shovel to uproot mallows in established beds.

Medicago lupulina

Black medic

Diminutive black medic hardly looks as if it could be a major frustration to gardeners, but this little, yellow-flowered clover relative is tenacious. It is also tough to uproot, despite the shallowness of its taproot. The bright yellow flowers dotted along its stems draw attention in lawns, disrupting from the clean sweep of green. Black medic quickly insinuates itself into lawn grass and runs rampant in garden beds, and may also crop up in gravel driveways or cracks in paving. Because of its generous seed production, it's vital to catch black medic when it's still young.

Pinpoint this common weed by its ground-hugging habit, its clover-like leaves on long, wiry stems, and its bright yellow bumbles of flowers. The flowers are borne for weeks or months, with new buds forming almost constantly as older blooms mature into heads of brown seeds. Growth habit varies: Seeds may sprout in fall with plants growing over winter and flowering in spring, like other winter annual weeds, or it may be a perennial presence in the backyard.

- A prostrate plant with long stems that stay at soil level.
- Central leaflet is stalked while side leaflets occur close to the stem.
- Leaves are shaped like three-leaf clovers, and are less than an inch across.
- Spheres of tiny, bright yellow flowers, like tiny clover blossoms.
- Seeds turn black when ripe.
- Skinny taproot with many fibrous side roots to help anchor it.

fact file

LIFE CYCLE	usually annual or biennial, but may also be perennial
SITE, SOIL & SEASON	sprouts in any sunny space; grows in almost any moist to dry soil; blooms spring to fall and may stay green into winter
DISPERSAL	seed
ULTIMATE HEIGHT	slinks close to the ground; creeping stems can reach 2 feet outward
OTHER NAMES	none

Although you are never going to view black medic as what you would call desirable, you can choose to look on the bright side if its little, unwanted yellow heads keep popping up unexpectedly. While trying to rid your garden of it, concentrate on its flowers and foliage, which are, after all, very pretty; consider how its seeds have some value for birds and rodents; and think about the nitrogen-enriching effect it can have on your soil.

■ **GARDEN USE** Black medics have tiny sacs, or nodules, of nitrogen attached to the roots, which increase the nitrogen content of your soil. Its deep root systems also help reduce compaction.

Don't call for this medic when you're feeling poorly. Although its name seems to suggest healing abilities, it actually refers to its geographical origins. The "medic" aspect stems from the Greek word for its relative alfalfa, which originated in an ancient country called Media, near present-day Iran. Black medic is tenacious and requires much patience to eradicate by organic methods, especially when it insinuates itself into lawn grass.

■ **HAND PULL** Pull only when the soil is thoroughly moist. Use a dandelion digger for extra leverage at the root. Compost the nitrogen-rich plants.

■ **SPOT HERBICIDE** Apply appropriate product to black medic plants, following directions on the label.

■ **PRE-EMERGENT HERBICIDE** Treat lawns according to label directions to keep new black medic plants from sprouting.

Myosotis spp.

Forget-me-not

Many gardeners welcome the exuberant, self-sowing tendencies of these perky blue flowers. But in regions with cooler summers and around water, forget-me-nots can actually achieve the weed list. It's the annuals that are most problematic. They shed seeds freely, and the seeds spread fast as water carries them downstream. In the garden, forget-me-nots require little effort to get back in bounds.

Forget-me-not plants are nondescript, but the flowers are instantly recognizable. The tiny blooms are borne in a curling spike that curls at the tip like a scorpion's tail. Most have bright, light blue flowers sporting a yellow eye in the center of each blossom. Bloom lasts for months. Allegedly, the leaf is as soft as a mouse's ear, in case you can find a small rodent patient enough to let you test for yourself.

- Tiny, five-petaled blossoms are spaced closely along the end of each flowering stem.
- Flowering stems are strongly downward-curled at the tip, forming a coil at bud stage that looks like a sleeping snake or a scorpion's tail.
- Leaves vary according to species but are usually softly furred, long and narrow, with a round tip.
- Plant form may be a tidy clump or a sprawl of loose-branched stems.
- Seeds form as flowers drop off along the stem; held outward on very thin stems, they become more widely spaced and noticeable as the flowering stem elongates.
- Thrives in water as well as in average garden soil.

fact file

LIFE CYCLE	weedy species are usually annual
SITE, SOIL & SEASON	often along or in water; wet to average soil in sun to shade; blooms in spring for several weeks
DISPERSAL	seed
ULTIMATE HEIGHT	most species are about 1 foot tall, and tend to relax into mounded clumps
OTHER NAMES	mouse ear, scorpion grass, snake grass

Friend?

Forget-me-nots are not likely to crop up in your yard unless a stream or other natural waterway runs through it. Usually they start out as desired garden plants, as they are perfect for planting around spring bulbs. Although you may soon have a much bigger crowd of plants than you intended when you sprinkled the first seeds, forget-me-nots are hard to stay mad at: Their bright blue (and occasionally pink or white) flowers provide a modest but charming backdrop for bigger garden flowers—so make the most of them. Hand pull, hoe off, or mulch over any unwanted plants.

- **GARDEN USE** Collect stems before seeds fall. Sprinkle them over an area newly planted with daffodils or tulips; they will soften the bare stems of the bolder flowers. Enjoy their serendipity as they self-sow among other ornamentals, or let them line a garden pool or spill over a shady rock wall. Transplant misplaced seedlings to the area around a faucet or birdbath, where they will thrive in the extra water.

Onopordum acanthium, other spp.

Scotch thistle

Large, spectacular and ultra-spiny, the Scottish national symbol has dramatic presence, even among other members of the attention-getting thistle family. A native of western Europe, it has spread by windborne parachute seeds that have sailed into the western United States, where it is vilified as a noxious weed. Occasionally it may take root in garden beds or driveways, or sneak into naturalized meadow gardens and dryland gardens. Several similar species are grouped under the name "Scotch thistle."

Scotch thistle lives up to its nickname of "giant thistle." A single plant may tower 9 feet tall and 6 feet wide, and leaves may reach up to 2 feet long and a foot wide. Gray leaves, cut into coarse, spine-tipped lobes, form a rosette the first year of this weed's life. In the second year, an erect yellow stem emerges, flagged with noticeable "wings" on the sides, and softly furred as well as stoutly spined. The flowers, in the typical thistle shape, may be white or purple.

- Giant-sized, branching, spiny plant.
- Leaves are covered with wooly or cottony hairs, which make them look gray-green from a distance.
- Main stems can be up to 4 inches wide at the base.
- Big, yellow spines on leaves.
- Flowers are borne either solitary or in groups of two or three at the branch tips.
- Blossoms may be dark pink to lavender purple, and are held within a big, bulbous base.
- Flower heads mature to fluffy white seedheads, each seed attached to a plume that will carry it off on the breeze.
- Most common in regions with dry summers.
- Thick, strong taproot may reach a foot deep.

fact file

LIFE CYCLE	biennial; sometimes annual
SITE, SOIL & SEASON	sunny sites; average to dry soil; blooms in summer
DISPERSAL	seed
ULTIMATE HEIGHT	to 9 feet
OTHER NAMES	giant thistle

Lore has it that the Scotch thistle saved Scotland. Vikings were sneaking up for attack when they stumbled into a patch of the prickly plants. Their cries of pain alerted Scotland's defenders, enabling them to save the country from takeover!

- **CULINARY USE** Artichokes are the unopened buds of a thistle plant, and Scotch thistle can be eaten this way. But harvest and preparation call for extreme caution. If you try it, steam until tender and eat with lemon butter; do not consume the immature tuft of flowers (the "choke," so-called for good reason).

- **GARDEN USE** Garden thistle is still enjoyed occasionally as a garden ornamental. Its towering height, huge leaves, and contrasting gray color all grab the eye. It's a great companion for ornamental grasses and casts a cool glow in an all-white garden.

Dense stands of the huge, prickly plants can cut off cattle from grazing land and even from water, which is why this plant is so reviled in the western part of America. Scotch thistle spreads super-fast, thanks to its windborne seeds. The plants quickly colonize any area where they find an undisturbed roothold.

- **SHOVEL** Slice off the rosette below soil surface, removing every single leaf. Dispose of it in the trash.

- **HERBICIDE** Spot treatment with an appropriate herbicide is also effective, although repeated applications are usually necessary. Dispose of the remains in the trash to prevent accidental prickings.

- **BIOLOGICAL CONTROL** Research is underway to find a natural pest of the Scotch thistle.

Oxalis stricta, other *Oxalis* spp.

Yellow wood sorrel

A familiar weed to anyone who has ever mowed the grass or weeded a garden, yellow wood sorrel (*Oxalis stricta*) is one of the most widespread weeds in the world. The rate at which it reproduces and its reappearance, year after year, make it less than welcome in most backyards. But at least it usually shows up as scattered plants, rather than in solid stands. It's your choice whether to fight the inevitable or learn to tolerate this commoner. Other *Oxalis* species are rarely troublesome in the home garden or lawn; they are less adaptable and less vigorous, and usually embraced when they do turn up.

Look for a dainty nosegay of clover leaves, usually folded instead of opened flat, topped by many yellow, five-petaled blossoms, and you've found yellow wood sorrel. The members of the *Oxalis* genus are unrelated to the much bigger, coarser sheep sorrel (*Rumex* spp.), but they do share the same sharply sour flavor when a leaf is nibbled—a clue to the presence of oxalic acid. Toxic in larger amounts, the tangy acid makes sorrel leaves a treasured (but sparingly used) ingredient to spark up salads of usually bland wild greens.

- The clover-shaped leaves are often partially closed.
- The half-inch-wide flowers are dandelion-yellow.
- Plant grows as a bouquet of stems, each about 6 inches tall, with leaves and flowers held on threadlike stems.
- Flowers mature to long, skinny, erect seedpods, at first green but turning brown as they ripen.
- Seedpods split with force, ejecting many brown seeds.
- Roots are taproots; stems also root near the main plant.

fact file

LIFE CYCLE	perennial
SITE, SOIL & SEASON	highly adaptable; sunny, moist to dry soil; blooms spring through fall
DISPERSAL	seed
ULTIMATE HEIGHT	to 6 inches
OTHER NAMES	Indian sorrel, sheep clover, sheep sorrel, sourgrass

Foe?

Ubiquitous *Oxalis* hardly ever shows up in numbers large enough to crowd out desirable plants. In flower beds, you can appreciate it as a determined wild thing and let the plants grow, or you can evict it. In lawns, however, it's an undesirable, because its height and color affect the uniform appearance of a well-groomed greensward. Wood sorrel is also fond of cropping up in gravel driveways and between pavers. Hand pulling is surprisingly difficult; the plants usually snap off at ground level, leaving the perennial roots to resprout. Use hand tools to gain the advantage and remove the plants entirely.

- **DANDELION FORK** Firmly grab a cluster of the *Oxalis* plant stems in one hand and use a dandelion digger to pry out the root from the lawn or garden bed. Compost what you manage to uproot.

- **TROWEL** Use the same method as with a dandelion fork. Shake off extra soil, then compost.

- **PRE-EMERGENT HERBICIDE** Apply an appropriate product to prevent yellow wood sorrel from infesting the lawn. Follow label directions.

- **SPOT HERBICIDE** Use an herbicide to spray or dab stray *Oxalis* plants in paving cracks or gravel areas.

Phytolacca americana
Pokeweed

This huge plant is striking in both form and color, the perfect ornamental citizen—except that you'll never have just one. Tolerate a pokeweed plant past fruiting stage, and next year you'll have dozens or hundreds to deal with.

A mature poke plant is no challenge to spot—its sheer size, along with its thick, brilliant magenta stems (in fall) and its drooping clusters of black berries are the giveaway. Even the leaves of younger specimens can reach 12 inches long.

- Flowers are small, whitish green, arise near upper leaves, and usually go unnoticed among the forest of foliage.
- Juicy, black berries leave purple stains when smashed.
- Unique rank odor evident when the foliage is bruised.
- Sparingly branched stems can be 4 inches in diameter.
- Leaves are long, pointed ovals, held on the branches by stems that themselves can be 4 inches long.
- Roots are huge taproots, up to 6 inches in diameter and several feet deep.

fact file

LIFE CYCLE	perennial
SITE, SOIL & SEASON	sun to shade; adaptable but most common in deep, fertile, moist to dry soil; dies back to root in winter, but dead skeleton persists
DISPERSAL	seed dispersal by berry-loving birds
ULTIMATE HEIGHT	usually 5 to 6 feet, but can reach 12 feet
OTHER NAMES	inkberry, poke, poke sallet, skoke

Pokeweed supports many songbirds with the insects on its foliage and more so with its immense bounty of juicy fruits. The berries ripen at the time of fall migration, succoring many hungry songbirds on the move. Flocks of robins, cedar waxwings, bluebirds, tanagers, and many other species are drawn to a plant of ripe fruit. Berries not eaten during the fall are collected over winter by birds, mice, and other wildlife. The earliest spring shoots are also eagerly sought by human diners, who cook the greens like spinach. Beware of experimenting, however: Poke contains several deadly poisons.

- **GARDEN USE** Pokeweed is too prolific to plant in any but the wildest gardens. If you have a corner where it and its many offspring can go wild, drop a few berries there or nurture the seedlings that will no doubt show up. The purple stems are outstanding with bleached ornamental grasses in fall.

- **WILDLIFE** Let a few plants grow in a meadow garden or shady woodland garden, and you'll be repaid by sightings of fabulous songbirds.

Poke is poison, although this didn't stop early settlers and Indians from eating and using the plant. Its leaves, roots, and seeds are tainted with powerful toxins that can kill an adult human being in short order. If you come from a long line of wild foragers and know when to pick and how to prepare the plant, continued good luck. If you're an interested novice, never mind—too many safe edible weeds exist to risk this one. Because of its toxicity, poke is dangerous to harbor if you have small children, to whom the berries are very tempting.

- **SHOVEL** Dig deep to sever the roots and lift the plant. Move the carcass aside, then dig again to extract broken pieces of root, which can sprout new plants. Wear long sleeves and gloves to handle poke. Dispose of plant parts in the trash and avoid touching skin until you wash thoroughly.

- **HAND PULL** Single scattered seedlings are easy to dispense with by simple hand pulling when they are less than about 2 feet tall; the taproot pulls out with one satisfying yank. Dispose of plants in the trash.

- **HOE** Scrape off flocks of seedlings with a swipe of the hoe blade just below the surface of the soil.

Plantago spp.
Plantain

Plantains are ultracommon weeds of grassy areas as well as gardens. Broadleaf plantain (*Plantago major*) and English plantain (*P. lanceolata*) are the two major culprits, sneaking into yards across North America, accompanied by a few other similar species. All have thick, low-growing rosettes of leaves, from which erupt a group of flowering stems at bloom season. These are an annoyance to lawn lovers because they rise above the grass.

Plantain leaves may be wide or narrow, but all have strongly pronounced veins that run the length of the leaf, creating distinct ridges that gave the plants the nickname "dog's ribs." At flowering time, the stems become topped with tiny, nubbly, closely packed flowers and seed capsules. The two most widespread species are easy to discern at this time, because their form is very different.

- *P. major* produces wide, rounded oval leaves with sturdy stems; *P. lanceolata* bears slender, long leaves.
- *P. major* has flowering spikes covered from the top to near the bottom with packed green nubbles; *P. lanceolata* has mostly bare flowering stems, with only a pointed, conelike cluster at the top of the bare stem; fuzzy white flowers open in rows from bottom to top.
- Leaves of *P. major* are smooth and have a slight gleam; leaves of *P. lanceolata* often have a dusty look.
- Wooly plantain (*P. patagonica*), a southwestern species, resembles *P. major* but has softly furred leaves and flowering stems.
- Roots are fibrous.

fact file

LIFE CYCLE	perennial
SITE, SOIL & SEASON	sun to partial shade; almost any soil; flowerheads emerge in summer to fall
DISPERSAL	seed
ULTIMATE HEIGHT	leaves are low; stalks to about 10 inches
OTHER NAMES	*P. lanceolata:* buckhorn plantain, chimney sweeps, dog's ribs, hock cockle, lance-leaved plantain, rub grass; *P. major:* broadleaf plantain, dooryard plantain, round-leaved plantain, whiteman's foot

Plantains are useful forage plants for wild and domestic animals. Rabbits, pigs, horses, and other herbivores are fond of the tasty foliage. Plantains also figure in herbal lore, and are still used in folk and modern medicine. Psyllium seed, the basis of Metamucil laxative, is harvested from *Plantago afra,* a Eurasian species. Buckeye butterflies and some moths use plantain plants as a host for their caterpillars, which devour the leaves.

- **HERBAL USE** Turn to the pages of Shakespeare's *Romeo and Juliet,* and you'll find Romeo himself recommending plantain for a shin injury. The leaves have astringent properties, and thus cool minor cuts and scrapes. Try it yourself by mashing a plantain leaf and holding it against poison ivy rash or a bee sting. In several minutes, you should notice a lessening of pain and itch.

- **CHILDREN'S GAMES** Before the days of television, kids would challenge each other with flower stalks of English plantain, each trying to knock off the "head" of the other's stalk.

Plantains followed along in the footsteps of man, taking root along with the expanding civilization. Today they are one of the most common garden pests, flourishing in the rich soil of vegetable plots and flower beds as well as staking a claim in sunny lawns. The plants are surprisingly easy to evict, especially if you use a hand tool for leverage aid.

- **HAND PULL** Firmly pull up young or established plants, giving a twist of your wrist as you exert pressure. Work only when the soil is moist.

- **DANDELION FORK** In lawns, use a skinny, bladed dandelion fork to help lift plantains from the grass. Poke the tool at an angle beneath the plant, and grasp the leaves in one hand while you pry with the tool. Compost the weeds.

- **TROWEL** Use a sturdy trowel to lift plantains from flower beds. Shake off the soil, then toss the weed on the compost pile.

- **SPOT HERBICIDE** If hand pulling is unsuccessful or infestation is severe, apply weedkiller to plantains in cracks of paving or in gravel areas. Follow label directions.

Poa annua

Annual meadow grass

Thank your lucky stars if you're pestered by this annual grass instead of bermudagrass (*Cynodon dactylon*) and other spreading perennial pest grasses: Its small tufts are exceedingly easy to evict from gardens and lawns. Quick to sprout and flower, it shows up here and there in niches of open soil, often beside the doorstep, or in the gravel of driveways and mulch. Seeds sprout and grow throughout the year except during very hot weather, when the plants usually disappear for a few months.

This plant often goes unnoticed until it's in bloom, with small flowerheads radiating outward from the low, tidy tuft of grass. Although it can achieve a sizable height in rich soil, it is usually so small that it is overlooked completely—not a problem since it doesn't compete with other plants. To make sure of its identity, take a close look at the tip of a leaf blade: It's shaped like the prow of a mini canoe.

- Grows rapidly from seed; flowers in as little as six weeks.
- Most annual meadow grasses bloom in early to mid spring, but depending on when they germinated, they may flower any time through late fall.
- Flowers are held in a branching panicle; the flowering head is usually about ½ to 1 inch long.
- Seen from above, the flowers, which are lighter green than the foliage, radiate above the tufted plant like a loosely held, little bouquet.
- Roots are fibrous.

fact file

LIFE CYCLE	annual
SITE, SOIL & SEASON	sun to light shade; almost any soil; individual plants may be seen in bloom from spring through late fall
DISPERSAL	seed
ULTIMATE HEIGHT	usually low, growing to about 4 inches, but can reach 20 inches
OTHER NAMES	annual bluegrass, dwarf meadowgrass, low speargrass, May grass, six-weeks grass

Friend?

If annual meadow grass were rarer, or perhaps perennial, it would be a prized garden plant among connoisseurs of understated charm. The dainty tuffets are tidy and well-shaped, and the outward spray of flowers, although small in size, is noticeable even from standing height. If annual meadow grass doesn't crop up in just the right place, transplant the clumps before they are in flower: Lift beneath the plant with a wide-bladed trowel, settle in a more favorable spot, and water well.

- **GARDEN USE** This diminutive grass grows well in sun or shade, making it usable in all kinds of gardens. Enjoy its serendipitous appearance in shade gardens, where it offers fine texture to contrast with the usual hostas and impatiens. Or try it as an edging for a sunny border. For an interesting garden arrangement, use annual meadow grass as a companion for deep blue Siberian iris (*Iris sibirica* 'Caesar's Brother'), or let it dot a patchy lawn along with violets. Other good companions for meadow grass include: roses, perennial geraniums, pansies and violas (especially yellow, white, or blue shades), mini-daffodils, impatiens, bedding geraniums (especially salmon or bright red), and coral bells.

Foe?

Too bad all weeds don't behave like annual meadow grass! Although you may be pestered by a bountiful sprinkling of these small, thick tufts, you'll soon discover that they tend to "disappear" before you get too annoyed. That's because the life cycle of this plant is compressed into just several short weeks. From seed to bloom takes only six weeks, and the plant's demise follows soon after. Leave the plant in place, and it will soon mature and disappear on its own. Of course, it will also produce a crop of seed for additional plants next year, so you may choose to evict it instead of following the laissez-faire approach.

- **HAND PULL** Grasp the tuft at its base and give a quick yank to uproot the plant. Shake off any clinging soil and toss the plant on the compost pile.

- **HAND HOE** Use a sharp-bladed hand tool to lift out the tuft. Toss it upside down and leave it to decay in place, or gather the tufts for composting.

- **HOE** Remove several plants with a quick chop and lift. Compost, or let the remains decompose in place.

Polygonum spp., *Persicaria* spp.

Knotweed, lady's-thumb, smartweed

These plants are recognized as relatives by their distinctive, swollen, jointed stems, from which the genus gets its name (*Polygonum* means "many knees"). Depending on which source you consult, smartweeds may be listed as Polygonum or Persicaria as experts have reclassified them over the years.

Most of this clan share similar flowers, bearing long, thin, nubbly spikes of tiny blooms. In fall, the plants often take on an attractive, red color. Plants tend to spring up in numbers.

- Closely-packed spikes of tiny flowers appear to be a haze of color from a distance, rather than individual blossoms.
- Flowers are deep to pale pink or white.
- Flower parts keep color even while seed is maturing.
- Erect or drooping flowerheads are 1 to 4 inches long.
- Leaves are thin and pointed. Lady's thumb (*Persicaria virginiana*) bears a reddish-black, heart-shaped "fingerprint" on each leaf (some believe the Virgin Mary pulled up, tasted and threw away a plant, leaving her thumbprint on the leaf).
- Stems are long and usually sprawl along the ground, with flowering stems held up. Plants may also be tall, or climbing, depending on species.
- Taproot; some species also sprout roots along the stems.

fact file

LIFE CYCLE	most annual, some perennial
SITE, SOIL & SEASON	sun or shade; wet or dry soils and even in water; blooms summer through fall
DISPERSAL	seed
ULTIMATE HEIGHT	depends on species; may be prostrate to 3 feet tall
OTHER NAMES	arsesmart, beggarweed, birdweed, blackheart, devil's shoestring, false buckwheat, heart's ease, knotgrass, lover's pride, pull-down, red shanks

These widespread weeds are a prime source of food for songbirds. Species with showy flowers also are ornamental in the garden; their form is best suited for casual plantings. In years past, the young shoots and roots were added to the diets of various peoples, and the abundant seeds were eaten whole or ground for flour. Herbalists once used the plants to treat various "female disorders," including menstrual problems, but their possibly irritating juice is too risky to experiment with.

- **WILDLIFE** This is an important winter food for small animals. Sparrows, finches, and many other birds nibble the seeds from fall through winter. If you tolerate smartweeds and knotweeds in areas like meadow gardens, you're likely to increase your fall and winter bird sightings.

- **GARDEN USE** To add a relaxed line and late-season color, allow a few smartweeds and knotweeds to wend their way among perennials. Lady's thumb (*Persicaria virginiana*) is a showy species for shade gardens, with white flowers that spray outward like fireworks. The shorter, pink-flowered Pennsylvania smartweed (*Polygonum pensylvanicum*) makes a colorful partner in front of fountain grass (*Pennisetum* spp.) and other bleached, fall-color ornamental grasses.

Take comfort in your fight against these weeds: Everybody has them. Seeds linger for years in soil or are spread by birds, so the plants crop up everywhere. Most are not frustrating to control: Hoeing, mulching, or competition from other plants quickly put them in their place. A notable exception is prostrate knotweed or knotgrass (*Polygonum aviculare*), which is common in less-than-perfect lawns, along driveways, and in paving cracks. A ground-hugging species, it has an unusually deep taproot and tough, wiry stems, making it hard to hand pull. Unfortunately, so-called "smartweeds" won't boost your I.Q.: Arsesmart (*Persicaria hydropiper*) and others get their name from the propensity of some species to cause bare skin to sting and burn (watch where you sit—or what you use for cleanup—was the lesson quickly learned from arsesmart). A toxin in the leaves does the trick, and in olden days the plants were used to bring fish to the surface in distress. It's tricky to tell one species from another, so it's better to play it safe and use gloves to handle these plants.

- **HAND PULL** Gather the stems at the point where they emerge from the soil, then pull with a steady pressure. Collect and dispose of any stray stems, which may root.

- **HOE** Scrape off crops of seedlings with the blade of a hoe, slicing just below soil surface. Hoe out established plants with a chop-and-lift motion.

- **MULCH** Pile 2 inches of mulch over seedlings or young plants, and they are quickly discouraged.

- **SPOT HERBICIDE** Apply to plants in cracks of paving, where it is important not to disturb the brick or other paving. Spot herbicides also are useful in gravel areas. Follow label directions.

- **IMPROVE THE LAWN** Repair any bare patches in your lawn to prevent colonization by knotweed (*Polygonum aviculare*). Or, just be thankful for the greenery it brings to tough conditions.

Portulaca oleracea

Purslane

Purslane's road map to success is written in its leaves: The tart, tasty leaves are plump and juicy, full of stored moisture to keep the plant lush green through even the worst dry spells. This ground-hugger usually crops up in sunny flower or vegetable gardens, or wiggles its way into patios or the cracks in paved paths. It's one of the least objectionable weeds, both because of its understated good looks—which make it worth consideration as a summer groundcover—and the ease with which it can be evicted. Because it grows so low to the ground, you probably won't even notice the plant until it has already formed a good-sized mat of foliage. And then you're likely to mistake it for an invited garden guest. Spring azures and other small butterflies adore the flowers.

The rounded, juicy stems break easily. The five-petaled flowers are readily overlooked, because their small size—only ¼ inch across—and pale yellow color get lost among the leaves. You need to be an early bird to catch them in the first place: They're open for only a few hours in the morning.

- Rounded to oval leaves are about an inch long and have a unique, thick, fleshy appearance, similar to those of the jade plant houseplant but lighter green in color.
- Leaves appear singly on stems but clustered at tips.
- Smooth, juicy stems sprawl outward from the main root and may extend to 10 inches.
- Seeds form in small capsules that open in a unique way, best appreciated with a magnifying glass: The lid of the capsule opens neatly to release the small dark seeds.
- Broken bits of stem or leaves may take root if they fall on bare ground.
- Killed by frost, purslane withers to nothing and disappears as the water that gave it substance evaporates.

 fact file

LIFE CYCLE	annual
SITE, SOIL & SEASON	dry soil in full sun; blooms are barely noticeable
DISPERSAL	seed
ULTIMATE HEIGHT	prostrate
OTHER NAMES	pressley, pursley, pussley

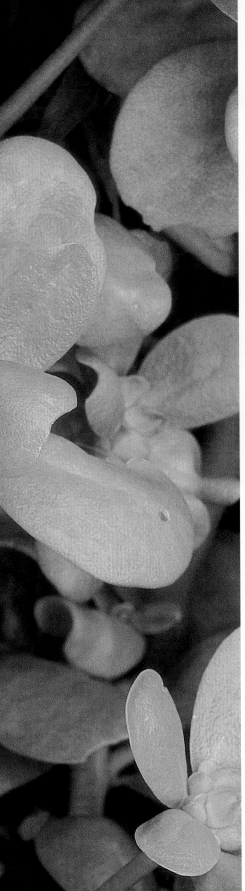

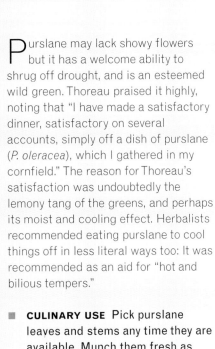

Purslane may lack showy flowers but it has a welcome ability to shrug off drought, and is an esteemed wild green. Thoreau praised it highly, noting that "I have made a satisfactory dinner, satisfactory on several accounts, simply off a dish of purslane (*P. oleracea*), which I gathered in my cornfield." The reason for Thoreau's satisfaction was undoubtedly the lemony tang of the greens, and perhaps its moist and cooling effect. Herbalists recommended eating purslane to cool things off in less literal ways too: It was recommended as an aid for "hot and bilious tempers."

■ **CULINARY USE** Pick purslane leaves and stems any time they are available. Munch them fresh as you garden, for quick, easy refreshment. Scatter leaves and bite-size stem pieces in green salads for a juicy, tart crunch, or steam as you would spinach. Go one better than your foodie friends and serve potatoes mashed with steamed purslane instead of garlic. As more adventurous foods gain in popularity, purslane is showing up at American grocery counters, but it has been popular in Europe, China, India, and Mexico for many centuries.

■ **GARDEN USE** An ideal plant to encourage in a hot, sunny garden, where it adds a welcome, cooling touch of green at ground level during the dog days of summer. Its mat of foliage has a softening effect on flagstone patios, although the juicy leaves crush easily under foot traffic. Grows well in containers, too; plant it in a pot with yellow pear or red cherry tomatoes for instant salad fixin's.

■ **WILDLIFE** Purslane's seeds are small, but songbirds, chipmunks, and other small animals nevertheless seek them out. Other birds also may nibble at the leaves, especially during dry spells when water is scarce.

Purslane has a life cycle that runs in fast motion. Within a few weeks after sprouting, the plant is already ripening seed. Its survival-of-the-species instincts are finely honed, too—not only does it sprout roots from any overlooked bit of leaf or stem, but it also continues to ripen its seeds even after the plant is pulled from the soil. Usually, however, the plants are not numerous enough to cause serious infestation problems.

■ **HAND PULL** The plant takes little effort to pull from moist soil, but in hard, dry ground the stems are likely to snap off, leaving the roots to regrow. Weed it out after a thorough watering or a rain. Be careful to remove every bit of plant that breaks off during the operation; like many other succulent plants, purslane will easily root from pieces of stem or leaves that fall to the ground.

■ **HOE** If you have a good eye and a sure swing, you can uplift entire clumps of purslane with one swift stroke. Remove from the garden so they don't reroot.

■ **MULCH** Cover even mature plants with 2 inches of organic mulch or with a piece of cardboard. The plants will quickly die when blocked off from all light.

■ **SPOT HERBICIDE** If you are unable to hand pull purslane from gravel or paved areas, you may decide to spray or dab it with an appropriate weedkiller, being sure to follow label instructions.

Potamogeton spp.

Pondweed

Unless you have a water feature in your yard, you'll never have to concern yourself wth the presence of pondweeds in your garden. These plants are strictly aquatic, growing with their stems completely underwater. They supply homes for snails and shelter for minnows, as well as food for water dwellers, and a natural check on the balance of nutrients in the water. But in a backyard pool or pond, they can quickly wear out their welcome, due to their habit of fast growth.

Pondweed is rooted in the mud at the bottom of a pool, but the bulk of the plant floats gracefully near the water's surface. Many branching stems travel in all directions below the surface, forming a willowy thicket of thin, flexible stems. Leaf shape varies according to species, but in most species the leaves are long and ribbony. Flowers are packed onto spikes and mature into brown, sometimes spiny seeds.

- Leaves may be attached to their own stems or snugged tightly to the main stems; floating or submerged.
- Leaf veins run lengthwise.
- A usually stringy or hairy leaflike structure is attached at the base of each leaf or leaf stem.
- Flowers are held above water to be pollinated by wind.
- Under a magnifying glass, flowers have a repeated four-parted structure, reminiscent of kaleidoscope patterns.
- Seeds have a prominent "beak" at one end; they may be brown, red, or grayish.
- Fine, short aquatic roots occur at joints along the stems.
- Underground roots are often creeping, extending the plant's territory in the body of water.

 fact file

LIFE CYCLE	perennial
SITE, SOIL & SEASON	aquatic; thrives in streams, ponds, garden pools, and other bodies of deep or shallow fresh water
DISPERSAL	seed; bits of broken-off plants
ULTIMATE HEIGHT	stems, which are submerged, may reach 3 feet long
OTHER NAMES	*Potamogeton foliosus:* leafy pondweed *P. nodosus:* American pondweed *P. pusillus:* small pondweed

Friend?

Not as frou-frou as some species of aquatics, such as the frilly parrot's feather, pondweed is a rugged American native worth inviting to a garden pool. It will give fish a place to hide from predators like herons and raccoons, and it will help oxygenate the water.

■ **GARDEN USE** Drop a start of the plant into a pool, and nature will take it from there. Commercial distributors also sell seed specially weighted in clay balls so that it sinks and roots quickly. The spiky flowers are a pleasant contrast to water lilies and other larger surface plants.

■ **WILDLIFE** Ducks, marsh birds, and shore birds eat the plants and seeds. Fish seek out the plants to devour the many small water creatures living among the vegetation. Sago pondweed (*Potamogeton pectinatus*) produces tubers below ground that are a favorite food of pintails, teal, and many other ducks.

Foe?

Pondweed multiplies fast, and once in your pond it's difficult to get out. Seeds are likely to arrive on the feet of visiting wildlife, however, so your best course is to learn how to manage it once you recognize its sinuous strands. In large ponds, control is practically impossible because of the dangers of herbicides to aquatic life; eventually, the succession of vegetation in the pond will swing toward a more balanced state.

■ **RAKE** Use a metal rake or special-purpose water garden tool with a long handle to remove excess pondweed from the water. You're likely to snag snails and other aquatic life with the weeds, but all will decompose into nutritious compost when tossed onto your pile. Combine well with other vegetation to prevent unpleasant odors.

Potentilla spp.

Cinquefoil

Purse your lips and say it the French way: "Sank foil." It means "five leaves," and those five lobes of each compound leaf—count 'em—are the identifying characteristic of these varied plants. It's easy to be charmed by cinquefoils, but many a gardener has cultivated one of these weeds and been disappointed as they have a very brief burst of bloom.

The leaves of cinquefoils look like an outspread hand. The leaflets are arranged in a widespread, rounded outline and have saw-toothed edges—quite like a strawberry leaf at first glance. The blossoms are borne singly or in loose clusters, and flowers are usually yellow. Over 500 species of cinquefoil roam the world, so habit varies considerably.

- Plant is erect, sprawling, or ground-hugging form, depending on the species.
- Rough cinquefoil (*P. norvegica*), a common species, has leaves that appear three-parted; the other two leaflets are small and separated from the rest.
- Leaves are paler on the undersides than on top, sometimes with a silvery cast below.
- Flowers have five petals, interspersed with pointed green "calyx lobes" that are nearly as long as the petals.
- A short, shaggy tuft of many stamens is in the center of each flower.
- Plant is related to roses and strawberries, and some species, including *P. recta*, bear fruits. Flowers of the non-fruit-bearing species mature into bunches of dry seeds.
- Taproot; running stems may extend above ground.
- Dead stems remain over winter; new growth reappears from the root in spring.

fact file

LIFE CYCLE	biennial or perennial
SITE, SOIL & SEASON	usually in full sun; in average to dry soil; blooms in summer
DISPERSAL	seed, spreading stems or runners that root at tips
ULTIMATE HEIGHT	varies by species; many are about 2 feet
OTHER NAMES	creeping Jenny, finger leaf, five-fingered grass, five fingers, starflower, tormentil

Friend?

In days of yore, those with an aching tooth were exceedingly grateful to cinquefoil, which was used as a soothing mouthwash, among other useful remedies. As well as being good for your health, cinquefoils can contribute well to a wild or informal garden. Specialists have now selected or hybridized various representatives for garden use.

- **GARDEN USE** Old field cinquefoil (*P. canadensis*), an American species, has lovely, sulfur-yellow flowers, big enough to make a pretty show with blue chicory and other field flowers of early summer. It also adds unusual color to a cottage garden bed of bachelor's buttons and annual poppies. Cinquefoils have a strongly independent streak: They grow where they want to and rarely stay where you put them. Sprinkle seeds or transplant young plants, and hope for the best.

- **HERBAL USE** To soothe toothache or help heal mouth sores, steep two to three teaspoons of fresh cinquefoil (*P. canadensis*) in a cup of water for 10 minutes, strain, and cool. Swish in your mouth, then spit. Nicholas Culpeper, author of the authoritative seventeenth-century *Herbal,* was a staunch advocate of cinquefoil: "Let no man despise it because it is plain and easy," he wrote; "the ways of God are all such."

Foe?

Potentilla means "little powerful one," but fast spread is the main reason that cinquefoils end up on weed lists. Some species, including plants sold as ornamentals, colonize hospitable ground quickly by sending out spreading stems and roots. This makes them unwelcome in tidy gardens and in lawns. Despite their colonizing tendencies, cinquefoils are not all that difficult to keep in bounds or to eradicate.

- **HAND PULL** Yank taller cinquefoils with old-fashioned muscle power by grabbing the single stem and giving a swift, hard pull. For low growers, gather stems in your hand and pull with a sharp twist.

- **DANDELION FORK** The thin, sturdy, forked blade of a dandelion digger will give you extra leverage for lifting out the root. This tool is useful in beds and lawn because it won't disrupt plants growing nearby. Shake off soil, then compost the remains.

Friend?

This cosmopolitan plant is native to three continents: North America, Europe, and Asia. People everywhere have embraced it as a medicinal aid throughout history. In the home garden, heal-all is not much of a threat as a weed. It's swiftly dispatched with hand pulling, should it slink into an area where it's not wanted. The cheerful flowers and long bloom season make it welcome for added color and texture in shady lawns or gardens where the choice of ornamentals is limited.

- **GARDEN USE** Heal-all transplants easily. It thrives in moist, shady to partly shady areas, where it won't bother competing with other perennials. It is particularly nice along the edges of beds or to flank a wood-chip path. In sunnier gardens, heal-all is still a charmer, although not a commanding presence among the bigger, bolder citizens.

- **HERBAL USE** Hard to believe a humble weed would hold such renown that it was deemed to heal all, yet this modest weed was said to "make whole and sound all wounds, both inward and outward" (Gerard, *The Herball or General Historie of Plantes,* 1597). Try its astringent properties yourself next time you get a cut in the garden: Steep two teaspoons of bruised, fresh leaves in one cup of water for 10 minutes, then cool and pour the water over the wound. Allow to air dry. Repeat two or three times a day as needed.

Prunella vulgaris

Heal-all, self-heal

A modest plant, heal-all creeps along the ground, raising stems topped with short spikes of blue-purple flowers now and then throughout the milder months. It often shows up in shady areas, nestled among hostas and ferns like a woodland native, but it also gets a roothold in sunny lawns and beds. Improved cultivated varieties are marketed for garden use.

Heal-all is reminiscent of its relative, the groundcover *Ajuga*. Highly adaptable to demanding conditions, heal-all clings even tighter to the ground than normal when a lawn mower or foot traffic threatens its existence, its leaves becoming smaller and thicker. The mat of foliage helps protect individual leaves within the clump. In bloom, heal-all's rich deep blue to purple flowers are its trademark.

- Square stems that root where they touch the ground.
- Chubby flowerheads, 1 to 2 inches tall, at tips of stems.
- Tubular, mint-family flowers are two-lipped, with the lower lip curving backward like the blade of a sickle.
- Blossoms are held in groups of three in the cluster, with each group backed by a bristly, rounded bract.
- Long season of bloom, with new flowerheads produced during the entire growing season.
- Flowerheads turn green, then brown, as seeds develop.
- Roots are fibrous.
- Often evergreen in winter, usually acquiring a reddish tinge during cold weather.

 **fact file**

LIFE CYCLE	perennial
SITE, SOIL & SEASON	shade to sun; moist to average soil, struggles in dry soil; blooms spring through fall
DISPERSAL	spreading, rooting stems; seed
ULTIMATE HEIGHT	a crawler; rises no more than about 6 inches from the ground
OTHER NAMES	all-heal, bluecurls, brownwort, carpenter's square, cure-all, heart's ease, hookweed, sicklewort

Ranunculus spp.

Buttercups

Cheerful yellow buttercups are over-enthusiastic wildlings. So, unless you enjoy a meadow garden well away from other beds, you'll want to keep your yard clear of these.

Buttercups gleam in sunshine like melted "butter." Single flowers are held in branched clusters at the ends of slender, erect stems. The toothy, lobed, three-parted leaves are deep green, and, in some species, even stay green through winter.

- Plants may sprawl or stand upright; roots are fibrous.
- The five petals curl upward, forming a shallow "cup."
- In the center of each flower is a mass of short stamens.
- When petals fall off, a spiky ball of seeds forms.
- Seeds have a pointed or hooked "beak" at the top end.

fact file

LIFE CYCLE	perennial
SITE, SOIL & SEASON	sun to shade; usually found in loose, fertile soil, but spreads fastest in moist soil and also thrives in average garden conditions; blooms from spring to early summer
DISPERSAL	seed; spreading roots
ULTIMATE HEIGHT	to 3 feet, depending on species
OTHER NAMES	crowfoot, gold cup, horsegold, king's cup, yellowweed

In a naturalistic planting, buttercups are a gardener's good friend because they will spread rampantly among other plants. In times past, various species were sometimes employed as a last-ditch cure for syphilis and other ailments—but use in medicine is no longer an option, now that less dangerous alternatives exist.

- **GARDEN USE** If buttercups are present on your property, enjoy their sunny yellow blossoms along creeks or in a meadow garden, where they can roam at will. They are invasive, but other meadow plants are even more so; buttercups will not usually choke out their neighbors.

Buttercups are best to admire from a distance, when they cloak pastures and meadows in a golden glow. If they finagle their way into your yard, remove them as soon as you spot them because problems will only multiply. Creeping buttercup (*Ranunculus repens*) is the most common invader of lawns, where it nestles out of reach of the mower. Besides their territorial habits, buttercups can be injurious: *R. acris,* a widespread weed, has acrid juice that may cause painful blisters in the mouths and digestive tracts of animals (or humans) that eat it. One unique use of a buttercup (*R. sceleratus,* or cursed buttercup) was noted in the nineteenth century by George Don in *A General System of Gardening and Botany:* "The bruised herb is said to raise a blister, which is not easily healed, and by which strolling beggars sometimes excite compassion."

- **HAND PULL** Almost always the first line of defense against weeds, hand pulling is an effective way to remove scattered buttercup plants. Pull out the main root, then remove any other rooted offshoots. Monitor for future seedlings.

- **HOE** Use a long-handled hoe to chop and lift out isolated plants in cultivated beds.

- **SPOT HERBICIDE** To kill plants in the lawn, apply an herbicide following label directions.

Friend?

Foe?

Amazingly enough, poison ivy has a lot to recommend it, with a few big "ifs." If you already are hosting a vine; if it is in an area of the yard where passersby are safe from contact; and if you have no pets to bring the oils home on their fur, you may choose to let it grow. You'll gain a spectacular show of fall foliage and the joy of watching birds come to feast on the berries. Bluebirds, the most desirable bird to American birdwatchers, adore poison ivy fruits. They will travel miles to reach the feast.

■ **WILDLIFE** An established poison ivy vine will attract birds and other animals year-round to its tangled stems, which serve as shelter and nest sites. When berries ripen, you may see woodpeckers, robins, cedar waxwings, grosbeaks, tanagers, and of course bluebirds gobbling the fruit of this weed. Songbirds and other wildlife depend upon the white berries for fall and winter food.

Individual degree of susceptibility to poison ivy varies widely, with some breaking out in a severe rash at the slightest contact and other lucky folks completely impervious to the effect. Don't be too smug if you never get poison ivy: You can develop sensitivity to the plant even after many years of immunity. Pets and livestock can also spread the rash by carrying the toxic oil on their fur and transferring it to their owners. You may choose to evict this troublemaker whenever you spy it in beds and borders, or in other niches where it may have gained a roothold. Vines grow slowly at first, so there's ample opportunity to pull them out before they get established.

Before you begin weeding, arm yourself with a widely available commercial product made by Tecnu; it removes the oil after contact and helps prevent a severe rash. Use the product as directed, after your weeding session.

■ **HAND PULL** Hand pulling, with or without the aid of a dandelion fork, makes quick work of young poison ivy vines and seedlings. Protective clothing is a must. Wear long sleeves and gloves to tackle poison ivy. A good trick is to slip your gloved hand inside a plastic grocery sack, pull out the plant, then turn the bag inside out so that the vine is in the bag ready for disposal in the trash.

■ **SPOT HERBICIDE** Poison ivy is tough to get rid of once it's settled in, because its roots spread far and wide. Repeated applications of herbicide are necessary. Choose a product labeled specifically for poison ivy and follow directions.

Rhus radicans

Poison ivy

Contact with any part of poison ivy can cause an intensely itching rash of small blisters. The plant may appear as groundcover, shrubs, or woody vines, but the leaves always consist of three leaflets.

■ Three oval but pointed leaflets, as long as 4 inches each; leaf edges may be ruffly, scalloped, or straight.

■ Leaves are reddish when they first appear in early spring.

■ Fall color is intense, blazing red, red-orange, and yellow.

■ Clusters of small, greenish white flowers are easy to overlook, especially on vines in the trees.

■ Small, white berry clusters form in late summer, stay into winter, and are most noticeable when leaves drop in fall.

■ Dark brown vines may look hairy due to aerial rootlets.

■ Old plants have thick vines, with no leaves at the bottom.

fact file

LIFE CYCLE	perennial
SITE, SOIL & SEASON	full sun to shade; in wet soil or dry; vines are visible year-round; leaves drop in fall
DISPERSAL	seed-containing berries are eaten by wildlife, then deposited everywhere
ULTIMATE HEIGHT	can climb to 20 feet or more
OTHER NAMES	cow-itch, markry, mercury

Rosa multiflora
Multiflora rose

One of the less-than-stellar achievements of the U.S. Department of Agriculture (USDA), multiflora rose was introduced to North America as a wildlife conservation aid. It worked only too well: Birds and animals, who came for its winter berries, spread its seeds far and wide, turning the plant into a pasture and roadside pest so severe it's on several noxious weed lists. Its seedlings usually appear in home gardens, too. Look out for it in flower beds, or creeping along fences, walls, or buildings.

Masses of small, white flowers so dense that they cover the bush are the identifying characteristic of a multiflora rose at bloom time. In winter, the bare branches are decorated with sprays of small, red rosehips, as abundant as the flowers. When the plant is not in bloom or in berry, it's tricky to separate it from other species of roses.

- Multitude of white flowers borne in long, densely packed clusters.
- Sweet-scented, five-petaled flowers, an inch or less wide.
- Nine-leaflet compound leaves, each leaflet with serrated edges.
- Smooth stems, but downward-pointing thorns occur where leaves meet stems and on undersides of leaf stems.
- Arching or climbing with support.
- Clusters of small (about ½ inch long or less) spherical to ovoid, red fruits, or rosehips, replace faded flowers.
- Rosehips held throughout winter on bare branches.

 **fact file**

LIFE CYCLE	shrub
SITE, SOIL & SEASON	sun to shade; moist to average soil; highly adaptable; blooms in early summer
DISPERSAL	seed distributed by berry-eating birds and other animals
ULTIMATE HEIGHT	isolated shrubs reach 5 to 6 feet tall before they bend into an arching mass of canes; plants with support may climb to 15 feet
OTHER NAMES	none

Friend?

Multiflora rose scents the night air with a sublime fragrance. Unlike many garden roses, it is very easy to grow. Since you will probably have seedlings to contend with anyway, you may want to consider letting one or two develop into garden plants, which offer beauty both in summer bloom and winter berry.

- **GARDEN USE** Before coddling a multiflora rose, check with your USDA extension agent to see whether its existence isn't outlawed by law in your community. In the garden, train canes against a tree or on a trellis for a more controlled effect. Multiflora roses are also fast-growing, sweet-smelling privacy hedges, or windbreaks.

- **WILDLIFE** This weed is ideal for birds and small animals. Its thorny canes keep them safe from predators, making its bushes a favorite nest site for songbirds; and its hips provide food all winter long.

- **HERBAL USE** Collect the ripe, vitamin C–rich rosehips, and dry them on a screen. To make tea, crush the dried berries with a rolling pin and use about one teaspoon per cup of boiling water. Steep for about 10 minutes; sweeten if desired.

Foe?

In the home garden, multiflora rose seedlings usually invade flower beds or pop up by fences, stone walls, buildings, or near birdfeeders. The plants are difficult to control if infestation is severe, but on a small backyard scale, a sturdy shovel usually gives you the advantage.

- **SHOVEL OR HOE** Dig deep with a shovel or grubbing hoe to ensure that you remove the entire root. Dispose of remains in the trash.

Rubus spp.

Bramble

The term "bramble" is used to refer to a wide range of *Rubus* species, including weedy ones as well as cherished fruit crops. But given the right conditions, all can spread where they are not wanted to become troublesome weeds. Brambles are most troublesome in regions where they flourish in the wild: The Pacific Northwest, for instance, is notorious for its ground-covering blackberries, which sneak out of wild lands to terrorize tidy gardeners anywhere within reach. But brambles can crop up in just about any garden, brought in as seeds in the digestive tracts of birds and animals.

Brambles usually grow as dense bushes with an arching, mounded shape, but they can also crawl along the ground. Their long, flexible stems are usually unbranched, and sprout quickly and in quantity from a central growing point. Stems are usually thorny, although some cultivated varieties have been bred for lack of thorns. A few species, including wineberry, have almost furry stems clothed in many soft, short spines. Flowers mature into fruits that may be black, purple, red, yellow, or orange, depending on the variety.

- Leaves are usually three-parted, occasionally five-parted, with each leaflet being a pointed oval.
- Five-petaled flowers are usually white, surrounding a central yellow tuft.
- Flowers mature into juicy fruits, each one made up of many flesh-covered seeds.
- Foliage is evergreen or deciduous, according to species.
- Canes persist in winter.
- Branching taproot; running roots are tough and pale.

fact file

LIFE CYCLE	perennial shrubs
SITE, SOIL & SEASON	well-drained soil; sun to shade; flowers in early summer; fruits summer to fall
DISPERSAL	seed; running roots; branch tips may sprout roots where they touch the ground
ULTIMATE HEIGHT	varies according to species; most are arching shrubs to about 6 feet tall
OTHER NAMES	blackberry, raspberry, dewberry, and many other "berries"

In *Song of Myself,* Walt Whitman wrote: "I believe a leaf of grass is no less than the journeywork of the stars … and the running blackberry would adorn the parlors of heaven." Many a gardener and stroller would agree with him: A handful of sun-warmed berries is ambrosia on a summer's day. Thanks to the plant's fast growth and bountiful fruit production, you can start a bramble patch and enjoy a harvest the following summer. Birds and other wildlife are also big fans of brambles. The bushes provide vital shelter, nest sites, and plenty of food.

■ **GARDEN USE** Give brambles a patch of their own, far from ornamental gardens, so that you can mow off strays with the lawn mower and not worry about them infiltrating ornamental beds. Many gardeners choose to grow brambles in controlled plantings, training the canes along wires or taking the time to prune them yearly for easier harvest.

■ **WILDLIFE** Brambles are one of the earliest permanent plants to move into meadow gardens, and they quickly take over from the other tough meadow flowers that preceded them. Allow some brambles to grow in a wild corner, or mow them periodically to keep them somewhat in control, and you'll be rewarded with great bird watching; more than 60 species of birds enjoy the luscious fruit, and may nest in the bushes.

In the bramble-friendly climate of Washington and Oregon, entrepreneurs make a career out of blackberry control, advertising their services in newspapers and the Yellow Pages. That's a clue to the difficulty of eradicating a determined onslaught of these fast-spreading plants. For a limited outbreak, elbow grease is the answer, but to reclaim severely infested land, you may decide to turn to chemical warfare.

■ **SHOVEL** Wear stout leather gloves and a thick jacket to protect against scratches; the thorns can be vicious. Tie long hair back, too, to keep it from getting snarled in the canes as you work. Prune off as much top growth as you can to make it easier to get to the root of the problem, then dig deeply around the base of the plant with the shovel, lifting upward as you go. Pull the roots out of the soil, shake off clinging soil, and dispose of them in the trash. Use your hands to follow any running roots that spread outward, and uproot those too. Monitor the area to watch for new plants that may spring up from overlooked roots.

■ **HERBICIDE** Spray plants with an appropriate product, which is specifically labeled for bramble control. Repeated applications may be needed.

Rumex crispus, Rumex spp.

Curly dock

Curly dock (*Rumex crispus*) is the main annoyance among this group of weeds, with other species filtering in as lesser culprits. This weed has a habit of cropping up in less-than-perfect lawns, as well as in the usual hiding places among garden beds and along walls and buildings.

A coarse weed of significant, physical stature, curly dock has long, tough, weedy-looking leaves that live up to its name: They twist about the stalk like pennants wrapped around a pole. Each leaf may be up to 2 feet long and about 4 inches across. Flowers are individually tiny, but held in dense, branching clusters.

- Basal leaves may be heart-shaped or rounded, or long and thin, and they have wavy or curling edges. They are enormous and often wooly underneath.
- Above the lowest leaves, the foliage is long and narrow, with pointed tips and an unusual habit of wavy, ruffled edges and curling growth.
- Leaves are sour, indicative of the plant's acid content.
- Tall, smooth flowering stem is sparsely leafed, with leaves becoming smaller and straighter toward the top.
- Vertical stalk holds upward-curving side branches of greenish blossoms, which turn reddish at maturity.
- Flowers mature to brown seeds, enclosed in papery husks, dangling loosely on short, thin stems.
- Deep, fleshy, yellow taproot is often branching.
- Seed stalk persists through winter. Basal leaves also remain green (sometimes tinged with red) except in severe winter cold.

 fact file

LIFE CYCLE	perennial
SITE, SOIL & SEASON	usually full sun; in moist to dry soil; adaptable to various soil types; rosette of evergreen leaves
DISPERSAL	seed dispersal by birds and wind
ULTIMATE HEIGHT	leaf rosette about 1 foot; flower stalk to 3 feet
OTHER NAMES	sheep sorrel, cow sorrel, curled dock, dock, field sorrel, sour dock, sourgrass, sourweed, winter dock, yellow dock

Friend?

Wild-greens enthusiasts appreciate the sour flavor of curly dock leaves, except for young growth, which is often bitter. Heavy clay or compacted soils also benefit from dock's presence, because the strong taproot increases the air spaces and allows water to penetrate. The plant can also be used to soothe skin problems: In rural Kentucky, the plant was once called "out-sting."

- **CULINARY USE** The leaves are best sliced sparingly into green salads; cooked greens become gluey, like okra. The simmered greens add a bite to cream soups and casseroles, but give them a mucilaginous texture.

- **HERBAL USE** Smash a curly dock leaf in your hands and hold it against nasty mosquito bites to stop the itch.

Foe?

Curly dock doesn't give up without a fight. Deep digging is needed to extract the roots, which will sprout new growth if broken pieces remain in the soil. Remove the plants as soon as you see them in lawn grass or in flower and vegetable gardens. Once the tenacious root takes hold, it takes muscle to pry the plant out of the soil.

- **SHOVEL** Check the handle strength of your shovel before you dig a mature plant—you'll need every bit of power you can command. Dig deeply a few inches from the growing point, lopping off top growth if needed for easier handling. Remove soil and tug on the plant to gauge where the roots go. Dig up all branches of the roots. Shake off the soil and dispose of the root and all its pieces in the trash. Monitor for new sprouts from overlooked pieces of root.

- **DANDELION FORK** The stout, skinny blade works well to extract young plants. Push it in at an angle near the base of the plant, and simultaneously pull on the top growth with one hand while you lever out the roots with the other.

- **SPOT HERBICIDE** If your digging strength is limited, apply spot herbicide as directed on the label. Be sure to choose a product whose label specifies that it controls dock. Repeated applications may be needed.

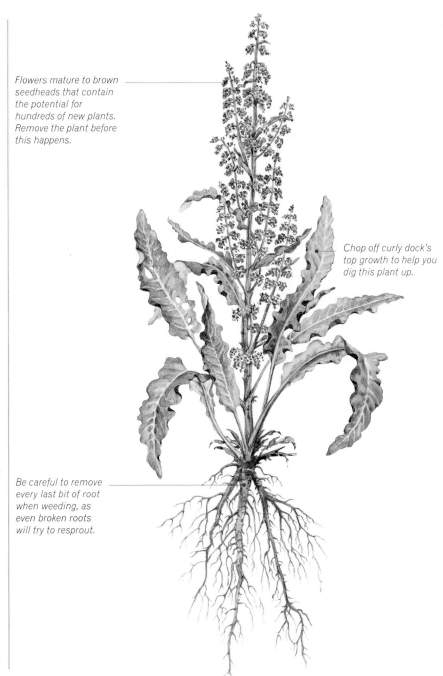

Flowers mature to brown seedheads that contain the potential for hundreds of new plants. Remove the plant before this happens.

Chop off curly dock's top growth to help you dig this plant up.

Be careful to remove every last bit of root when weeding, as even broken roots will try to resprout.

Senecio spp., *Packera* spp.

Groundsel, ragwort

Some Senecio species are now classified as Packera so you may find them listed under either name, depending on your reference. With their golden flowers, butterweed (*Senecio triangularis*), golden ragwort (*Packera aurea*), and tansy ragwort (*S. jacobaea*) are perky enough for the garden; whereas groundsel flowers never look like more than fluffy, dirty white, closed-up flowers past their prime.

Most ragworts and groundsels are recognizable by their leaves alone, which is all you'll have to go on until bloom time. In most species, the leaves are elongated, with many lobes and indentations, all edged with zig-zag teeth. The plants are usually about knee height, with a single stem arising from a few basal leaves, usually unlobed. Some species—notably stinking groundsel (*S. viscosus*) and tansy ragwort (*S. jacobaea*)—have a rank smell. At bloom time, these weeds are easier to identify because of their trademark many-flowered clusters of small, aster-like blossoms.

- Leaves usually rounded to oval at the base of the plant.
- All other leaves are finely cut and elongated; at the top of the flowering stem, they are much smaller.
- Flowers are mostly small, flat, yellow or whitish daisies.
- Root is a thin, weak taproot or cluster of taproots.
- Seeds are surrounded by fine, white hairs that act as fluffy parachutes to get airborne.
- Basal rosettes may remain green in winter.

 fact file

LIFE CYCLE	annual/biennial
SITE, SOIL & SEASON	mostly in sun; in almost any moist to dry soil; blooms in spring, summer, or fall, depending on species
DISPERSAL	seed
ULTIMATE HEIGHT	most species are about 2 feet tall or less
OTHER NAMES	*Senecio vulgaris:* chickenweed, ragweed; *Packera aurea:* female-regulator, golden ragwort, golden senecio; *Senecio jacobaea:* stinking Alexanders, tansy ragwort

Friend?

Unless you're a farmer, ragworts and groundsels are usually only a mild and occasional annoyance. These weeds deserve a place in both the historical herb garden and the casual flower garden—or at least a few seconds of appreciation before you toss them on the compost heap.

■ **GARDEN USE** Let ragworts and groundsels grow at will in naturalistic meadow gardens, and encourage ragworts among informal flowers for their dash of bright color. Golden ragwort (*Packera aurea*) is particularly showy, as vivid in color as goldenrod (*Solidago* spp.), but a much earlier bloomer; it's beautiful with blue bearded iris. Do behead the plants, though, before the flower clusters mature to fluffy white seeds, or your opinion of golden ragwort may change from friend to foe in years to follow.

■ **WILDLIFE** Many small wasps, bees, butterflies, and other insects visit the daisy-like flowers. So a few groundsel or ragwort plants in your yard will make life easier for these pollinators.

■ **HERBAL USE** Too risky to experiment with, these weeds are nevertheless interesting for their historical uses. *P. aurea,* an American native plant, was used by American natives to induce abortion and relieve menstrual difficulties; *Senecio vulgaris* and *S. jacobaea* had similar applications. Today we know that liver damage can result from the alkaloids in these plants.

Foe?

These weeds may occasionally appear in enough quantity to cause consternation. Fortunately, the plants uproot easily when hand pulled, even at maturity.

■ **HAND PULL** Unless you're the proud owner of a ragwort plantation (in which case, call in the tractor to turn them under), you can swiftly eliminate the weeds by hand pulling. Compost if flowers haven't matured.

Setaria spp.

Foxtail grass

One of the most common roadside weeds, foxtail grass frequently pops up in gardens, too, often thanks to birds, which are very fond of the nutritious seeds that see them through the winter. Foxtail needs open space to grow well, and will not usually compete with turfgrass except in poor, patchy lawns. Because songbirds have learned to rely on foxtail seeds for winter food, these wild grasses are a favorite with wildlife gardeners. The straight or arching seedheads also are beautiful in casual fall bouquets.

The bristly brush of the seedhead looks exactly like its "foxtail" namesake. Yellow foxtail (*Setaria glauca*) holds its seedheads straight up, while those of green foxtail (*S. viridis*) are gracefully arched and so thickly furred that they're a delight to stroke.

- Usually unbranched, with several stems springing from a single cluster of roots.
- Each long, flat leaf blade may be up to a foot in length; leaves are shorter near the top of the plant.
- Bristly flowerheads appear in summer through fall—erect at first, they lengthen and arch in green foxtail, but remain vertical in the yellow species.
- The densely packed seeds are green or yellow, maturing to brown; hundreds are borne on each spike.
- Plants turn tan after seeds mature and remain standing until they yield to weather.
- Roots are a fibrous cluster.
- May appear singly or in a thick stand.

 **fact file**

LIFE CYCLE	annual
SITE, SOIL & SEASON	sun; almost any well-drained soil; blooms in summer, seedheads persist through winter
DISPERSAL	seed
ULTIMATE HEIGHT	to 4 feet
OTHER NAMES	bristly foxtail, foxtail millet, pigeon grass; *Setaria faberii:* Faber's foxtail; *S. glauca:* yellow foxtail; *S. viridis:* green foxtail

Friend?

Birds would have a hard time getting through the cold months without the banquet of foxtail grass seeds found in wild places and gardens. You can attract native sparrows, finches, and other lively little birds by letting these wild millets grow in naturalistic gardens. The seedheads of green foxtail add grace to bouquets and perennial gardens, too.

- **DECORATIVE USE** Clip the stems of seedheads, either green or brown, and put in a container without water. Ensure you shake seedheads well before you bring them into the house so that the seeds have all dropped out. Green foxtails will soften to a paler sage-green hue, while tan seedheads add warmth and a softening line to dried arrangements of orange Chinese lanterns (*Physalis alkekengi*), yarrow (*Achillea*), strawflowers (*Bracteantha*), and other everlastings. You can also include green seedheads in bouquets with other flowers, in water; try them, for example, with zinnias for a striking combination.

- **WILDLIFE** Enjoy foxtail in meadow gardens or in a discreet, weedy corner. By the end of winter, all that will remain is the nibbled stems of the seedheads, since small birds and animals are especially fond of the seeds.

- **GARDEN USE** Foxtail has a knack for wriggling in among perennial flowers. Its arching seed sprays are lovely with most tall, late-season flowers.

Foe?

Foxtail grass is a fast grower that can quickly overshadow seedlings and young vegetable, flower, or herb plants. Its roots grow swiftly, too, spreading a fibrous network that can disturb nearby plants when you try to remove it. Foxtail grass can even sneak into less-than-perfect lawn areas, and it is also apt to spring up in gravel driveways and among plantings of cotoneaster and other groundcovers. Each seedhead holds the makings of hundreds of potential new plants, so be sure to evict the grass before the seeds mature, or you risk creating major problems for yourself next year. An old-time method for controlling "pigeon grass," as it was then called, was to turn sheep loose to graze in the infested area. However, lacking a few woolly Dorsets, your best bet is good old-fashioned hand labor.

- **HAND PULL** One quick yank and foxtail grass is history. When soil is moist, grasp the plant at its base and pull strongly to extract the roots. Shake off soil, and add the weed to the compost pile.

- **HAND HOE** Scrape young plants off the soil with a sharp blade, or chop and lift older plants. Shake off soil, then compost the remains.

- **HOE** Chop and lift at the base of the plant. Shake off soil, then add to the compost pile.

Solanum spp.

Nightshade

Potatoes, tomatoes, peppers, and eggplants were deemed poisonous fruits when Europeans brought samples home from America, not because of their color but because they belonged to a genus of plants treated with wary respect: the death-dealing nightshades. Nightshades contain toxic alkaloids, especially in their fruit, although the plants were once employed as herbal cures.

Densely leafy plants, nightshades often exhibit a noticeably rank smell when you brush against their foliage. Leaves are smooth and pointed, and usually very simple, although *Solanum dulcamara* has an added fillip of two smaller leaflets at the base of the much larger central leaf. Habit varies depending on species.

- *S. dulcamara* is a weakly climbing vine that forms a jumbled mass of leafy stems, while *S. nigrum* is a much bushier, more branching plant that usually relaxes into a sprawl with maturity.

- Flower shape is unique and even peculiar: The flowers look like stars from underneath (similar to those of eggplant), but the petals are often strongly bent backward, exposing a pointed center.

- Flowers are white or deep purple, depending on species.

- Flowers are borne in open branching clusters.

- Leaves are smooth and simple, with long pointed tips.

- Fruits are clusters of smooth, fleshy, glossy but soft berries, spherical or ovoid in shape. They are shining red in *S. dulcamara*, black in most other species.

- Roots are usually taproot with branching fibrous roots.

fact file

LIFE CYCLE	perennial, annual
SITE, SOIL & SEASON	shaded areas; rich, moist soil; flowers in summer
DISPERSAL	seed
ULTIMATE HEIGHT	*S. dulcamara:* vine to about 5 feet; *S. nigrum:* sprawling plant 2 to 3 feet
OTHER NAMES	bitter nightshade, blue berry, deadly nightshade, hound's berry, poison bittersweet, poison flower, snakeberry, stubble berry

Friend?

Nightshades are usually uncommon weeds, except in undisturbed niches along fences or outbuildings, where they may get a good start before you notice them. Their dense foliage makes an eye-pleasing backdrop to white or pastel flowers. Do not use them medicinally nowadays, and always wash hands thoroughly after handling. Some country folk make pies and other foods from the ripe berries of *S. nigrum* and the very similar *S. americanum*. However, it's best to stick to cultivated fruits if you don't have a personal heritage of harvesting nightshades.

■ **GARDEN USE** If you are sure children—or visitors, for that matter—won't be tempted by the fruits, cultivate the climbing *S. dulcamara* as a curiosity, for its unusual, purple flowers and bright red berries. Its leafy stems do a good job of hiding a chain-link fence and can also act as a tangle of groundcover on a steep bank.

Foe?

Deadly poison is the main reason to avoid nightshades. Keep your garden safe for friends and family by eliminating these potentially dangerous plants or keeping them strictly off-limits to children and visitors.

■ **HAND PULL** Wear gloves to avoid possible contamination by alkaloids. Cut back top growth to about 6 inches, just enough for a secure handhold. Apply firm, steady pressure to extract the roots.

■ **SHOVEL** Use a long-handled shovel for easier removal of established plants. Remove most of the top growth first, using a string trimmer or pruners, so you can see where the stems emerge from the roots.

Sonchus spp.
Sow thistle

A native of Europe, sow thistle is a common pest in garden beds, gravel driveways, and even in lawns that are patchy enough for it to get a start in.

Even though its leafy rosette does not appear dangerously armed, this plant is painfully prickly. In the first stages of its growth, the plant forms a leafy rosette. This is soon followed by an emerging flowering stem that soars skyward.

Sow thistle looks a bit like a cross between a wild lettuce and a thistle. And its leaves are like a bigger, wilder version of those of the dandelion, but lighter green in color.

- Leaves are coarsely toothed, and up to 1 foot long.
- Leaves are spined at the tips, and are often twisted and curling.
- Leaves are arranged alternately on the stem.
- Stem may be branched or unbranched, and is smooth and hollow between the joints.
- Stem gives a milky juice when broken, which is where sow thistle gets its alternative name, "milky tassel."
- Flowers are small, pale yellow daisies; they are about an inch across and are borne in clusters.
- Seedheads are highly noticeable, producing bountiful white fluff, which is visible from a distance.
- Root is a taproot.
- Plant dies after seeds disperse.

Friend?

Sow thistle is safe to eat, but tastes bitter. Pigs, however, enjoy the leaves, which is where the weed gets its common name. In the past, sow thistle was used to "prolong virility in gentlemen," as a popular antinarcotic, and also to help break addiction in the days of opium dens. Perhaps its day may roll around again, but let's leave that decision to the experts.

- **HERBAL USE** It's best to simply appreciate sow thistle in the wild, since it replicates too rapidly to be a good garden guest. Little research has been done into the chemical properties of the plant, so no matter how tempted you are to experiment with a possible alternative to Viagra, avoid home experimentation.

Foe?

Sow thistle sneaks into garden beds almost everywhere, and usually reaches appreciable size before it's noticed and consequently evicted. It also has limited practical use, so is one to reject from the garden.

- **HAND HOE** Chop off the top growth of sow thistle before it goes to seed. If the plant regrows from the root, repeat the treatment.

- **SHOVEL** Dig and lift out the plant. If not yet in bloom, dispose of on the compost heap; otherwise, toss in the trash since the flowers can mature to seeds even after the weed is uprooted.

 **fact file**

LIFE CYCLE	annual
SITE, SOIL & SEASON	almost any soil; full sun; may be seen in bloom spring to fall, depending on when the plant sprouted
DISPERSAL	seed, borne by the wind on little parachutes
ULTIMATE HEIGHT	to 10 feet
OTHER NAMES	hare's thistle, hare's lettuce, low thistle, milk thistle, milky tassel

Sorghum halepense

Johnsongrass

Introduced to America as a hay plant, this tall grass soon leaped out of its farm fields to spread in yards, gardens, and fields of other crops. The plant is on the noxious weed list of many states and counties. It shoots up extremely fast after rain. Its fat roots are very difficult to eradicate completely.

This giant grass grows taller than head height, with leaves up to two feet long. In summer, flower clusters appear atop the plants in open panicles that may be two feet in length. The plant is usually tattered by the time it flowers, and stems often collapse under the burden of the seedheads. Although you may host only a single plant of the grass at first, you will soon be hosting an ever-growing colony.

- Leaves are ½ to 1 inch wide, with a pronounced white rib down the center.
- Grows in single stalks, usually spaced a few inches apart.
- Stem may be 2 inches in diameter at soil level.
- Stem and leaves are often streaked with red or brown.

- Underground rootstocks are thick, brittle, and white, sometimes marked with pink.
- Flower clusters have long, wavy hairs on each spikelet.
- Seeds are reddish brown.
- Dead stalks persist in winter, although they may collapse in a pile; new growth appears in late spring.

 fact file

LIFE CYCLE	perennial
SITE, SOIL & SEASON	sun; almost any soil; blooms midsummer through fall
DISPERSAL	underground creeping rootstocks; seed
ULTIMATE HEIGHT	usually about 5 to 7 feet
OTHER NAMES	Cuba grass, Egyptian millet, maiden cane, Syrian grass

Even if you live far from farming country, you may find johnsongrass in your yard, courtesy of seed-spreading birds. Attack this weed on sight, even if it seems to be remaining in one spot: Beneath the soil, its insidious rootstocks are colonizing as far as they can reach. Hand pulling won't work; the weed's stems snap off in your hand, leaving roots to resprout. Even if you can pull out the main clump, you're bound to break off any rootstocks that have already moved outward; new plants are likely to spring up from them with a vengeance.

- **SHOVEL** Cut back top growth to a few inches above soil level for easier handling. Then dig deep to lift out the main plant. Follow any spreading rootstocks and dig those out too. Then place the soil from the area into a sieve and painstakingly remove all bits of root you can find. Monitor the area and repeat as often as you see new growth. Collect all bits of root and dispose of remains in the trash, not on the compost pile. Repeated attention is time-consuming but successful.

- **SPOT HERBICIDE** Apply a product that specifically lists johnsongrass on the label. Repeated applications may be necessary.

Foe?

Stellaria media

Chickweed

Any gardener who hasn't had to deal with chickweed is probably gardening in the desert. One of the most ubiquitous weeds, this diminutive troublemaker quickly grabs empty vegetable beds or bare nooks and crannies of ornamental plantings or patchy lawns. It's a winter annual, so you'll notice seedlings in fall and green plants all winter long. Plentiful as it is, chickweed is easy to eradicate—at least until next year. It's also welcome despite its weediness, because it's often the first flower of the year in bloom. Better yet, this one is edible—and good for you, too, being rich with vitamins.

Chickweed has itty-bitty flowers, very small leaves, and slender stems, but it grows in large, vigorous clumps, so you won't miss it. By late winter, it's a definite presence in the vegetable garden and other sites, thanks to its habit of growing during the colder months. To distinguish this species, look for a many-stemmed plant with pointed, wide-bottomed leaves on dainty stalks, and diminutive, starry, white flowers. As night approaches, you can witness an intriguing survival mechanism: The paired leaves fold toward each other, to protect tender new growth.

- Freely branched stems come from a central root cluster.
- Leaves are paired, and are oval with pointed tips.
- Leaves and stems are light, bright green.
- Tiny flowers are borne singly in leaf axils and in small clusters at stem tips.
- Flowers are white, with five notched petals backed by a larger star of softly furred green sepals.
- Seeds are held in oval pods on threadlike stalks.
- A mass of fibrous roots supports the plant.
- Plant yellows and dies after setting seed.

 fact file

LIFE CYCLE	annual
SITE, SOIL & SEASON	sun to partial shade; moist soil but highly adaptable; blooms late winter to spring
DISPERSAL	seed
ULTIMATE HEIGHT	usually about 6 inches
OTHER NAMES	chicken weed, common chickweed, starwort, white birdseye, winterweed

Friend?

With its mild "green" flavor, chickweed is a wild green that will give you great satisfaction to serve in salads—a fitting end for a plentiful weed. You'll also be feeding your family and friends a sneaky dose of vitamin C, along with vitamins B_6 and B_{12}, potassium, iron, magnesium, and lots of other healthful goodies. It all adds up to lots of power from a pesty plant. Medicinally speaking, chickweed was used to soothe the stomach and bowels. It has a diuretic effect that has caused it occasionally to star in "natural" over-the-counter weight-loss products.

- **CULINARY USE** Harvest the fresh plant before it flowers. Gather the stems in one hand and snip them off an inch or two above ground level with ordinary scissors. Rinse and use fresh in salads.

- **HERBAL USE** Steep two to three teaspoons of fresh leaves in one cup boiling water for about 10 minutes. Sweeten as desired and sip as often as you like— though, as with any herbal preparation, not habitually. Also note that chickweed stimulates urination.

Foe?

Chickweed may be a fact of gardening life, but that doesn't mean you have to like it. In mild-winter climates, its presence is a great excuse to get outside during the off-season for a bout of vigorous hoeing. In cold-winter areas, avoid the temptation to rush the season (you run the risk of compacting the soil by walking on it when wet), and wait until just before planting time to eradicate the chickweed crop.

- **HAND PULL** This is a successful method to use in loose soils, where the fibrous roots of chickweed give up without much struggle. Shake off excess soil, and then toss on the compost pile.

- **HOE** Use a long-handled hoe in open beds, or a hand hoe in tight quarters. Chop and lift out the clumps, shake off the soil, and compost the plants.

- **MULCH** Apply a 2-inch layer of grass clippings, compost, or other fine mulch at the end of the gardening season in fall to block the emergence of chickweed seedlings, or to smother those that have already sprouted.

Symphytum officinale

Comfrey

A garden plant gone bad, comfrey is usually a pest only in limited areas, either in the garden where it got its start or in neighboring wild areas or backyards. Popular among herb gardeners, it should be considered a permanent member of the garden when invited in. That's because the roots are very difficult to remove entirely, and new plants will continue to grow from neglected bits left behind. Its presence can add a touch of bold to dainty-looking plants in an herb garden.

Comfrey's roots are unmistakable, with their black outsides and white insides, but it's the top growth you'll be seeing first. Big and bristly are the watchwords for this tall herb. The plant forms a large clump of basal leaves and sports several angular stems flagged with large, relatively narrow leaves. Comfrey plants have a bristly look because of the stiff, short hairs on their leaves and stem. The flowers emerge in a coil and hang downward, reminiscent of Virginia bluebells (*Mertensia virginica*). The flowers are similar to that wildflower in color, too, with pinkish buds soon opening to blue blooms.

- Leaves are elongated and rough to the touch.
- Stems are thick and have sharp angles along the edges.
- Flowers are borne at the tips of stems, and open blue from pink buds.
- The flowering tip curls down and under, and the blossoms are pendant.
- In cold winters, the plant dies back completely. Old flowering stalks collapse.
- Roots are thick and deep. They have a black covering over a fleshy, white interior.

fact file

LIFE CYCLE	perennial
SITE, SOIL & SEASON	adapts to sun or shade; almost any soil, even wet areas; flowers summer through fall
DISPERSAL	seed; spreading roots
ULTIMATE HEIGHT	up to 4 feet
OTHER NAMES	blackwort, bruisewort, healing herb

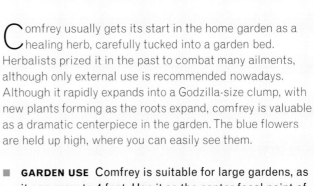

Friend?

Comfrey usually gets its start in the home garden as a healing herb, carefully tucked into a garden bed. Herbalists prized it in the past to combat many ailments, although only external use is recommended nowadays. Although it rapidly expands into a Godzilla-size clump, with new plants forming as the roots expand, comfrey is valuable as a dramatic centerpiece in the garden. The blue flowers are held up high, where you can easily see them.

■ **GARDEN USE** Comfrey is suitable for large gardens, as it can grow to 4 feet. Use it as the center focal point of raised beds planted with more delicately textured herbs, or let its blue hues tower over shorter plants. The tall stems may get floppy, but a few garden stakes will help them stand up straight.

■ **HERBAL USE** Comfrey leaves are recommended by herbalists for bruises and sores, but the plant is bound to gain fame among baby boomers for its alleged ability to keep skin looking youthful. To give it a try: Dry the roots, chop off a small piece, and mince or food process it into two to three teaspoons of fine pulp. Then tie it into a cheesecloth packet and drop into bathwater. Enjoy a soak and check the results for yourself!

Foe?

Anyone who has ever attempted to get rid of a clump of comfrey will have less than kind things to say about this weedy herb. Its tenacious roots have a habit of resurrecting themselves and sprouting new growth, despite repeated digging. Comfrey has also strayed to wild places, where it settles in diverse habitats, including along streams, at shady woods' edges, and on dry, sunny roadsides.

■ **SHOVEL** Deep, repeated digging is the organic gardener's only hope for removal of this weed. Cut back top growth before tackling, for easier access to the root. Sharpen the shovel blade so that it slices through the meaty roots more easily. Dig all around the main plant, then lever it from the soil. Follow any roaming roots and remove those, too. Dispose of top growth on the compost pile, but put the roots in the trash so they don't come back to haunt you. Monitor the plant's former site and remove any new shoots immediately.

■ **SPOT HERBICIDE** Apply an appropriate weedkiller to the plant. Watch for signs of new growth and repeat as often as necessary.

Taraxacum officinale

Dandelion

Common almost everywhere lawns are found, the dandelion is a familiar sight in early spring, when its yellow flowers announce the season. Its foliage, a ground-hugging rosette of dark green leaves as jagged as a lion's tooth ("dent de lion," as the French say), is also easily recognizable. One of the most abundant as well as widespread weeds, dandelion sports parachute-equipped seeds that sail away gracefully in the mildest breeze, aiming for any sunny bit of ground, where the deep, tenacious taproot will quickly take hold in open places. It's impossible to shield your yard from dandelion invasion, but there is much that you can do to keep the weed under control or indeed to eliminate it each year. The appearance of the dandelion changes over its lifetime:

- A dandelion starts life as a single-stem plant, with leaves growing in a cluster. The leaves are green but are often tinged with red in winter.
- In early spring, plump buds form on short stems near the center of the rosette; flower stems start to elongate. The many-petaled, fluffy, bright yellow flowers appear mostly in spring but also sporadically throughout the year. Flowerheads close up on dreary days and at dusk, reopening when touched by sunshine.
- At maturity, the spent flower closes up into a cylindrical mass of silky hairs and seeds. The flower stem lengthens even more to raise the seedhead above surrounding plants so that the wind can freely disperse the seed.
- When the seeds are ripe, the seedhead opens into a ball of soft white fuzz made of hundreds of tiny parachutes, each tipped by a small seed.

 fact file

LIFE CYCLE	perennial, often evergreen
SITE, SOIL & SEASON	sun; adaptable but prefers well-drained soil; year-round with peak bloom in spring
DISPERSAL	seed
ULTIMATE HEIGHT	ground-hugging, but seed puff rises 12 to 18 inches tall
OTHER NAMES	swine snout, blowball, wild endive

Dandelions are undeniably cheery after a long winter. A scattering adds country charm to your lawn, and the deep-rooted plants coexist well with grass. Leaves add an interesting, slightly bitter tang to salads and soups, and the flowers are famed for making wine. Dandelion also has a long history as a medicinal herb.

- **HARVEST** Gather leaves anytime, slicing just above soil level. Wash, separate, and chop the leaves for culinary or herbal use. Dig the root in late summer. Wash and use fresh, or dry for two weeks.

- **CULINARY USE** Young leaves have the mildest flavor; older leaves are more bitter. Chop into bite-size pieces before adding to salads, tossing with boiled potatoes, or stirring into soups. Boil leaves as you would spinach; the greens make a tasty side dish with ham. Steep older leaves for a bitter tea. For wine, gather fresh flowers in early morning, before nectaring insects are active.

- **MEDICINAL USE** Dandelion is brimming with iron, potassium, vitamin A, and other healthy compounds, which is why it is a popular "spring tonic" among country folk. Traditionally used for liver ailments, dandelion juice pressed from the leaves or an infusion of the root is a strong diuretic. Tea made from the leaves may also help combat insomnia as well as soothe indigestion.

Dandelions multiply generously, sowing themselves and blowing in on the wind from neighboring yards. When not in flower, their presence creates a patchy appearance in a smooth lawn. Because flower buds are held so close to the soil, you can't mow them off, and once the buds form, their stems will keep elongating even if you behead the blooms. Hand weeding is tricky both because of the strength of the deep root and because a broken root left behind will regrow. Herbicides are effective, but they leave your lawn riddled with dying plants to be removed by hand.

- **HAND PULL** It's best to save hand pulling for young dandelions growing in the loose soil of flower beds or vegetable gardens. Leaves are apt to tear loose from the root should you attempt to yank out mature specimens. Twist as you pull to help break the root free.

- **DANDELION FORK** Also called a dandelion weeder, this hand tool lives up to its name. Plunge the skinny metal blade and shaft deep into the soil, right by the crown of the plant; lift the leaves if you're unsure of placement. Grasp the leaves in a bunch at the base, pry upward with the tool, and the root should pop out of the ground.

- **MOWING** This won't get rid of existing plants and can even encourage dandelions to spread by roots. Do mow to remove flowers before seeds form, though, as this may limit their offspring. Be sure to couple this with another method to discourage plants.

- **SPOT HERBICIDE** Spray anytime in their growing season, covering as much of their leaves as you can. Two applications may be needed. Protect grass with a shield, and spray only on a windless day.

- **CHEMICAL HERBICIDE** Apply a post-emergent weedkiller in spring or early fall, selecting a product that specifies dandelions. Be sure to follow directions.

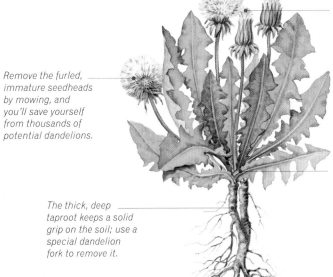

Once the plant has gone to seed, it will spread fast, so it is best to tackle the weed earlier in its life cycle.

Remove the furled, immature seedheads by mowing, and you'll save yourself from thousands of potential dandelions.

The leaves form a rosette atop the root and hug the ground, where they are safe from the mower.

The thick, deep taproot keeps a solid grip on the soil; use a special dandelion fork to remove it.

Trifolium spp.

Clover

Clover's three-part leaves have been a part of folklore and St. Patrick's day celebrations for centuries. White clover (*Trifolium repens*), a low-growing American native, and red clover (*T. pratense*), a taller European plant imported as a hay crop, are the most widespread and familiar. Red clover limits its invasions to garden beds and roadsides, while the lower-growing white species is one of the most common lawn pests.

Both white and red clovers (*T. repens* and *T. pratense*) bear the traditional shamrock leaf; the related white sweet clover and yellow sweet clover (*Melilotis alba* and *M. officinalis*) have more elongated leaflets in their three-parted leaves. *Trifolium* species bear flowers in a fat bumble shape, made up of dozens of individual florets. The sweet clovers (*Melilotis* spp.) have long, dainty spikes of tiny tubular blossoms. All clovers, however, boast a deliciously sweet, vanilla-like fragrance when the flowers are sniffed or the foliage crushed.

- Three-parted leaves may have pale or reddish markings.
- Leaves of white clover (*T. repens*) rise on long, bare stems from ground level; leaves of other species sprout from ground at base of plant and also branch from the stem.
- Flowers open from the base of the blossom first.
- Flowers may be white, pink, deep red, purple, or yellow.
- White clover flowers may be tinged with rosy purple in bud or when newly opened.
- White clover spreads into thick mats via aboveground stems that root along the way: red clover and sweet clovers usually stay in one clump.
- Foliage at the base of the plant may stay green through winter; top growth dies back after several hard frosts.

fact file

LIFE CYCLE	perennial
SITE, SOIL & SEASON	widely adaptable to various soils in full to part sun; blooms spring through fall
DISPERSAL	seed or spreading roots, based on species
ULTIMATE HEIGHT	depends on species; some hug the ground, others are knee-high or taller
OTHER NAMES	shamrock, cowgrass, sugar-plums, honeysuckle, lamb sucklings, Dutch clover (*Trifolium repens*)

American Indians knew white clover long before Europeans arrived, bringing other species to these shores. They may have enjoyed the sweet scent of the flowers and foliage, but they appreciated more the plant's usefulness as a welcome food. Clovers are legumes, high in proteins, vitamins, and certain minerals. Dried white clover (*T. repens*) went into stews and dried, pounded meat mixes, and the white flowers were also a sweet treat. During famines in Ireland, white clover flowers were dried and ground into flour. Red clover and the tall sweet clovers are pretty in a meadow garden, and as legumes, all species enrich the soil in which they grow with a nitrogen boost. Herbalists employ clovers in preparations for various ailments. Rabbits, horses, sheep, and other foraging animals adore eating clover, and nectar-seeking insects find a bounty in the plentiful blossoms.

■ **CULINARY USE** Limit recipe use to blossoms. Pick only the best blossoms since once the flowers begin to brown at the bottom, their taste becomes unpleasant. Try a good herb tea made from about two tablespoons of dried white clover flowers, steeped for 10 minutes and strained.

■ **HERBAL USE** Sip clover-blossom tea (see "Culinary Use," left) to soothe coughs. Red clover is also used medicinally, and has been a treatment in folk medicine for various cancers; now, scientists are giving its efficacy a second look after researchers discovered it contains a substance that may hold some hope for slowing the spread of breast cancer. However, do not experiment yourself with large doses of clovers or sweet clovers. They may contain coumarin or other chemicals, which are thought dangerous as they can cause drastic side effects such as hemorrhage.

■ **CRAFT USE** Dry fresh blossoms of red or white clover on screens in a shady, airy place, then tie into squares of loosely woven cloth to scent drawers of clothes or linens. Add dried blossoms or bits of blossoms to potpourri. Search for a four-leaf clover, press in an old phone book, and mount in a small frame for a good-luck gift on special occasions.

■ **WILDLIFE** Clover in bloom will make your yard a favored destination for honeybees and other nectar seekers. The leaves and blossoms are eagerly devoured by rabbits, groundhogs, and other small animals.

■ **LAWN INTEREST** White clover creates a lush, fragrant lawn that's a joy to mow. Its scattering of blossoms perks up the usual uniformity of lawn grass, and the perfume is delicious next to a patio or other outdoor seating area. Beware of bee stings, though: Springy, cool clover is wonderful to walk barefoot upon unless it's harboring honeybees.

White clover can take over a lawn almost overnight, it sometimes seems. Unfortunately for you, its running, rooting stems travel just as fast in the loose, rich soil of garden beds as they do in lawns. Because of its strong growth habit, even a tiny piece of this plant left behind after a weeding session is capable of fathering another invasion as soon as it regathers its strength and sends out new stems. Thankfully, red clover and sweet clovers are a lot easier to evict because they usually show up singly and do not spread.

■ **HAND PULL** Pull clover out of garden beds as soon as you see it. For taller clovers, grasp the plant at its base and pull upward with a twist to loosen the root. For creeping white clover, lift beneath the plant with your fingers to remove the main plant. Then remove any additional stems.

■ **HOE** Use a long-handled hoe to chop out taller clovers and to chop and lift clumps of white clover in vegetable gardens. Shake off any soil, then add to the compost pile.

■ **HERBICIDE** Treat infested lawn areas with an appropriate herbicide, as directed on the package. Spot-treat smaller outbreaks with a spray-on weedkiller to eradicate.

Tussilago farfara

Coltsfoot

With a long list of names like ass's foot and horse's foot, it's apparent that this plant looks like an animal's hoof, although just which animal is obviously a matter of opinion. Coltsfoot rarely shows up spontaneously in gardens. Usually it arrives by invitation, either because of its healing properties or its welcome early burst of bloom. The flowers look very much like dandelions, but the plant's habits are very different from that common weed.

The dandelion-like, yellow flowers appear on bare stems long before the leaves emerge from the soil. The blossoms open wide on sunny days, remaining closed in rain and in overcast weather. Coltsfoot leaves are relatively small when they first break the ground, but soon expand to a very large size; and their stems get taller too. Plants spread to form a dense groundcover.

- Sunny yellow, dandelion-like flowers when there are no leaves visible.
- Flowering stems are reddish, with overlapping scales.
- Flowers mature into fluffy white seedheads.
- Leaves are roughly the size and shape of a colt's foot when young; they mature to the size of a full-grown bull or draft horse's hoof, usually about 7 inches across, but occasionally reaching an elephantine 12 inches!
- Leaves have silvery undersides.
- Plants form solid stretches of foliage.
- Roots are pencil-thick, shallow, horizontal, and branching. They spread quickly in loose soil to expand the colony.

 fact file

LIFE CYCLE	perennial
SITE, SOIL & SEASON	sun to shade; prefers loose, dry soil; blooms in late winter or early spring
DISPERSAL	creeping roots
ULTIMATE HEIGHT	up to 1½ feet
OTHER NAMES	ass's foot, bull's foot, foal foot, horse's foot, sow foot

Friend?

Cheerfulness is a notable quality of coltsfoot. A patch of the sunny, yellow flowers makes a great welcome along a driveway—even if the neighbors do suspect you of harboring dandelions. The thickly knitted roots and dense leaves spell groundcover, and this plant lives up to that promise. It's happiest with room to roam, although not difficult to keep in bounds in the garden.

■ **GARDEN USE** Plant as a groundcover on slopes. Use in shade gardens for the bold punch of its big leaves. Or try it along a walk or path for the surprise of its seemingly overnight blooms.

■ **HERBAL USE** The ancient Romans sure knew their cures: Pliny suggested inhaling the smoke of the burning plant through a reed to cure a chronic cough, noting that "the patient must take a sip of raisin wine at each inhalation." By the end of the treatment, you'd probably have forgotten all about the cough! Although coltsfoot has been embraced for centuries as an herbal medicine, recent research shows that compounds in the plant cause cancerous tumors in rats. Ingestion of coltsfoot is therefore strongly discouraged, no matter what you learned at Grandma's knee about homegrown "cures."

Foe?

Coltsfoot is hardly a determined enemy. It readily yields the field when its roots are disturbed, although remnants may resprout in a last-ditch attempt at recolonization.

■ **HAND PULL** Use your fingers to lift the matted roots from the soil.

■ **HOE** Scrape out the roots with a long-handled hoe. Chop the soil to loosen it, and sift through with your fingers to remove broken pieces of root.

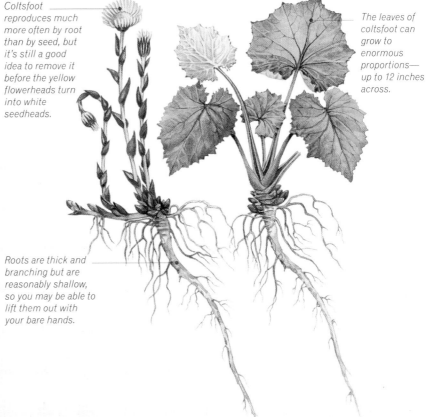

Coltsfoot reproduces much more often by root than by seed, but it's still a good idea to remove it before the yellow flowerheads turn into white seedheads.

The leaves of coltsfoot can grow to enormous proportions— up to 12 inches across.

Roots are thick and branching but are reasonably shallow, so you may be able to lift them out with your bare hands.

Urtica dioica

Stinging nettle

Stinging nettles are enjoying a renaissance among gardeners, thanks to their reputation as an irresistible host plant for the red admiral butterfly, and a renewed interest in herbal remedies. Back in good graces they may be, but the plants are still horrid to the touch: Their nefarious stems and leaves are armed with millions of tiny hairs, each of them a hypodermic needle in miniature. Brush against the plant, and a flurry of spines releases their venom into your tender skin, burning like fire. Amazingly, the plants have been used for centuries as edible greens, cooked up like spinach, and employed as a remedy for a host of ailments.

Reminiscent of mint, this square-stemmed weed grows in dense colonies, but that's where the resemblance ends. Stinging nettles smell rank, not minty, and they are immediately painful to the touch. Close inspection will reveal the aforementioned covering of fine, bristly hairs that carry the irritating toxin. Leaves are arranged on opposite sides of the stem, and the plant has a generally vigorous appearance. Male and female flowers are usually borne on separate plants. The flowers are green, and look like loose catkins drooping from the leaf axils near the top of the stems.

- Leaves are heart-shaped or pointed-oval, and are attached to short stalks.
- Stems are square.
- Stems looks bristly when viewed up close.
- Drooping "catkins" of green flowers hang from leaf axils.
- Grows in thick stands.
- Multiplies rapidly by running roots.

 fact file

LIFE CYCLE	perennial
SITE, SOIL & SEASON	moist to dry soil, sun to shade; blooms in summer
DISPERSAL	seed; running roots
ULTIMATE HEIGHT	to 3 feet
OTHER NAMES	nettles

Friend?

Nettles were once used for all sorts of purposes: clothing, medicine, food, and even as a reputed cure for baldness. Modern herbalists are once again experimenting with the plant, touting its use as a hairwash to add shine and maybe stimulate hair follicles. Wild foragers and country folk still enjoy a dish of nettle greens, although the safety factor of eating the cooked foliage is open to dispute. Butterfly gardeners, too, cherish the presence of the plant, which practically guarantees an improved population of fluttering wings in the garden.

■ **WILDLIFE** The red admiral butterfly lays its eggs on the plant, whose foliage is then devoured by the caterpillars. Orioles collect strong white fibers from the stems of winter-weathered plants to use in nest construction.

■ **CULINARY USE** Collect fresh leaves, wearing gloves and long sleeves. Boil or steam them until tender (cooked leaves lose their sting), and eat occasionally as a vitamin-rich wild green.

■ **COSMETIC USE** Collect some fresh leaves and simmer a cupful in a quart of water for 10 to 15 minutes. Steep for 10 more minutes, strain, cool, and use the liquid as a rinse after shampooing to enhance your hair's shine.

Foe?

Tracking the botanical invasion of America in the seventeenth century, John Josselyn, in *An Account of Two Voyages to New-England,* made a list of "such plants as have sprung up since the English planted and kept cattle in New-England.... Nettle stinging," he noted, "was the first plant taken notice of." And why? The punch this plant packs is alleged to have killed hunting dogs that blundered into the weeds and to have caused a blistering rash on human skin that can last for days. Luckily, nettles show up only occasionally in the garden, and when they do, they are fairly painless to eradicate—as long as you wear gloves! Shady areas seem to be most attractive to nettles, so watch for their unwanted appearance in woodland gardens. Moist soil alongside streams or ponds may also be the first line of an invading force.

■ **HAND PULL** For a limited patch of nettles or a few isolated plants, don protective clothing and hand pull when the soil is moist.

■ **SHOVEL** For a larger nettle problem, mow the area with a lawn mower, bagging clippings for the compost pile. Loosen the network of roots with a shovel, then pull with gloved hands.

■ **HERBICIDE** Apply an appropriate product as directed. Treat isolated plants with spray-on herbicide, shielding nearby desirable plants.

Drooping green flowers make it easy to identify nettles, but also indicate that the plant will soon launch its seed.

The minuscule hairs on the stems and leaves make for a nasty sting, so get your gloves on before you attempt to remove any stray nettles in the yard.

Even if the top growth is mowed off, it is best to hand pull the root system afterward to prevent the weed from spreading further.

Verbascum thapsus
Mullein

Mullein has "please touch" written all over it. The felted, gray leaves are like velvet to the touch, making this an ideal plant to include in a garden for the visually impaired or for children. The big, silvery rosettes are elegant enough to invite into the most formal garden. At flowering time, mullein changes personality and goes from a neat ground-hugger to a skyscraper, with its erect, flowering spike. The plants may drift in from wild areas, but usually as isolated specimens. Mullein was once a staple in herbalists' remedies.

Finally, a super-easy weed to pin a name to! Mullein looks like nothing else. In its first year, before flowering, it forms a thick clump of long, pointed leaves that are an outstanding silvery gray and have a velvety touch. At bloom time, a stiff, tall spike emerges, with a poker of sulfur-yellow blossoms. The plant dies after setting seed, but the dark brown skeletons remain vertical well into winter.

- Big (up to 1 foot long), floppy leaves, covered with soft, wooly hairs that give the leaves the feel of flannel.
- Leaves arranged in a circular rosette before flowering.
- Flowering stem is thick and stiff, with blooms held closely together for about the top 10 inches of the spike.
- Inch-wide, five-petaled flowers are pale yellow.
- The leaf stalks of foliage on the flowering stem are modified with fluted ridges to enable them to cling to the stem.
- Seeds are held in capsules on the stalk.
- Deep taproot.

fact file

LIFE CYCLE	biennial
SITE, SOIL & SEASON	full sun; adapts to many soils except wet ones; blooms in early summer
DISPERSAL	seed
ULTIMATE HEIGHT	usually about 4 to 5 feet
OTHER NAMES	Adam's flannel, Adam's rod, candlewick, flannel leaf, miner's candle, old man's flannel, velvet dock

Friend?

Mullein is a statuesque beauty, well worth a place in the garden. Scatter seed in late summer, fall, or spring, and let it self-sow for future generations. Misplaced seedlings are very hard to transplant, due to the taproot, but they are easy to uproot if unwanted. Tiny thrips may infest the seedhead; they and other hidden insects are eagerly devoured by small woodpeckers and other birds.

- **GARDEN USE** Scatter mullein seed in the herb garden or among scarlet salvias and other flowers, or grow it in a cool garden of silver foliage and white flowers. The gray foliage is perfect for cooling strong, warring colors, such as magenta and orange.

- **WILDLIFE** Downy woodpeckers, chickadees, and titmice scour the seed stalks of mullein in search of insects in both fall and winter.

- **EMERGENCY LIGHT SOURCE** Mullein earns its "candle" nicknames not only because of the candelabra effect of its flowers but also because the entire flowering stalk was dipped in suet and used as a torch in days of yore: a good thing to keep in mind during rolling blackouts!

Veronica spp.

Speedwell

Good things come in small packages, as the saying goes, but so do pernicious weeds—and to lawn lovers, speedwells rank among the worst. Usually they appear in quantity rather than as isolated plants. They infest lawns and spread fast, as their name suggests they should, staying so low to the ground that a lawn mower doesn't touch them. They may also move into flower beds or gravel driveways and among pavers. The name "Paul's betony" refers to their herbal use; Paul of Aegina was a seventh-century physician.

Sky blue or true blue flowers, miniature leaves, and a creeping habit are the hallmarks of the weedy speedwells. They bloom early in spring, often in the company of chickweed and purple dead nettle. Leaves vary in shape according to species, of which there are more than 200, many of them prized garden plants. The worst weed offenders are thyme-leaved speedwell (*Veronica serpyllifolia*) and common speedwell (*V. officinalis*).

- Trailing stems may be erect or prostrate.
- Flowers are blue, but vary from pale to deep blue depending on species.
- Flowers have four petals.
- Leaves may be thin and pointed, rounded and scalloped, or other shapes, depending on species; they are generally less than ½ inch long.
- Stems are thin, and the plant has a dainty look.
- Flowers form in leaf axils and at tips of stems.
- In severe infestations, the flowers may create a powder-blue dusting on lawns.
- Roots are fibrous.

fact file

LIFE CYCLE	annual, perennial
SITE, SOIL & SEASON	sunny to lightly shaded lawns; many soil types; blooms in spring
DISPERSAL	seed, rooting stems
ULTIMATE HEIGHT	ground-hugger, rarely reaching 4 inches tall
OTHER NAMES	*V. serpyllifolia:* thyme-leaved speedwell, Paul's betony; *V. officinalis:* common speedwell, gypsyweed

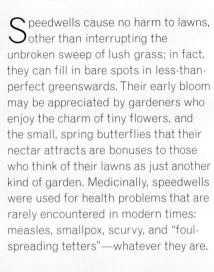

Speedwells cause no harm to lawns, other than interrupting the unbroken sweep of lush grass; in fact, they can fill in bare spots in less-than-perfect greenswards. Their early bloom may be appreciated by gardeners who enjoy the charm of tiny flowers, and the small, spring butterflies that their nectar attracts are bonuses to those who think of their lawns as just another kind of garden. Medicinally, speedwells were used for health problems that are rarely encountered in modern times: measles, smallpox, scurvy, and "foul-spreading tetters"—whatever they are.

- **WILDLIFE** Let speedwells nestle among your lawn grasses to attract small butterflies and other nectaring insects. They are particularly attractive to the diminutive "blues," a group of butterflies that are hard to see when their wings are closed but simply breathtaking in color when they open their wings to flit to another blossom.

- **CRAFT USE** Speedwells are just the right size for pressing in an old telephone book. They flatten easily and dry quickly, retaining their color. Use the finished product to decorate notecards.

Although many gardeners are enchanted by the fairy-size flowers and their beautiful color, speedwell plants are too small to be valued players in the garden. If you find them an annoyance in the lawn, you can crowd them out by improving your turf, or raise your mower blade so that grass shades them out.

- **HAND PULL** Weed out of ornamental beds by gathering the stems and giving a firm tug to the roots. Shake off the soil and toss the plants on the compost pile.

- **PRE-EMERGENT HERBICIDE** Choose an appropriate product and apply to lawn areas according to label directions.

Xanthium spp.

Cocklebur

A regionally abundant pest, cocklebur is rarely seen in some areas and all too common in others. It invades garden beds and farm fields, and thrives in vacant lots. The burrs are the business end of this plant: They are armed with hooked spines that stick as stubbornly as burdock to clothing and animals. The now extinct Carolina parakeet used to relish the seeds, which it extracted after cracking the burr with its strong, curved beak; in fact, John James Audubon painted these colorful, small parrots in the act of dining on cockleburs for his *Birds of America* series. When the birds were hunted to extinction, the weeds proliferated.

The tall, bushy plant has large, wedge-shaped leaves, but you may not work out exactly what it is until the burrs appear in late summer to early fall. Clustered thickly at leaf axils, the leaves persist on the plant into winter. Cocklebur may grow singly or in thick stands, where many seeds have dropped.

- Big, bushy plant that has one to several erect stems.
- Stems are ridged and may be spotted with purple. They are often hairy.
- Leaves are relatively simple in shape: a wide wedge with shallow lobes and serrated edges.
- Male and female flowers are borne in separate clusters; males at the top, where they can shed pollen onto the female flowers in the leaf axils below.
- Flowers are small, and female flowers are held in hairy, spiny, closed structures that mimic the shape of the mature burrs.
- Burs mature to brown in fall. Two seeds are contained in each burr.
- Root is a taproot.

fact file

LIFE CYCLE	annual
SITE, SOIL & SEASON	sun to shade; widely adaptable to soil; blooms in summer
DISPERSAL	seed
ULTIMATE HEIGHT	3 feet
OTHER NAMES	butterbur, lesser burdock, sheep burr, small burdock

Foe?

Unless you like the painstaking chore of picking burrs off your clothes and out of your pets' fur—and don't mind the irritating, almost invisible spines they leave behind— you'll want to uproot any cocklebur plants you may be hosting. Keep an eye on undisturbed areas, such as brushy corners, along fences and buildings, or in established perennial beds. Always dispose of burrs you remove from yourself or others in the trash; do not toss them aside in the yard, where they might grow.

- ■ **HAND PULL** Old-fashioned elbow grease is a swift solution to these big weeds—when they're young. As the plant matures, tools will make the job easier.

- ■ **TRANSPLANTING (OR POACHER'S) SPADE** Use this narrow-bladed shovel to dig out cockleburs among close ornamental neighbors. Compost if they haven't yet set seed.

- ■ **SHOVEL** One deep thrust of the blade should be all it takes to evict an established plant. Compost if it hasn't yet set seed. To remove a plant with burrs, protect yourself with leather gloves and lop off the top growth with long-handled pruners. Gingerly pick up the plant and drop it into a trash bag. There's no need to dig out the root, it won't regrow.

Using weeds

It's a scary thought: inviting weeds into the garden instead of keeping them out. By following the advice in this chapter, you'll learn how to judge the potential beauty—and the potential harm—from any weed that catches your eye. You'll find suggestions for using weeds in almost every style of informal garden, then learn how to make plantings appear controlled even when they're "full of weeds." You'll also learn the benefits of weed gardening, and how just a few simple tricks will keep your weed garden from making the neighbors uneasy. And you'll see that it's not just in the garden that weeds can be useful—but in the kitchen, in the medicine cabinet, and for crafts. The guidelines in these pages will help you make a good assessment of potential for every weed you meet.

Gardening with weeds

Flowers, form, winter architecture—weeds can add beauty and character to your garden as invited guests. A slope of goldenrod and wild asters, a scattering of fresh-faced daisies in the grass, a bower of fragrant honeysuckle over your porch, and tiny scarlet pimpernel and speedwell flowers to delight lovers of miniatures: Weeds bring it all home.

CHOOSING WEEDS

Keep in mind that when it comes to weeds, personality is much more important than good looks. No matter how pretty a plant is, it's no prize if it causes you hours of catch-up to corral stray progeny.

Informal or naturalistic gardens are best for weeds because of their know-no-bounds nature. Weeds that grow lanky or bare-legged will fit in among the informal plantings, perhaps leaning over lower-growing annual flowers or weaving between them to offer an interesting texture or contrasting color. Meadow gardens are ideal for pretty flowering weeds or grasses, which can be allowed to spread at will, competing with other aggressive plants. Shade gardens can benefit from blooming or ground-covering weeds, some of which thrive in conditions that are difficult for garden plants. Formal gardens are usually not suitable for weeds, since this style depends on well-behaved plants of polite habit.

SOIL CONDITIONERS

Despite their reputation as drawbacks in the garden, weeds can have positive effects, too. They work in several ways to improve your soil, making it more hospitable for the garden plants that follow. Dock and other tap-rooted weeds push through soil, opening and increasing air spaces and improving drainage, even in dense, compacted clay. Shallow-rooted, ground-hugging weeds such as ground ivy act as a groundcover to prevent erosion. Chickweed and other winter annuals shield the surface of bare garden beds from erosion, and help prevent crusting of sandy and silty soils. Clover and other leguminous weeds give the soil a boost of nitrogen, increasing soil fertility. What's more, pulling weeds benefits garden plants by loosening the soil around them so that roots can grow more easily.

WEEDS FOR WINTER INTEREST Seedheads that stand through most of the winter make your garden more interesting, while adding height to the sleeping winter landscape.

READ YOUR WEEDS

Some gardeners believe a preponderance of particular weeds, and a lack of others, can provide clues to soil conditions such as fertility, moisture level, and pH, all of which you may want to correct to improve your lawn or garden. These are indicated by the presence of various weeds:

- *Wet soil* Yellow nutsedge, dock, beggarticks, heal-all
- *Dry soil* Dyer's woad, thistles, shepherd's purse, mullein, knapweeds, Bermudagrass, purslane
- *Lean soil* Shepherd's purse, mullein, black medic
- *Fertile soil* Henbit, dead nettle, dandelion, clover
- *Shade* Garlic mustard, ground ivy, Japanese honeysuckle, nightshade, poison ivy
- *Compacted soil* Annual bluegrass, goosegrass, knotweed, mouse-ear chickweed
- *Acidic soil* Sorrel, crabgrass, annual bluegrass, Carolina geranium, plantain
- *Neutral soil* Chickweed, dandelion, wild mustard
- *Alkaline soil* Poppy, woody aster, sagebrush

WEEDS FOR INFORMAL GARDENS

Most styles and designs of garden have at least a corner for a few welcome weeds, but you can take things a little further in a laid-back, informal garden. Choose weeds with a relaxed form and appealing flowers or seedheads that will add color to your casual garden. You'll find that they combine well with annuals, perennials, or herbs.

WEEDS FOR FLOWERS

Garden weeds can be an unexpected delight as well as a headache, bringing forth their delicate, pretty flowers and attracting visitors such as bees, butterflies, and moths. The flowers may not generally be as showy as garden flowers, but they certainly add color to the mix—and they're free! Pick some for indoor bouquets, too: Queen Anne's lace or fleabane are pure country charm in a pottery jug; tiny blue speedwell and scarlet pimpernel are delightful in a thimble!

WEEDS TO COVER GARDEN STRUCTURES

For fast coverage, nothing beats a weed. Some flowering vines will self-sow or grow back from the root year after year. Given a vertical support, multiflora rose will clamber vertically against a trellis (with ties for added support) or into the branches of a tree. The deadly nightshade vine can also be a beauty, despite its well-earned reputation as a poisonous weed. Other climbers that will happily take to whatever climbing obstacle you put in their path are bindweed, Japanese honeysuckle, and morning glories.

WEEDS FOR GROUNDCOVER

Bare ground loses moisture to the air on sunny days and soil to erosion when it rains. A healthy groundcover of living plants will conserve moisture and prevent erosion, and weeds can be good candidates. Buttercups, clover, lungwort, ground ivy, moss, and heal-all all spread into thick colonies, generally not as dense as garden plants sold for that purpose but still providing an area of green over bare ground.

WEEDS FOR WILDLIFE GARDENS

Increase the liveliness of your garden by planting weeds that offer food, shelter, or other benefits to songbirds, butterflies, and other interesting creatures. An inexpensive magnifying glass will give you a real eyeful of the diverse visitors and inhabitants of the weed patch (see table, above right).

FAVORITES WITH THE YOUNG Children are often attracted to the diminutive size, bright colors, and abundance of garden weeds. They also love to be included on hunting expeditions for interesting creatures among the weeds.

weeds that attract wildlife

WEED	USE
Brambles	Birds and animals eat fruits; shelter, nest site
Buttercups	Flowers attract butterflies
Chickweed	Songbirds eat seeds
Coltsfoot	Butterflies visit flowers; seed fluff used in nests
Dandelion	Butterflies visit flowers; songbirds eat seeds
Fleabane	Flowers attract butterflies
Forget-me-not	Flowers attract butterflies
Foxtail grass	Songbirds eat seeds
Heal-all	Flowers attract butterflies and hummingbirds
Knotweeds	Birds eat seeds; butterflies visit flowers
Lamb's quarters	Songbirds eat seeds
Mallows	Flowers attract butterflies
Moss	Birds use moss to build nests
Mullein	Woodpeckers eat insects in seed stalk
Multiflora rose	Birds and animals eat berries; shelter; nest site
Pigweed	Songbirds eat seeds
Plantain	Rabbits eat leaves
Pokeweed	Songbirds eat fruits
Queen Anne's lace	Flowers attract butterflies
Stinging nettles	Host for caterpillars of red admiral butterfly
Yarrow	Flowers attract butterflies

Weed-gardening techniques

Plan your weed garden carefully to eliminate as much "weeding" as possible. Choose plants that grow well together and coexist happily for years, without the need for much human intervention. Expect the planting to change over the seasons, as one weed or another asserts temporary dominance. If you maintain a laissez-faire attitude, you'll notice your weed garden eventually begins to assume a very different character, as plants move in of their own accord. In nature, this process is called succession, and eventually results in a landscape that has reverted to its original character: young trees in a region that was once forest; chaparral in arid areas; and so on.

To keep the original character of the planting, guide your weeds so that the plants you prefer are favored. That may mean—yes—weeding your weed garden.

CONTROLLING SEEDS

The only sure way of keeping weeds from dropping their seeds is to snip or mow their flowering stems before the seeds form. The old-fashioned skill of scything or its modern counterpart, the string trimmer, are efficient aids in controlling seeds. Slice your weeds off at half-height after flowering but before they set seed. You can leave them in place as a mulch if your weed garden tends toward the wild side, or gather the remains as valuable nitrogen materials for the compost pile. The cut-back weeds will push out new growth and may even flower a second time. For more on weed control, see Chapter 4.

Realistically, however, most of us are apt to get forgetful when it comes to removing potential seedheads. Birds, mice, and other creatures will help out by devouring a huge number of the seeds, but seedlings will still spring up in abundance. For the least labor-intensive solution, pile on the mulch to prevent seeds from sprouting. Most will suffocate beneath a 2-inch layer of grass clippings or another type of mulch (see pages 154-157), thereby contributing their remains to building better soil. Control measures that you practice in other garden areas will also work in your weed garden: hoeing, hand pulling, or, as a last resort, chemical warfare (see pages 160-63).

KEEPING WEEDS IN CHECK Instead of disposing of grass clippings and fallen leaves in the trash, rake them up and use as a mulch to prevent unwanted plants from inveigling their way into your weed garden.

choosing a location

Unless you're planning to convert your entire yard to a weed garden, you'll want to select a site with forethought.

Keep the planting as far away as possible from more traditional beds, because seeds will drop and roots will spread.

A sunny site is best for most weeds.

Most weeds grow best in well-drained soil, but they are highly adaptable to soil types.

Keep the garden away from property lines, so that weeds don't infiltrate your neighbors' yards.
(See also right, "Controlling Spreading Roots.")

CONTROLLING SPREADING ROOTS

Weeds with takeover tendencies that spread themselves through far-reaching roots, including those listed for groundcover purposes, are the most difficult to keep in bounds. These plants won't recognize where your weed garden ends: instead, they'll merrily push right on through into the lawn or, worse yet, other garden areas. To prevent their spread, depend on barricades. Install a barrier of metal or strong plastic strips in the soil, deep enough to keep the roots from going underneath in their colonizing attempts. Although it may seem like overkill, a 12-inch-deep strip will save you headaches in years to come. Anything shallower is likely to be just a temporary challenge to determined roots.

Use a continuous strip or commercial types of barricade made with closely interlocking ends so that weeds can't infiltrate between sections. Allow at least 2 inches of the barricade to extend above the soil level, to discourage those tentacle-like roots from sneaking out of bounds over the top.

Even with a barricade in place, you will still need to monitor the area for escapees. Rigorously root out or chemically spot-treat any weeds that make the leap or sow themselves onto the wrong side of the area.

MEADOW GARDENS

Most gardeners have tried the "meadow in a can" dream at least once, usually with less than satisfying results. The first year, the planting is as pretty as the picture on the package, but by year two, the garden has gone to weeds. By carefully selecting the weeds for a meadow planting, and augmenting them with a dash of colorful bloomers from a "meadow garden" can or packets of wildflower seed mix, you can enjoy the best of both worlds.

Begin planning your weed-enhanced meadow garden in summer to fall, when you can gather seeds of weeds for future plantings. Choose weeds that reproduce abundantly, so that less desirable characters are crowded out. Explore natural meadows in your area so you can see which plants coexist happily—Mother Nature is a top-notch garden designer! Weeds with aggressive roots and those that self-sow with a vengeance are the top candidates for your meadow garden. Clip seedheads into a labeled paper bag and store in a cool, dry place.

In fall or spring, prepare the area as you would for any garden, by removing existing vegetation and loosening the soil. Scatter your seed liberally, just before a rain if possible. Cover lightly with a scattering of dry grass clippings or straw to keep birds from eating the seeds. Transplant additional desired weeds into the garden anytime during the growing season. Even plants in bud can be successfully moved by

MAKING FINE TILTH If you are creating a weed garden from scratch, first prepare the soil by digging it over and raking it to establish the best conditions for your seedlings.

best weeds for meadow gardens

Besides the weeds listed below, other wildlings will no doubt appear in your inviting meadow, springing up from seeds in the soil or brought in by wildlife. You're likely to see asters, goldenrod, chicory, and other common flowering weeds of open areas cropping up. Enjoy the surprises!

WEED	HABIT	COMMENTS
Annual meadow grass	Annual	One of the many attractive grasses to add visual grace and a backdrop for flowers
Beggarticks	Annual	Search out *Bidens aristosa* or *B. pilosa,* two members of the genus that lack the barbed seeds of this group; they have billows of golden flowers that attract butterflies, followed by bird-favored seeds
Bindweed	Annual	Cheery white mini-morning glory flowers wind their way up taller weeds or recline along the ground
Buttercups	Perennial	Determined root spreader to wash the meadow with melted-butter color in spring
Cinquefoil	Annual, perennial	Pale yellow flowers that resemble old-fashioned single roses appear in spring
Clover	Annual, perennial	Bundles of purple, white, or red sweet-scented flowers attract butterflies and other insects; foliage is manna to rabbits
Dock, sheep sorrel	Biennial, perennial	Valuable late summer presence, thanks to its tall spikes of brown seeds, which persist all winter and provide food for birds and animals
Fleabane	Annual	Abundant branches crowned by clusters of tiny fringed daisies in white, pink, or lavender; attracts butterflies
Foxtail grass	Annual	Fat, fuzzy, arching seedheads add beauty and are a favored food for songbirds
Horsetail	Perennial	Primitive plants with leafless green stems; some species almost fernlike, others tall and spare
Jimsonweed	Annual	Statuesque branching form, like an open shrub; trumpet flowers attract hummingbirds
Knotweeds, smartweeds	Annual	Many strings or clusters of white or pink flowers; often acquires good red fall color in foliage and stems
Mallows	Annual, perennial	Bushy plants or sprawlers with flowers in pink or white; attracts butterflies
Morning glory	Annual, perennial	Beautiful wide trumpet flowers in white, blue, purple, and rose, often with contrasting eye, on a vining plant
Mullein	Biennial	Rosette of soft, gray leaves from which emerges a tall spike of pale yellow flowers. Seedhead persists all winter, adding vertical interest and providing food for woodpeckers and other birds
Pigweed	Annual	Eye-catching red stems at the approach of fall; seeds attract finches and other songbirds
Pokeweed	Perennial	Birds will do the planting honors; the plant's pendant clusters of purple-black fruits are a favorite. Imposing shrublike form; thick stems turn vivid magenta in fall
Queen Anne's lace	Biennial	Feathery foliage and delicate white flowers that attract butterflies
Teasel	Biennial	Strongly vertical form with dramatic seedheads that persist all winter
Wild garlic, wild onion	Perennial	Sweet-smelling (non-oniony!) flowers that attract butterflies
Wild lettuce	Annual	Tall plant with wicked-looking (but soft) spiny leaves; the mostly bare flowering stem is topped with a wide cluster of tiny white or blue flowers. Worth including for its attraction to seed-seeking finches
Wild mustard	Annual	Pretty sulphur-yellow flowers that perk up the garden beginning in late winter; attracts butterflies
Yarrow	Perennial	Late spring to fall color; attracts butterflies

keeping soil around the roots and "muddying in." Fill the planting hole with water, let drain, and fill with water again before setting a transplant in place.

As your meadow changes from season to season, you'll also enjoy getting to know other plants that manage to wiggle their way in. Remove dastardly interlopers like thistles and knapweeds, which are banned from cultivation in many areas. Be aware that a meadow is really a place of transition: Unless you live in an arid area or natural grassland, shrub and tree seedlings will soon appear. Native peoples used fire to discourage the succession process, but you can control young woody plants by mowing in late winter to early spring to keep your meadow garden from reverting to woodland.

GRASS MAKES THE GARDEN

Natural meadows get their grace from the mix of grasses among the flowering plants. An easy way to incorporate grass is simply to let lawn grass mature among the flowering plants. Fescue, bluegrass, and other varieties all have interesting seedheads and graceful habits when they are allowed to grow to their full potential. If you're planning a meadow where lawn currently exists, allow some sections of the turf to remain in place. It will not only save you time and labor, but also add to the effect of the garden.

ILLEGAL WEEDS

In order to protect crops and pastures and prevent environmental disasters, federal, state, and sometimes local government agencies develop lists of "noxious weeds." These plants are considered dangerous characters, and must be controlled, even in your own yard. In general, you can count on thistles being flora non grata in most areas; they are a serious pest on farmland. In the West, knapweeds are high on the list of villains.

Listen up: Traditional gardening and lawn practices are usually not in danger of violation, but the increased popularity of more naturalistic landscaping may make you a lawbreaker. Before you let your yard go *au naturel*, check with your local governing body and search the Internet for state and federal noxious weed lists of plants considered serious pests. Local agencies may also require weeds to be removed or cut when they reach a certain height, even if they are not on the least-wanted list.

GRACEFUL GRASSES A combination of grass species provides a subtle backdrop for more showy weeds (below left). The seedheads of many grasses (below right) are particularly stunning on a dewy morning.

Weed-garden design

Take your tips from Mother Nature when designing with weeds. Look at wild places for plants and combinations that appeal to you. Use your own good eye, too, when you decide to invite selected weeds into existing or planned gardens of other flowers. Cast a critical eye upon:

- *Form* The dramatic seed spike of dock, for instance, adds a strong vertical punch to filmy cosmos foliage. Creeping purslane is appealing among paving stones.
- *Texture* Stout, ruffled burdock foliage may be just the textural accent you need among a planting of fine-textured alyssum or grassy-leaved daylilies. Flannel-soft rosettes of mullein leaves are so appealing you may be inspired to clip the flower stalk when it begins to form and enjoy the plant as a low-growing accent.
- *Color* Consider foliage and flower color, plus any winter color a weed may offer. Sheep sorrel, for example, provides dramatic dark brown seed spikes that stand all winter long, while foxtail grass bleaches to a platinum blonde. A flurry of white English daisies brightens a shady garden or lawn.

NEIGHBORHOOD STANDARDS

We've been trained so well to consider weeds as pests that a garden with—or entirely of—weeds can inspire alarm. Before your neighbors start giving you nasty glances, take steps to make your weed garden look as if it's in control.

- *Neat* Keep the edges of the planting neat. A clearly demarcated edge of the garden shows your guiding hand is in charge, and border the planting with lawn or wood chip mulch for a firm sense of start-and-stop.
- *Straight edges* Design your beds with straight edges. Straight lines effect an attitude of formality, even if the plants within are wild in their habits.
- *Boundaries* Back the planting with a solid, manmade boundary. A fence, sidewalk, driveway, or wall lends a strong sense of control.
- *Paths* Divide large weed gardens with wide, well-defined paths. Not only will this trick make your garden appear groomed, but it will also give you a better view of your weeds and their visitors.

THE NATURAL LOOK Allow pretty weeds such as English daisies to intermingle with your ornamentals to create a charmingly relaxed cottage garden feel.

weeds for shade gardens

WEED	USE
Buttercups	Rampant spreaders, but a good groundcover choice in wilder shade gardens
Forget-me-not	Looser form and fewer flowers than in sun, but still worth inviting into the shade garden for spring color
Ground ivy	An all-too-eager groundcover, but harmless to hosta and other robust companions; pretty blue flowers in late spring look good with little bulbs and mini-daffodils
Heal-all	Reminiscent of ajuga, although not as dense a groundcover
Horsetail	Striking architecture from the bare-stemmed species; soft texture from branching species, which look like a forest of mini-pine trees
Moss	Learn appreciation for smaller plants by exploring the wonderful variety of textures and forms of mosses
Smartweed	Shade-adapted species vary from tall types with firework-like flower sprays to tiny creepers

- *Ornaments* An imposing planter or statue, or a pedestal birdbath or gazing globe, announces to passers-by that this is an intentional garden, not a lowly weed patch.
- *Transition* If you want to soften the transition zone between traditional flower beds and a weed garden, choose weeds of complementing texture and color to the other plantings, and plant them in sweeps or groups of the same kind.

Situate your weed collection in the backyard or another discreet area if possible. If the front yard is your only choice, however, start small and pay extra attention to creating an appealing design. Talking to your neighbors is a huge help in keeping relationships friendly. Tell them why you value weeds, and what you hope to gain from your new garden. They may even be inspired to start their own planting.

NATURAL LANDSCAPING

A naturalistic style is perfect for weeds because they're probably growing in the very landscape you're attempting to evoke. Start by experimenting with native plants that may be too exuberantly self-propagating for a more traditional garden. Because a naturalistic design requires less fussing than other styles, you're bound to find unexpected seedlings cropping up here and there. Let them grow until you learn to recognize them, so that you can encourage those you want and oust those you don't while they're young.

Use natural elements like logs, stumps, and rocks as accents. To further enhance your natural style, make curving paths, instead of using the more formal feel of straight lines and prune trees and shrubs only to remove dead wood or interfering branches or to enhance their natural shape.

SHADE GARDENS

Volunteer plants—okay, weeds—that pop up in shade gardens deserve a careful look before you cast them out. The list of ornamentals, especially flowering ones, is much shorter for shady than sunny sites, and weeds may hold potential. Uproot poison ivy, of course, but consider giving unfamiliar weeds a trial period before you give them the heave-ho. Foliage and form are the pluses of these shade-loving weeds, which add variety to the planting in a shade garden. A few also contribute a burst of bloom to brighten shady places.

Weeds that are already established in your shade garden are likely to be those with spreading roots, including ground ivy, goutweed, and heal-all. While some gardeners make it a matter of honor to eradicate every trace of these fast spreaders, others treat them as groundcovers, and plant hostas and other shade ornamentals among them.

Ornamental plants themselves can achieve weed status in shade gardens: Consider dame's rocket, English ivy, and honesty (lunaria), which now infest natural woodlands, and lungwort, a prized plant in many American gardens that is treated as a weed in the moist, shady, cool gardens of the Pacific Northwest and England.

SUNNY GARDENS

Gardens situated in the sun harbor a greater diversity of weeds than shaded sites, which is both good news and bad news: You'll meet many interesting weed species in a sunny garden, and you'll have lots more weeds to keep under control. It's best to evict at first sight any weeds that spread quickly by creeping roots; plants such as buttercups, Jerusalem artichoke, goutweed, and ground ivy will quickly overrun the garden. Those that spread moderately by roots, such as yarrow, are considerably easier to keep from crowding out your other plants.

Self-sowing weeds flourish in a sunny garden. Follow the usual control methods, beginning with mulch, to keep them at a reasonable level.

SOFTENING THE EDGES Weeds are perfect for creating a "lived-in" look in your garden. The fast-growing habits of many species make them perfect for softening the straight edges of a newly laid path (below left). Mosses will quickly cover garden structures and ornaments (below right), so even the newest additions to your garden will soon look at home.

Healing weeds

HISTORY OF HERBAL USE

Humans have been using plants for medicinal purposes since the dawn of time. We have always been plagued with cuts, toothaches, labor pains, and other discomforts. As time passed, each culture developed its own list of tried-and-true favorite remedies, based on the plants that grew in the neighborhood. Nomadic people spread the word and sometimes the plants themselves. Native American tribes, for instance, shared and traded plant roots, berries, and other preparations between each other and later with European colonists, who brought their own plants from abroad and embraced Native American treatments as well.

Modern medicine has been with us only for a hundred years or so, but since its advent, herbal remedies have been left in the dust, forsaken for manufactured drugs bought at the pharmacy instead of medicinal herbs picked in the field. Although herbalists have been with us all along, the lore and lure of herbal medicine have been making a strong comeback in public perception only during recent decades.

Herbal remedies made from weeds or other plants should not take the place of good medical care, but you may find a few uses that combine compatibly with other treatments, or can be used on their own. A caution: To avail yourself of the best old and new remedies medical science has to offer, always tell your doctor about any herbal treatments you are using, whether purchased or homemade.

SAFE WEEDS FOR HERBAL USE

The making of prescription and over-the-counter medicines is like following a detailed recipe, with every ingredient and step of preparation spelled out to the last detail. That's why each bottle of decongestant, for example, has the same effect on the body as any other bottle on the shelf.

Herbal treatments tend to be less controlled, especially the homemade kind, the preparation of which is more like home cooking than manufacturing—a pinch of this, a big handful of that, and stir until done. They're also based on plants, whose chemical active ingredient content can vary depending on the influences of weather, growing conditions, and the genetic makeup of the particular plant. With herbal treatments, guesswork is part of the process, and that's what gives them the potential for risk. Weeds may be all-natural, but that doesn't mean they're safe to use medicinally. Plants can cause side effects, poison you, or cause lifelong ill effects just as surely as manufactured chemicals.

Used in moderation and treated with respect, however, weeds can be a ready source of care for minor ailments. For more extensive use, and with more chemically potent weeds, it's best to leave the preparation in the hands of experts.

SLEEP WELL AT NIGHT The mullein plant (*Verbascum thaspus*), especially the flower parts, have been used for centuries as an herbal drink to induce sleep. See page 142 for instructions on how to make an infusion.

safe weeds for occasional herbal use

Each of these weeds has a long history of helping humanity, and they are considered safe to employ as long as you follow the instructions closely. To be sure of your identification, turn to the directory section (pages 18-129). For hints on storing excess weeds, see page 144.

HERB	PART USED	USE	PREPARATION
Burdock *Arctium lappa*	Leaves	Skin abrasions, poison ivy	Crumple a leaf between your hands to break the leaf veins and release the juice. Apply leaf directly to irritated skin until the itch is relieved, usually within a few minutes. Burdock may cause allergic symptoms in those sensitive to the Asteraceae/Compositae families (including ragweed, marigold, and daisy); if you experience any skin irritation, discontinue use.
Chickweed *Stellaria media*	Leaves	Skin irritations, constipation	For skin problems, crush a handful of leaves and plaster to skin. For constipation, stir 3–4 tablespoons of fresh foliage and stems into 8 cups of water, bring to a boil and simmer until reduced to 2 cups of liquid. Strain, cool and drink 1 cup warm. Repeat in 3 hours if needed.
Chicory *Cichorium intybus*	Root	Constipation	Scrub and boil a 3-inch piece of fresh root in 2 cups water for 5 minutes, strain, and cool. Sip ½ –1 cup of the liquid daily. Chicory may cause allergic symptoms in those sensitive to the Asteraceae/Compositae families (including ragweed, daisy, and marigolds); if you experience any chest pain or breathing problems, discontinue use.
Coltsfoot *Tussilago farfara*	Leaves	Coughs, hoarseness	Steep 2 teaspoons of leaves in 1 cup of water for 10 minutes; strain, sweeten, and sip warm. Drink no more than 1 cup per day for no more than 3 days. Coltsfoot may cause allergic symptoms in those sensitive to the Asteraceae/Compositae families (including ragweed, daisy, and marigolds); if you experience any chest pain or breathing problems, discontinue use. Coltsfoot may have a negative effect on the liver in large or regular doses due to alkaloids in the plant, and may cause cancer, so regular ingestion is strongly discouraged.
Curly dock *Rumex crispus*	Leaves	Boils	Crumple a leaf in your hand and apply it to the sore spot. Leave in place for 10 minutes. Repeat daily if required.
Dandelion *Taraxacum officinale*	Leaves, flowers	Wart remover	Dab the juice from a broken leaf end or a flower stem onto the wart. Allow to dry. Repeat daily until wart disappears. This weed may cause allergic symptoms in those sensitive to the Asteraceae/Compositae families (including ragweed, daisy, and marigolds); if you experience any skin irritation, discontinue use.
Heal-all *Prunella vulgaris*	Leaves	Sore throat	Steep 2 tablespoons of fresh leaves in 2 cups of water. Strain, cool, and use as a gargle as often as needed.
Mullein *Verbascum thapsus*	Flowers	Respiratory inflammation	Steep 1 teaspoon fresh flowers in 1 cup water. Strain and sip an hour before bedtime.
Multiflora rose *Rosa multiflora*	Hips	Vitamin-C boost (true of all rose hips)	Crush dried rose hips with a rolling pin. Tie hips in cheesecloth and steep for about 15 minutes to make tea, using 1 tablespoon crushed hips per cup of water. Sweeten with honey to taste.
Plantain *Plantago major*	Leaves, rootstock	Insect bites, toothache	Crush fresh leaves and apply to insect bites. Chew the fresh, rinsed root to relieve tooth pain as needed. Some people are allergic to this species.
Purslane *Portulaca oleracea*	Leaves, stem	Iron and potassium boost	Nibble on a stem or use in salads. Use judiciously in the diet.
Queen Anne's lace *Daucus carota*	Root	Heartburn, acid stomach	Process several rinsed roots in a juicer. Drink ½ –1 cup, undiluted, as needed. Queen Anne's lace has occasionally caused kidney irritation, neurological effects, and photosensitivity. It is also vital to be certain of your identification, as this weed is easily mistaken for the highly toxic poison hemlock. Do not use unless absolutely certain of its identity.
Stinging nettle *Urtica dioica*	Root	Hair restorer	Use gloves and do not touch plant parts to bare skin. Boil about 2 teaspoons fresh, rinsed root in 1 cup water for 10 minutes, then steep for an additional 10 minutes. Cool, strain, and pour over scalp.

Preparing a remedy

Be absolutely confident of your identification of a weed before you attempt to use it in an herbal treatment. Just to be on the safe side, you may want to start your medicinal experiments with weeds used externally.

If you've never experimented with homemade herbal or weed treatments before, you'll likely be surprised at the small quantities recommended for ingestion: A teaspoon a day of a certain preparation is often all that's recommended. This is because boiling and other methods of preparation create a concentrated content. Don't be tempted to increase the recommended dosage in an attempt to speed up your recovery; you might find that overdoing the cure will make you feel worse than the original ailment.

Preparations

The healing powers of natural remedies can be released only if the material is prepared in the correct manner, so that the active ingredients of weeds are made available to the body in the most appropriate form. Here follows a brief glossary of the most widely used medicinal preparations. Before getting started, check the weed's identity in the weed directory (see pages 18-129) and use only the amount recommended.

making an infusion

This is the easiest method to make a mild herbal tea, sometimes called a tisane or an infusion.

1 Check the amount you can use safely (normally about 1 teaspoon dried herb or 2 teaspoons fresh leaves) and place in a teapot, bowl, or pitcher. Cover with 1 cup of boiling water and leave for 10 minutes.

2 Strain the liquid into a cup or glass and add sweetener to taste. Store leftovers in a covered container in the refrigerator; it will keep for several days.

making a decoction

Similar to the tisane, this preparation harnesses the goodness in an herb's roots.

1 Wash the plants thoroughly to remove any traces of dirt or insects. Discard any unwanted bits of the plant, and roughly chop the rest. Try to retain as much moisture and sap as possible.

2 Place the weeds in an enamel or stainless steel pan and cover with cold water. You will need 1 pint of water for every 2 ounces of weed parts. Bring to the boil and simmer, covered, for 10 minutes.

3 Pour the liquid through a strainer into a container to remove any hard pieces of weed. Top off to make 1 pint with fresh water. Allow to cool before use.

making a poultice

This preparation helps the body absorb compounds through the skin.

1 Mix flour and warm water to form a thick paste, then stir in the dried or fresh weeds and apply immediately to the skin.

2 Secure a cloth or bandage over the area. A hot water bottle placed on the poultice will help keep the heat in longer. Keep on until pain, itch, or swelling is relieved. A poultice is often effective after only 10 minutes; it can be kept on for longer if desired, and remoistened with very warm water as needed. Wash off residue with water afterward.

making a compress

Soak a clean cloth (linen, gauze, and cotton are all good) in a hot tisane or decoction, wring out, and apply immediately. If necessary, change when the liquid cools.

HARVESTING AND STORING

When to harvest depends on which part of the plant you're picking (see "harvest season", below). The aim is to gather the leaves, flowers, or roots when they are rich with the acids, proteins, and other chemical compounds that give them their healing power. If you would like specific advice on how to harvest and store a particular weed, turn to the directory section (see pages 18-129).

If you want to preserve your pickings, there are two main methods of doing so—drying and freezing. Air drying is the most popular way. Hang loose bunches of leafy stems upside down; hang roots right side up where air can freely circulate, out of direct sun. This is also the best method for plants you wish to use for ornamental arrangements. This method will allow the plant to keep its form better because it may take several weeks for the moisture to fully evaporate.

You also can experiment with drying weeds in your oven or microwave. Preheat an oven at the lowest setting, lay your plants on a baking tray, and place inside with the door ajar.

freezing weeds

Rinse your weeds thoroughly, then gently dry them between two sheets of paper towel.

You can either place them directly into resealable freezer storage bags or pack them into rigid plastic boxes, separating the layers with non-stick baking parchment.

Be sure to label your freezer bag or box clearly so you can identify the leaves at a later time.

harvest season

Gather weed leaves for herbal use just before flowering, when the leaves are fully mature in size. Or pick individual leaves anytime you need them. To harvest large amounts of a certain weed twice a season, cut it back to half its height or to ground level in early summer; it should have enough time to regrow and provide a second cutting several weeks later.

Harvest flowers as soon as possible after they have opened. Pick them early in the morning, before insects are out and about, to reduce the time spent cleaning the flowers before use.

Dig roots in fall. Photosynthesis, which occurred in the weed all summer, will have plumped up the roots with stored food, including the medicinal compounds you're after.

Collect fruits and seeds when they ripen to their mature color (see the weed directory, pages 18-129). As harvest time nears, monitor closely so you can catch them before they fall.

Leave them to dry for up to five hours, checking every half hour. To dry weeds in a microwave, begin with a brief cycle of no more than 30 seconds on a medium setting and adjust until the weeds are dry but not brittle. Microwaves vary a lot so you will need to experiment to find the correct drying time. Keep note of your results so you can duplicate them.

Moisture, heat, and light are the enemies of stored herbs because they can cause deterioration of plant chemicals. Keep your dried herbs in airtight containers, including glass jars or metal tins. Plastic kitchenware is fine for short-term storage, but some plastics release their own gases that may interact with the herbs. Roots stay freshest in the vegetable bin of your refrigerator, where they will last for at least three months, or even longer for those with a low-water content.

Freezing edible weeds can preserve their flavor for up to six months for use in cooking. Once frozen, however, they cannot be used in fresh salads or as a garnish. Rinse your weeds thoroughly, then gently dry them between two sheets of absorbent paper towel. You can either place them directly into resealable freezer storage bags or pack them into rigid plastic boxes, separating the layers with nonstick baking parchment. Be sure to label your freezer bag or box clearly so you can identify the leaves at a later time.

Edible weeds

Eating weeds harkens back to a time when spring was eagerly greeted as the season of fresh greens. Then, salads weren't called salads; they were known as "greens."

Weeds are still as tasty as ever, even if most of us buy our greens at a store when we have no fresh ones to pick from our gardens. Still, for that feeling of living off the land and discovering a new taste on the table, it's fun to try out the flavors of backyard weeds.

KNOW WHAT YOU'RE EATING

Learning what weeds you can eat is only half of the wild-food quest because first you must be able to identify them. In the old days, plant knowledge was passed down from family members, so that young children as well as grandparents could be trusted to gather spring greens. If you weren't lucky enough to have had weed expert and forager extraordinaire Euell Gibbons as your grandpa, you'll have to depend on books to hone your identification skills. The cardinal rule, which cannot be stressed enough, is to be sure you know what it is before you put it in your mouth. See "danger: poisonous weeds." page 147, for a list of some dangerous weeds to avoid nibbling on at all costs.

WHEN TO PICK

The younger the leaf, the milder the flavor. As chicory, dandelion, and other greens mature, their leaves turn from a slightly bitter tang to a flavor that's too strong for most palates. Enjoy wild greens when they're young. Older leaves are still valuable for adding flavor and nutrients to soups and other cooked dishes, or you can chop them into small pieces to give an extra tang to your salads.

The chemicals in certain weeds can build to toxic levels as the plants mature. Pokeweed is most notorious for this effect. Well-known as a spring green by country people who learned the old ways, it is edible only when the shoots are just beginning to emerge from the ground. Later, the whole plant is tainted with toxins. Even when picked young, it can sometimes cause stomach pains.

FOR EXTRA TANG Incorporate a selection of weed leaves into your regular salad to liven up the lettuce. Many weeds have a delicious peppery flavor, similar to arugula.

It is important to play it safe when foraging for weeds. Always be absolutely certain of your identification. Be sure to pick weeds from clean areas not exposed to dogs or cats, and avoid gathering weeds near roads, where exhaust toxins may have settled. Also take care that you pick only unsprayed weeds that have not been treated with chemicals. Then, when it's time to eat your harvest, start with just a nibble. Unfamiliar foods, even if they are deemed edible by experts, may cause tummy upsets.

USE CAUTION

safe weeds for eating

WEED	PART TO EAT	TIME TO HARVEST	PREPARATION
Burdock *Arctium lappa*	Root	Spring, before flowering	Wash and slice for a nutty, mildly sweet flavor in casseroles, soups, and sautés. Use judiciously in the diet. Popular vegetable in Japan. Avoid if pregnant or allergic to Asteraceae/Compositae family.
Chickweed *Stellaria media*	Leaves, stems	Winter to spring	Gather before flowering and eat in salads; mild, undistinguished flavor. Use judiciously in the diet.
Chicory *Cichorium intybus*	Young leaves, root	Leaves, spring; root, late summer to fall	Add leaves to salads or soups for bitter tang; roast root and grind for teas or coffee flavoring. Eat as much of the leaves as you like, but exercise moderation with the root, which has a mild laxative effect, until you see how your body reacts.
Dandelion *Taraxacum officinale*	Young leaves, tight flower buds	Any time	Add to salads or cook as greens; interesting bitter flavor. Use judiciously. Avoid if allergic to Asteraceae/Compositae family.
Garlic mustard *Alliaria petiolata*	Leaves	Spring	Slice into thin strips for strong garlic flavor in salads or with pasta. Use judiciously in the diet.
Japanese honeysuckle *Lonicera japonica*	Nectar	Summer to fall	Pinch green tip of flower tube and slowly draw out pistil, which will collect a drop of nectar on the filament for a tiny taste of sweetness. Use judiciously in the diet.
Japanese knotweed *Fallopia japonica*	Shoots	Early spring, when shoots are about 6 inches tall	Discard any leaves. Slice and steam as with asparagus and add to rice; the sour, tart, rhubarb-reminiscent flavor is also good in fruit pies. Used as a vegetable in Asia. In large quantities (more than a cup), it has a mild laxative effect. Contains Resveratrol, which research has shown to be beneficial in preventing heart attack.
Lamb's quarters *Chenopodium album*	Leaves	Any time	Use fresh in salads or simmer in soups; tasty in quiche as a spinach substitute. Use judiciously in the diet.
Multiflora rose *Rosa multiflora*	Hips	Fall to winter	Gather red, ripe hips in fall and dry for use in tea. Use judiciously in the diet.
Purslane *Portulaca oleracea*	Leaves and stems	Any time	Use fresh in salads for a sweet-sour flavor. Use judiciously in the diet.
Queen Anne's lace *Daucus carota*	Root	Fall to early spring, before flowering	Wash and chop for soups or to add a mild carrot-flavored crunch to salads. There is a very small risk that it may cause kidney irritation, neurological effects, or photosensitivity. It can also be mistaken for the highly toxic poison hemlock, so be sure of your identification.
Shepherd's purse *Capsella bursa-pastoris*	Basal leaves	Spring to summer	Cut into bite-size pieces for a peppery tang in salads. Do not eat too large an amount, as there is a risk of heart palpitations.
Sorrel *Rumex acetosella*	Moderately young basal leaves	Spring	Sorrel has been used in cooking for generations, yielding such specialties as French sorrel soup and cream sauces for fish, but the oxalic acid in the plant may have negative effects on the liver if eaten regularly or in large quantity. Enjoy its lemony flavor no more than once a week, in moderation. The flavor is intense, so use a single tablespoon of chopped leaf in soups, sauces, or salads.
Stinging nettle *Urtica dioica*	Young leaves	Spring	Simmer or boil, as for spinach; eat in moderation and only occasionally. Mild, "green" flavor. Never eat nettles raw.
Wild garlic, wild onion *Allium spp.*	Leaves	Spring to summer	Chop and scatter over rice, pasta, and vegetables as a garlic/onion substitute. Use judiciously in the diet.
Yellow wood sorrel *Oxalis stricta*	Leaves	Any time	Scatter in salads for a sharp, sour-lemon flavor; a single leaf nibbled on a hot day is refreshing. Eat in moderation (no more than once a week). Research into the effects of the plant's oxalic acid suggests we might be better off not ingesting it, since the acid can aggravate gout or affect the liver when eaten liberally.

AN ALTERNATIVE TO COFFEE A cup of chicory root "coffee" or chicory-enhanced regular coffee each day is a good starter dose.

TRICKY TABLE WEEDS

Pokeweed is often listed as an edible weed, but the timing of harvest is extremely important. Picked at the wrong time, the risk of an adverse reaction to pokeweed is so strong that you should make it a plant of last resort unless you've learned firsthand how to pick and use it safely.

Sorrel and yellow wood sorrel require a different kind of caution. These weeds contain high concentrations of oxalic acid, which can cause kidney damage if you eat too much. Eaten in very small amounts, and only occasionally, the body can handle oxalic acid, which is present in spinach and Swiss chard, too. So, it's best to use these weeds as flavor accents rather than main courses.

Stinging nettles also can be boiled as a green, though their hypodermic-like plant hairs can cause irritation or damage to internal organs, so it's best to keep your intake down. If you're concerned about whether a particular plant is edible, check the weed directory (see pages 18-129), and if there is no mention of its culinary uses or there is a warning against its ingestion, don't take any chances and steer clear of consuming it.

danger: poisonous weeds

WEED	METHOD OF EXPOSURE	EFFECT
Cocklebur	Internal	Vomiting, weak pulse, lowered body temperature, spasms, coma, death
Jimsonweed	Internal	Hallucinations, coma, convulsions, death
Milkweed	Internal, external (sap)	Internal: cardiac distress, death external: irritating to severe itching and burning
Nightshade	Internal	Hallucinations, stomach distress, convulsions, death
Poison hemlock	Internal	Respiratory distress, violent convulsions, death
Poison ivy	External (all plant parts)	Severe itching, blistering rash
Poison oak	External (all plant parts)	Severe itching, blistering rash
Pokeweed	Internal	Diarrhea, vomiting, spasms, convulsions, death
Spurge	External (sap)	Burning, blistering rash; scarring of skin
Water hemlock	Internal	Respiratory distress, vomiting, diarrhea, convulsions, loss of sight, death

LAMB'S QUARTERS Use the leaves of this weed fresh in salads or simmer in soups; it is tasty in quiche as a spinach substitute. Use judiciously in the diet.

FEEDING ON WEEDS

Like all produce, weeds are best eaten fresh when they are most flavorful and nutritious. As mustards and dandelions begin to brighten the landscape, it's fun to bring their tangy leaves in to liven up the table offerings and to enjoy a change of flavor that's closely connected to the changing seasons.

For fresh use, simply clip off whatever leaves you need from plants that have not been exposed to pesticides or herbicides. Avoid picking near any roadways, too, because of possible contamination from vehicle exhaust.

Rinse the leaves thoroughly just before serving, and chop into inch-long pieces to make eating easier and to distribute the flavor throughout a mixed salad. Add fresh weeds to lettuce or spinach salads.

Toss clean, chopped leafy weeds, such as garlic mustard, wild onion, and dandelion, with hot pasta before you top the dish with sauce; remember to save a few chopped leaves to garnish the dish. Cooking lessens the flavor and often turns weeds into mush. It also reduces their size, so pick plenty because, like spinach, they "cook down." Stir them into soups or stews for the last several minutes of simmering, or chop for casseroles. Strew chopped leaves on home-assembled pizzas before baking. (For ideas of how to put your weeds to culinary use, see table on page 146.) A traditional dish, a

"mess of greens," consists of whatever the country cook knew was edible, mixed together, and boiled to tenderness. Dandelion, wild mustard, lamb's quarters, and the young shoots of milkweed and pokeweed were all likely to be in the pot, although the last two are considered best avoided today.

Alongside calming and vitamin-rich medicinal teas, it is also possible to produce something a little stronger on the liquid side using your humble weeds. Dandelion wine and nettle beer have been enjoyed for centuries, and you, too, can have a go at producing your own brews at home.

STINGING NETTLES Next time you get attacked by these weeds, remember that they also have their benefits. They make a delicious brew, not unlike ginger beer, and are also tasty in soups.

how do weeds taste?

Some weeds, including sorrel, have a lemony tang. Mustards have a peppery bite, and most people find that dandelion and chicory are on the bitter side. Wild garlic tastes just like its name—rank and strong-flavored. But most weeds aren't very flavorful at all: They simply taste mildly "green," just like many varieties of lettuce leaves.

Weeds for crafts

The very qualities that give many weeds their distinctive lanky look—slender stems, few leaves, and well-separated or small flowers—also make them appealing in dried arrangements and botanical wall decorations. Some weeds are suited for potpourris, lending fragrant or colored foliage and blossoms. Many have interesting leaves that are standouts when pressed and used on notecards, bookmarks, or other paper crafts.

DRIED ARRANGEMENTS

It's the seedheads of weeds that are most decorative in a dried arrangement, which means that the best time to pick is after the plant has matured and dried to its natural end-of-season brown. For annual weeds like foxtail grass or shepherd's purse, that can be as early as late summer, but perennial weeds often hold their seeds until after frost.

Creating an arrangement couldn't be easier. All the supplies you need are to be found in your local craft shop or garden center. Use a single type of weed, or fill your container with a mix that pleases your eye. A rustic container usually looks best with the wildness of weeds.

POTPOURRI

Weed flowers add a dash of color to potpourris. Plus, every blossom you pick will eliminate at least a few potential offspring because it will never mature into a shower of weed seeds. English daisy, heal-all, purple loosestrife, and white clover are all pretty additions to a potpourri mix. Pick the blossoms soon after opening, dry, and add them to the more fragrant leaves of herbs like lavender, rosemary, and other aromatic plants that make up your potpourri. Give the combination a stir, followed by a few drops of any type of essential oil you like. Shake and keep in an airtight jar for several days to let the aromas marry and mellow. You could also mix in a little fixative, such as orris root, if you want to make the scent last longer.

Botanical art

One of the most attractive ways to turn a weed into a wonder is to frame the entire plant (except the root), or a flowering stem of the plant, as a piece of botanical art. If you don't own a plant press, slip the weed between the pages of an old phone book and weight it down with a couple of bricks. Plants vary in how long they take to dry. Check them after two weeks to see if they have lost all their moisture. Once your specimen is completely dry, position the dried weed on a piece of mat board (available at hobby and art-supply shops), cut with a craft knife so that it will fit your picture frame, and dab it into place with quick-drying, all-purpose glue. Add a small label, either handwritten on the mat board or written or typed on a separate strip of paper, with the weed's common and botanical names, and the date if you like.

After the glue has dried, assemble your matted composition in the frame, slipping in a small packet of silica granules (available at crafts stores) to prevent mold in damp weather, and it will be ready to hang.

DRYING WEED FLOWERS To make potpourri or dried arrangements, carefully place the flowerheads, such as these white clover flowers, on a drying rack and leave them in the shade.

Weed control

In this chapter, you'll learn how best to weed, using a combination of timing and technique. Preventing weeds from getting started is step one, and you'll find quick and easy tricks to reduce the number of potential pests on your property. You'll also discover an arsenal of techniques to attack any troublemakers that manage to sneak in past your defenses—and find advice on when and how to use each method, from the simplest yank-and-toss to powerful chemicals. Finally, because different areas of your yard— from beds and borders to lawn, patio, water garden, and driveway—are beset by different kinds of weed invasions, you'll find a handy guide tailored to the specifics of each part of your weeding needs.

An ounce of prevention

Since weeding is an activity best measured in time, not weight, let's change the old adage to "An hour of prevention is worth a week of cure." In fact, the news could be even better than a few hours of saved time. Depending on the methods you employ to prevent and control weeds, you may be able to reduce your weeding chores to a once a month session or even less frequently.

GET THEM WHILE THEY'RE YOUNG

Procrastination doesn't pay when weeding. The more time weeds have to grow, the deeper and larger their root systems become, and the more time and muscle power you'll need to pry them out of the soil. If you attack when they're tender young seedlings, you can slice off hundreds of potential problems with one quick stroke of a hoe or hand weeder. Young weeds are easy to smother with mulch, too, though it's always a good idea to hoe weeds into submission before you pile on the mulch. You may not get every last one, but the stressed survivors will probably lack the energy to break through the mulch and reach daylight again.

If you allow a weed to grow long enough to set seed, your problems multiply exponentially. A single plant of ragweed drops thousands of seeds, enough to keep you busy weeding for years. One overlooked dandelion puff can send hundreds of potential progeny parachuting to other parts of your yard.

Should you fall behind on weed patrol, at least make an effort to snip off seedheads when you see them forming. Dispose of them in the trash, not onto the compost heap where they may contaminate the finished material and, hence, sprout or spread once more wherever you use the compost in your yard or garden.

SMART COMPOSTING

Transforming weeds into prized compost is a gratifying process, but it can backfire quickly if you add any seeds to the mix. Unless your compost pile generates enough heat (at least 130°F) to bake seeds and tenacious perennial weed roots into oblivion, you will spread weed problems with every shovelful of compost you add to the garden. Avoid potential problems with these tricks:

WEED-FREE POTS Growing plants in containers is a great way to avoid weeds, because you have complete control over the soil and compost that fills them. Buy commercially bagged potting soil that is labeled as being sterile, and cover the surface with a layer of fine gravel or pebbles where fallen seeds can't take root.

- *Preparation* Clip off and dispose of weed seedheads in the trash. You then can toss the rest of the plant onto the compost pile.
- *Grass clippings* Don't empty your mower bag onto the compost pile if it includes weed seeds collected from the grass; put the contents in the trash instead.
- *Protection* Keep an eye out for weeds that sprout near the pile. If possible, keep your pile penned within a compost bin to prevent seeds scattering onto your treasure heap.
- *Regular care* Turn up the heat in your pile. Air and moisture are your allies, so use a garden fork to turn the pile every two to three weeks in summer, and spritz with a

Be careful when you are given plants from friends' gardens. The tentacles of tenacious weeds can wrap themselves around the roots of other plants and install themselves in your garden. So, examine the root clump of any passed-along plant before you plant it. Look for roots that don't match the plant's. You can usually spot creeping, wiry, or skinny, jointed roots among the roots of the desirable plant.

PASS-ALONG PLANTS

hose as often as needed to keep it moist. If your pile is already sprouting a healthy crop of weeds, just turn them under weekly and they will quickly turn into compost rather than weeds.

UNINVITED GUESTS

Weeds are sneaky all right, which is how they get a foothold in your garden to begin with. As we saw in Chapter 1, their nefarious tricks for spreading themselves across the land include hitchhiking on plants and people entering the garden, blowing in the wind, and even using the digestive systems of birds as transport and delivery services—deposited with a dash of fertilizer for good measure.

The bad news is you'll never keep weeds out of your yard altogether; the good news is that you can take simple steps to reduce the number of uninvited guests:

- *Be vigilant* Check the contents of nursery pots before you plant. Greenhouse and outdoor weeds can settle just as easily into potted soil as they do in the garden. Uproot any infiltrators before planting.
- *Check the small print* Read the label of grass seed bags before you buy. Those with a higher percentage of desirable seed—and a lower content of unidentified or weed seeds—are worth the higher price tag.
- *Contaminated seed* Birdseed is occasionally contaminated by field weeds such as burdock and cocklebur. If you notice unfamiliar seeds when filling your feeders, take a few minutes to pluck them out for disposal.
- *Pet care* Keep pets that roam well groomed. "Stick-tights" and burrs that hitchhike in pet fur will fall out or be pulled off and left on the ground in your yard—just as the sneaky weeds intended.

COVER CROPS AND SMOTHER CROPS

Weeds are most at home in open, disturbed soil, so they are less likely to colonize soil that is covered with healthy plant life. If you are thinking of leaving a cultivated patch of earth open for any length of time, such as over the winter, it is a good idea to plant a specific "cover crop," such as annual rye grass, to keep winter weeds from gaining a root hold. Some cover crops, especially leguminous plants such as clover or soybeans, will also improve the soil. They form a symbiotic relationship with certain types of bacteria, called rhizobia, which form root nodules and begin extracting nitrogen from the air, changing it into a form that plants can use. Other

plants, including mustard, will draw nutrients to the upper soil via their deep roots—in the case of mustard, breaking phosphorus into an easily absorbed form and then excreting it into the soil. First thing in spring, either mow down or turn your cover crop, usually a fast-growing annual. Allow three weeks for it to decompose, and proceed to plant your spring garden, which will benefit from the nutrients added by the cover crop.

Weed seeds need sun to sprout, so you can also discourage them by making sure the soil is shaded by overlapping foliage. All through the year, fill gaps in your ornamental beds with flowers to shade unplanted areas, plant a dense groundcover to smother unwanted weeds, or add salad greens to shade vegetable beds. For example, daylilies and creeping thyme can knit together into such a thick mat that

weed-free potting mix

If you would rather not buy potting soil, you can heat a small amount of garden soil to kill off any hidden weeds.

1 If you wish to make potting mix that is completely weed free, you can also sterilize it in an outdoor gas grill. Set the temperature level to low heat (300° to 350°F) and place an inch-deep layer of soil in a metal pan on the grill. Close the hood and heat for 30 minutes, stirring occasionally.

2 If you are using a charcoal grill, when the heat has died down to moderate (so you can comfortably hold your hand 4 inches above the coals for 10 seconds), place an inch-deep layer of soil in a metal pan on the grill, positioned 3 inches above the coals. Close the lid and heat for 30 minutes, stirring occasionally. After soil is cool, mix with peat or vermiculite to keep the texture light.

USEFUL PROTECTION Plant leafy greens such as lettuce (above) between crops to protect exposed soil and any underlying crops from weed attack. The fast-growing leafy salads create shade that prevents weeds from flourishing.

weeds have trouble competing for elbow room. Broad-leaved, fast-sprouting plants that are short in height and shallow rooted can be particularly effective as weed-smothering crops. Many gardeners look to lettuce, mustard, and other leafy annual greens to shade out weeds. Just remember to provide enough water for both the primary and the smother crop.

TURNING THE SOIL

Every time you set a spade in the soil, chop with a hoe, or pull a weed, you're setting the stage for the emergence of weeds. Each handful of soil holds a massive number of weed seeds, all waiting for the conditions they need to break dormancy.

A few weeds need highly specialized keys to unlock their sleeping seeds, such as heat from forest fires, but our most common lawn and garden weeds need only a bit of moisture, a crack of sunlight, and favorable temperatures to get them growing. Many weeds have evolved to sprout right on the soil surface; they drop from the parent plant to the ground and sprout soon afterward. Others surf their way into the sheltering earth on a rivulet of rainwater or free-fall through the fine cracks of freezing ground. When weed seeds are buried deep, they have little incentive to grow and usually

remain dormant until disturbed. Let these "sleeping dogs lie," and you'll reduce your weeding chores. Here are a few ways to do it:

- *Nip in the bud* Instead of pulling young weeds, slice off their tops and smother the struggling roots with mulch (see pages 154-157).
- *Focused approach* Practice using a slicing-off motion with your hoe instead of hacking at the soil. A once-a-week swipe at or just below the soil surface should take care of most weeds in the row.
- *Minimize upheaval* Dig planting holes individually for ornamentals and vegetables rather than turning up large expanses of soil.
- *Efficient work* Keep the blades of hand tools and hoes sharpened with a metal file or whetstone, available at any hardware or home-supply store. A sharp blade makes quick work of skimming off weeds at the soil surface.
- *Catch dormant weeds* After you turn new beds, wait a while before planting. Allow about 10 days for newly turned weed seeds to sprout, slice them off with a hoe, and repeat if possible. Then plant the bed.

MIRACULOUS MULCHES

Applying mulch is the number-one way to reduce the amount of time you spend weeding. It's easy, quick, inexpensive (or free!), and mulching only needs to be done a few times during the growing season. Mulch also works wonders for

solarizing

Laying a sheet of transparent plastic over a newly turned bed uses solar energy to heat and kill weed seeds in the upper inches of soil. This technique has enjoyed a burst of popularity in recent years, but the gains in reduced weeds may be outweighed by the loss of helpful microorganisms. As the plastic sheet focuses the sun's heat on the soil, worms, ground beetles, and other large creatures can move out of the way, but bacteria, fungi, and other beneficial organisms are stuck in the death trap. Other methods of reducing and removing weeds are healthier for your allies in the soil—and thus better for your plants. For advice on sterilizing your own potting mix on the outdoor grill, see page 152.

your soil, your plants, and for your water bill, making it a winning proposition for you and for your garden. The only losers are the weeds. This technique works well for most weeds, except for these: established perennial weeds, which have a tough root that will keep sending up determined shoots; weeds that spread by creeping roots or creeping stems, which will travel far outside the mulch to spring up again; vining weeds, which grow so quickly their stems can pierce through the mulch; and perennial grasses, which are accustomed to weathering tough times and can go dormant, only to rise again when mulch thins or is removed.

MULCHING NATURE'S WAY

In the wild, fallen leaves, pine needles, twigs and bark chips, dead plants, and other organic debris create a natural layer of decomposing organic material. This spongy, absorbent covering keeps the soil moist while attracting all manner of creatures, from earthworms to ground beetles, which aerate, fertilize, and condition the soil day after day.

In the domestic garden, we tend to change the natural order of things. We rake up leaves and remove dead plants, then add fertilizer to provide nutrients that would have been replenished naturally had we followed nature's plan. Our gardens may look tidy, but we've also managed to disrupt the natural cycle that keeps weeds at bay. Spreading mulch is a wonderful compromise. Mulch keeps your beds looking good and enriches the soil, just like natural debris would, because earthworms and other soil organisms are naturally drawn to the mulch and will carry it into the soil as they burrow.

Make your mulch deep enough to completely cover the soil, but not so deep that it smothers or shades your plants. A light scattering of mulch, applied by hand, is perfect for seedlings. As the plants grow, add more mulch to get better coverage. A 2-inch layer works well for most perennials,

shrubs, and trees. Mulch compacts over time, and warm, wet weather speeds up its decay. When you notice more than a few scattered weed seedlings popping up in the mulch, it's time to add a fresh helping.

BANISHING WEEDS WITH MULCH

Organic mulch is also a great weed deterrent when tiny weeds are beginning to appear. It works by burying them alive under damp barricades that prevent them from reaching light and air, so they simply waste away. Young weeds rapidly succumb beneath 2 inches of mulch, but older weeds require a deeper, more impenetrable covering, such as cardboard with more mulch on top to hold it in place. But beware: Tenacious perennial weeds can bide their time for a year or more under a covering, springing to life again as soon as a gap appears in the mulch. (For descriptions of the different life cycles of weeds, see pages 9-10.)

The smothering method may not work on weeds with creeping roots, such as bermudagrass and ground ivy. They can send out their roots for several yards, in a desperate attempt to escape the suffocation treatment. If you're concerned about using mulch on a particular weed, turn to its entry in the weed directory (see pages 18-129).

USE YOUR GARDEN'S PRODUCE One of the most effective mulches is simply a layer of twigs, fallen leaves, and bark chips collected from your garden. Cover your soil thickly to ensure that weeds are deprived of light.

WEEDS FOR WHICH MULCH IS INEFFECTIVE

CHOOSING A MULCH The table opposite will help you choose the best type for your garden. Clockwise from top left: bark chippings, gravel, shells, and small stones all look good in both ornamental and productive gardens.

TYPES OF MULCH

There are two sorts of mulch to choose from: organic and inorganic. *Organic mulches* are derived from any material that began life as a plant. Big garden, slim wallet? Turn to freebies like chopped leaves, newspaper, and grass clippings. Or, buy mulch by the truckload for significant savings over bagged products. Rice hulls, cocoa-bean shells, pomace (the pulpy byproduct of juice manufacturing), shredded cedar, and other by-products of regional agricultural manufacturing may be available at low cost.

Organic mulches eventually decompose and become part of your garden soil, adding nutrients and attracting beneficial organisms, which improve growing conditions. They are also best as weed preventives, because they are easy to renew when weeds begin to infiltrate—as they eventually will in all types of mulch.

Inorganic materials such as marble chips, river rocks, and crushed lava did not start out as living organisms, so they do not decompose, and therefore do not contribute to soil fertility. They do, however, look good and last forever. Gravel also improves drainage if it gets mixed in with the soil

benefits of mulch

A layer of mulch is the best gift you can give your garden—and yourself, too. Here are the benefits:

Less weeding is needed as mulch smothers young weeds and makes it difficult for new weeds to sprout. Any that do appear are easy to pull.

Less watering is required as mulch preserves soil moisture by protecting the surface from the sun and wind. Mulch slowly releases moisture to the soil below, and stabilizes temperatures.

Improved soil as a result of organisms attracted to mulch which work naturally to make soil loose and well aerated. Organic mulches also supply the soil with nutrients and encourage the activity of disease-fighting microbes.

A cleaner harvest is obtained as mulch prevents mud from splashing onto your edible plants.

at all. If you use an inorganic mulch, underlay it with a fabric weed barrier, a weed barricade of perforated plastic sheeting, or several layers of cardboard to save yourself from tedious hours of weeding the mulch!

To choose the best mulch for the job, refer to the chart (see page 157). Where appearance is important, it may be a good idea to use the same material throughout the garden for a unified effect. Light-colored mulches are a quick trick to brighten shady gardens. Attention-getting mulches, such as white marble chips, look best in more formal or stylized gardens, or to highlight a garden sculpture or special planting. Good organic mulches for vegetable gardens, such as straw, grass clippings, and compost, will also add nutrients to the soil and help produce a bumper crop.

a mulch for every garden

MATERIAL	WHERE BEST USED	APPEARANCE	ADVANTAGES	HOW TO APPLY
Wood chips, bark	Shrubs, trees, large ornamental beds	Coarse texture; large pieces; available in dyed colors.	Inexpensive, long-lasting. Cools the soil and blocks the loss of moisture.	Spread a 1- to 2-inch-deep layer over the soil. Renew large bark-chip mulch once a year or every two years. Wood chips may need renewing twice a season. Warm, wet weather hastens decay.
Shredded bark	Perennial beds	Fine texture, dark color.	Attractive backdrop for flowering or foliage plants. Cools the soil and blocks the loss of moisture.	Spread a 1- to 2-inch-deep layer over the soil. Usually needs refreshing every 6 months to a year. Warm, wet weather can hasten decay.
Grass clippings	Vegetable and herb gardens	Fine texture, easy to scatter around seedlings. Quickly ages to soft tan color.	Decomposes quickly to enrich soil. Cools the soil and blocks the loss of moisture.	Apply no deeper than 2 inches to prevent excess ammonia buildup during decomposition. Needs frequent renewal.
Wheat or oat straw	Vegetable gardens, roses, strawberries	Lightweight, inexpensive. Weathers to buff brown, then grayish tan.	Prevents diseases; keeps plants clean; suppresses weed seed germination. Cools the soil and blocks the loss of moisture.	Apply about 4 inches deep to prevent weeds. It will soon settle, with rain and watering, to a depth of 2 to 3 inches.
Dried leaves	Perennial beds, shade gardens, shrubs and trees that need acidic soil	Fluffy mulch that packs well without becoming matted.	Free and widely available; creates acidic soil conditions preferred by many plants. Cools the soil and blocks the loss of moisture.	Chop leaves with lawnmower. Spread chopped leaves over soil in a 2-inch layer. Needs fairly frequent renewal due to its fast decay.
Pine needles	Shrubs and trees that need acidic soil, strawberries, blueberries	Rich brown color and fine texture.	Cools the soil and blocks loss of moisture. Makes weeding very easy as roots just slide out.	Start with 3 inches and add a little more every few months, because needles break down slowly.
Evergreen boughs	Perennial beds, herb gardens in winter	Not attractive, but great for winter protection.	Discourages weeds; protects plants from wind and cold. Cools the soil and blocks the loss of moisture.	In early winter, place over perennials in a loose layer. Remove after last spring frost.
Newspaper and cardboard	Vegetable garden, perennial beds, shrubs	Should be covered with another mulch to avoid a littered look.	Blocks light to weeds; free and fast to apply. Cools the soil and blocks the loss of moisture.	Lay sheets over ground, over-lapping edges. Wet thoroughly before topping with more appealing mulch to secure.
Old carpet	Vegetable garden, paths, shrubs, trees	Top with attractive mulch, or leave exposed between vegetable rows.	Long lasting and long-wearing. Cools the soil and blocks the loss of moisture.	Cut to size with utility knife and lay on the soil, with the natural-looking burlap side up.
Gravel	Herb gardens, rock gardens	Light color, attractive texture	Facilitates drainage; keeps plants clean; radiates heat to cold soil. Blocks the loss of moisture.	Spread a layer of gravel at least 1 inch thick over a fabric or perforated black plastic weed barrier.
Crushed shells	Ornamental beds, shrubs, sidewalk edging	Light color, moderately fine texture. Adds brightness to shade gardens.	Keeps roots cool by reflecting the sun's rays. Blocks the loss of moisture.	Often available free or at low cost in areas where shellfish are commercially gathered or processed.
Stone, marble chips	Herb gardens, rock gardens, hillsides, specimen plantings	Smart appearance works well in formal gardens.	Cools the soil and blocks the loss of moisture.	Underlay with cardboard or other weed barrier to barricade weed seedlings.

Weeding techniques

Grab-and-yank is the way most of us attack weeds. It's fast and usually effective, but it's not always the best or easiest way to tackle the problem. Other methods may give you better results, depending on what kinds of weeds your yard harbors and their stage of growth. For specific advice concerning the particular mix of weeds plaguing your garden, turn to the directory section (see pages 18-129).

HAND PULLING WEEDS

All the new weeding tools on the market can't hold a candle to the best, most natural tool of all: your careful hands. The roots of some weeds can be surprisingly tenacious, though, even against the strength of your muscles.

Hand pulling works best with younger weeds and those with fibrous, shallow roots, such as chickweed, hawkweed, and crabgrass. If you find regular gloves too cumbersome when weeding, try latex medical exam gloves.

For best results, grasp the weed as close to the surface of the soil as you can (see below). To help free stubborn or deep roots, use a twisting motion as you pull. With spreading weeds, such as quackgrass or Canada thistle, try lifting the growing point at the base with a fork before attacking them with your grip to avoid breaking off the head of the weed, leaving the roots buried in the soil.

hand pulling
The best method for small weeds, allowing you to work closely.

1 Grasp the weed firmly as close to the surface of the soil as you can. Test the resistance of the weed by pulling upward gently. This should remove young seedlings. If you meet resistance, use a twisting motion as you exert upward force. If the weed stem is tough, wrap it around your hand for an even better grip.

HAND TOOLS FOR WEEDING

Short-handled tools can handle jobs that are too much for your hands, and they are easier to aim and control than a hoe. Use them for weeding in ornamental beds, where they can reach neatly between desirable plants to destroy the weeds.

There are two essential types of hand-weeder: a standard weeder for slicing and chopping and a taproot weeder for prying out deep roots. You'll use these tools a lot, so select the ones that fit your hand and feel well balanced. Look for tools in which the head and shaft are one continuous piece to avoid an early "broken neck" when the tool fails from metal fatigue. Good hand weeders will also have a certain amount of spring built into them so they can give and rebound when they hit rocks and other obstacles.

Keep hand tools sharp by using a metal file or whetstone on the blade; using a dull tool to slice off weeds is very frustrating. For tools used in special garden areas, such as water gardens or gravel gardens, turn to the section on weed control at home (see pages 165-171).

HOE-DOWN FOR WEEDS

A sharp-bladed hoe is a great tool for weeding large stretches of soil because it removes dozens of weeds with a single stroke. Hoes actually control weeds two ways—by chopping or slicing them off their roots and by stirring the top layer of soil. Thus loosened, more weeds cannot germinate, at least until the next rain.

A little practice will help you learn the stroke needed to slice shallow-rooted weeds off at soil level. Once weeds mature and acquire a tough stem, you'll need to use a chopping motion rather than the slicing stroke you use on flexible green-stemmed weeds. Much depends on the hoe itself, and there are many different kinds. If you are growing a large vegetable garden and anticipate doing lots of hoeing, try out the hoes before you buy. Settle on a hoe that works well with your natural swing.

Use your hoe to chop out entire clumps of shallow-rooted weeds, too. You can make quick work of chickweed in a vegetable garden, for instance, by using the hoe to hack and lift each weedy plant. Practice your stroke, aiming the blade close to where the weed's stems arise from the soil. If you hoe in the morning, by evening all the dead weeds will appear decidedly shriveled. Leave in place to die, where they will

TAKE YOUR PICK From left to right: A short-handed hoe, ideal for close work around delicate plants; a long-handed hoe to work over a large area of soil; and a flame-thrower, for killing isolated weeds that emerge between paving and on gravel paths.

decompose to add nitrogen to the soil, unless the weeds are those that spread by creeping roots, or grasses, which tend to reroot. Compost weeds only if they haven't yet set seed.

A hoe is ineffective against deep-rooted weeds such as dandelion and burdock, because it merely beheads the plant and doesn't pry out the root. To remove these weeds, invest in a good dandelion fork, which is a weeder with a long, sturdy metal shaft tipped with a forked blade. Some models add a lever-action refinement and a long handle, so that you can use the tool standing up. Drive the prongs down over the weed and then pull on the handle to draw up the lever, which locks the prongs around the taproot. Continue the horizontal movement of the handle to pull out the weed, root and all.

STRING TRIMMER

Many gardeners invest in an electric or gas-powered trimmer to use against tall, determined weeds, such as blackberries. Models of varying weights and capabilities are available; some have metal blades, as well as the usual whirling plastic string, for heavy-duty weed or brush cutting. If you have large weedy areas, a string trimmer is the fastest way to keep weeds in check, but it can injure bystanders or desirable plants, so operate with care.

GOING TO EXTREMES

Gardeners have come up with some truly ingenious ways of solving weed problems. In years past, salt was poured onto planting beds (it killed weeds, but also affected the desirable plants). Today, some gardeners are using a type of flame-thrower—a device that shoots out fire to burn weeds to a satisfying crisp. The dangers are apparent, but there's no

denying this is an effective method of getting rid of driveway or patio weeds. Of course, the roots of some weeds are likely to live through such treatment and sprout again, and the flames may damage or discolor paving. An alternative method to get rid of weeds sprouting between cracks in walks, drives, and patios is to simply pour boiling water on them. Deeply rooted plants are likely to come back, however, unless the hot water reaches the roots.

Tackling toxic weeds

Chemical weedkillers are your best bet for tackling poison oak and poison ivy, whose deep, tenacious, spreading roots are difficult to hand pull (see pages 160-163). Young single-stemmed plants are removable with a dandelion digger, but be sure to remove all of the root, which may travel surprising distances. Dress for battle when you fight poison ivy and poison oak. To weed out a very few young plants, wear long sleeves and gloves, and for extra protection slip your hand into a sturdy plastic bag. After weeding, do not touch your skin with clothes that have been in contact with the plant, and wash clothes immediately in hot water. Oak-N-Ivy Brand Tecnu Outdoor Skin Cleanser and Burt's Bees Poison Ivy Soap, both commercially available, are excellent products to have on hand after your weeding efforts to prevent the plants' toxins from irritating the skin.

redeem a weed

Weeds that haven't gone to seed are great for the compost pile. As they decompose, they enrich the compost with a good dose of nitrogen. Before tossing a weed on the pile, shake it to knock most of the soil clinging to the roots back into the garden.

Manufactured herbicides

Visit any discount store or garden center, and you'll find aisles filled with brightly-colored containers promising an easy answer to your weed problems. With all these products available, it's a wonder anyone still uses a hoe. But the unfortunate side of manufactured herbicide solutions is their potential for damaging desirable plants and the environment.

Because herbicides are intended to kill plants rather than animals, they are not considered as dangerous to handle as chemicals that kill insects. Most are nontoxic to insects and birds, but they should still be handled with care, and always in strict accordance with label directions.

There's no denying, however, that manufactured weed controls can make the chore much less labor-intensive, especially for killing large expanses of weeds for new bed preparation. Like manual weeding, manufactured controls require repeated applications.

A WEALTH OF OPTIONS There is a wide selection of herbicides on the market, and they can be an invaluable resource to the gardener if used wisely.

Safety

The following precautions will enable you to minimize the risks involved with using herbicides:

- *Protective clothing* Wear rubber gloves, long-sleeved shirts, thick pants, and boots. Protective face masks are also recommended when using spray-on herbicides.
- *Inhalation* If you accidentally inhale an herbicide, leave the area and take deep breaths of fresh air. If exposure is prolonged or intense, or if you develop symptoms such as wheezing, coughing, shortness of breath, or burning in the mouth, throat, or chest, see a doctor immediately.
- *Skin* If your skin comes into contact with the chemicals, immediately flood the affected skin with water and wash using soap. Remove any contaminated clothing quickly. If redness or irritation develops, consult a doctor.
- *Eyes* Should you get any herbicide in your eyes, flush your eyes with water or saline solution for approximately 20 to 30 minutes (taking out any contact lenses first), and call a doctor.
- *Ingestion* If weedkiller is ingested, take several glasses of water to dilute the chemical and immediately call a doctor, hospital, or poison control center.
- *Storage* Always keep herbicides in their original containers, out of reach of children. Make sure that the labels are well attached to the container so that there is no chance of mistaken identity and inappropriate usage.
- *Age* Check with your USDA county extension agent before using "left-over" herbicides from previous seasons; they may no longer be considered safe to use.

CHOOSE YOUR WEAPON

Whatever your weed problem, there is an herbicide to fill the bill. Each combination of active ingredients has been created with particular groups or species of weeds in mind. There are two broad categories of herbicides: pre-emergent and post-emergent. *Pre-emergent herbicides* prevent weeds from sprouting or act quickly to kill their first shoots; they also can stop garden and lawn grass seeds from sprouting. They are a good choice for annual weeds, including crabgrass, which live for only one year, because they drop their seeds to lie in wait for the right conditions for sprouting the following season.

Post-emergent herbicides act after weeds have already established themselves. They are therefore often used for perennial weeds, such as dandelions, which resprout each year. Also called contact herbicides, most post-emergent weedkillers work by being absorbed into the leaves, moving down throughout the plant and to the root. They work best when the weed is in a period of rapid growth but is still young. To help them stick to plants, labels often recommend dampening the area before applying the herbicide. For more information on how to use herbicide, see box below.

ORGANIC OR SYNTHETIC?

Chemicals are derived from both natural and man-made sources, but in general, gardeners use the word "chemical" to mean synthetic materials, concocted in a laboratory. "Organic" is used loosely to describe controls derived from natural sources, including plant, mineral, and animal origins.

Only two organic active ingredients—soap and corn gluten—are currently in use for weed control. Highly concentrated soaps control weeds by burning the foliage, but don't confuse them with insecticidal soaps, which can safely be applied to garden plants. For weed control in lawns, products made from corn gluten work like pre-emergent herbicides (see page 160). Applied in spring and fall with a spreader, corn gluten products help prevent crabgrass, dandelions, and other lawn weeds from sprouting.

MATCHING A WEED TO ITS KILLER

Manufactured brands of herbicides sold over the counter are legion—see the table (see pages 162-163) for more details. Each species of weed responds to different active ingredients in the herbicides, and the same is true of cultivated plants.

Before you buy an herbicide, carefully read the label to see if it will control the weeds that are causing your problems, and if it is safe to use around nearby cultivated plants. These plant lists are printed on the peel-off label attached to the front of the bottle, or they are printed on the bag.

Understanding herbicide label lingo

Broadly speaking, there are four weed categories that you'll find repeatedly mentioned on the labels of herbicides—annual grasses, perennial grasses, broadleaf weeds, and woody plants. Check the directory pages if you are unsure which heading particular weeds fall under (see pages 18-129). Be aware that many cultivated plants also will fall into these categories, and may be just as susceptible to the recommended herbicides manufactured with weeds in mind:

- *Annual grasses* Grasses or grasslike weeds that germinate, grow, and die within one year, such as crabgrass or annual bluegrass.
- *Perennial grasses* Grasses or grasslike weeds that re-emerge from the roots year after year, such as Bermudagrass or quackgrass.
- *Broadleaf weeds* Plants with wider leaves that do not resemble grass. Dandelion, plantain, chickweed, and dock are all broadleaf weeds.
- *Woody plants* Plants with tough, bark-covered stems, such as honeysuckle, poison ivy and poison oak, and wild brambles.

applying herbicides

Match the product specifically to the place targeted and the weeds you want controlled, and buy only the amount you need.

Use your herbicide only in the season instructed. Apply to plants only in the stage of growth recommended, and follow package label directions to the letter. Dilute soluble weedkillers strictly according to the instructions. Apply herbicides only at the rate recommended on the label.

Aim carefully to avoid killing nearby desired plants. Protect these plants using a plastic sheet for large shrubs, or smaller areas with plastic pails, cardboard boxes, or newspaper. For individual squirts, try crafting a collar from a plastic milk jug and placing it around the weed you are spraying.

Spray only on windless days to avoid accidental drift to nearby garden plants or neighboring yards. Ideally, rain should not be expected for at least two days from application. It is always wise to restrict the entry of people or pets until the chemical has dried.

herbicides

Use this table to help choose the right herbicide for your problem—but also take the time to read the label carefully before you buy.

TYPE OF GARDEN	WEED PROBLEM	ACTIVE INGREDIENT	BRAND NAMES	DESCRIPTION
Vegetables and other edibles, mixed flowerbeds, ground covers	Assorted weeds, mostly seedlings of annual species and a few perennial weeds	Trifluralin	Miracle-Gro Garden Weed Preventer, Preen	Pre-emergent. Liquid applied with lawn spreader, or as granules, gently worked into top of the soil early in the season to prevent weed emergence and kill seedlings as they germinate. Should control weeds for a full season.
Mixed flowerbeds, ground covers, shrub beds	Crabgrass, annual bluegrass, other grassy weeds	Fluazifop	Fusilade, Grass-B-Gone, Ornamec, Over-The-Top	A selective, systemic herbicide for the control of grass weeds in broad-leaved crops. Most effective when applied as a post-emergent herbicide, when weeds are still young. Translocates from leaves to the roots. Comes as a liquid concentrate or as a ready-to-use spray. Not for use on edible plants.
Lawn	Crabgrass and assorted broad-leaf weeds	Combination products containing MSMA; 2, 4D; Mecoprop; and Dicambra	Bayer Advanced Lawn, Scott's Turf Builder (includes fertilizer), Sta-Green Weed & Feed (includes fertilizer)	Selective post-emergent herbicides. Granules or liquid concentrate. Granules can be mixed with fertilizer. Not for use on edible plants or on certain grasses such as St. Augustine, carpetgrass, bentgrass, and dichondra.
Along fences, woodland trails	Tough woody weeds including poison ivy, poison oak, wild brambles	Triclopyr	Enforcer Bush Killer, Ortho Brush-B-Gone	Selective, post-emergent herbicide. Liquid concentrate, applied with a brush or spray bottle. It is absorbed systemically and is especially effective in periods of rapid growth. Will kill any plant that comes into contact with the spray.
Cracks in pavement, gravel driveways, other places where no vegetation is wanted	Annual, perennial and woody weeds	Glyphosate	Roundup, Kleenup, Ortho Triox	Broad-spectrum, post-emergent herbicide. Liquid concentrate or ready-to-use spray applied to plants is absorbed systemically and kills them over a period of 1 to 2 weeks. Apply as spot treatment with sprayer. Kills any plant that comes into contact with the spray.
Cracks in pavement, gravel driveways, other places where no vegetation is wanted	Annual, perennial and woody weeds	Diquat Dibromide diydrodipyrise pyrazinediium dibromide with Fluazifon	No-Pest Grass & Weed Killer, Spectracide Grass & Weed Killer	Post-emergent. Liquid concentrate or ready-to-use spray applied to plants is absorbed systemically and kills them over a period of 1 to 3 days. Apply as spot treatment. Will kill any plant that comes into contact with the spray.
Lawn, vegetable gardens	Annual and perennial weeds	Corn gluten, a by-product of corn processing	Safe 'N Simple, Earth Friendly, WeedFREE, W.O.W.!, Supressa, GreenSense, DynaWeed, Organic Weed-Stopper Plus	Powder or pelleted product applied with spreader. Works as a pre-emergent weedkiller on crabgrass, dandelions, smartweed, pigweed, purslane, lamb's quarters, and foxtail grass. Contains 10 percent nitrogen by weight, so it fertilizes as it prevents weeds.
Cracks in pavement, gravel driveways	Annual and perennial weeds	Soap, bleach	Ready-made as Weed-Aside	Post-emergent. The mixture is absorbed systemically and kills over 1 to 3 days. Perennial weeds may need more than one application.
Along fences, cracks in pavement, gravel driveways	Annual and perennial weeds	Lemon, vinegar	Burnout Weed & Grass Killer	Post-emergent. Kills any plant it touches but breaks down into inert ingredients once in the soil. Spot-treat weeds, spraying until leaves are wet. Tough weeds may need another spraying.

Always follow label instructions precisely when applying herbicides.

HEALTH CONCERNS	ENVIRONMENTAL CONCERNS
Can cause eye irritation and inflame skin on contact. Inhalation can aggravate the respiratory tract, while ingestion will irritate the gastrointestinal tract, and in serious cases may lead to convulsions and coma. (See "applying herbicides", page 161.)	Excess can leach into groundwater. Known to become concentrated in tissues of fish. Usually persists in soil for six months or less."
May irritate eyes and skin. Large doses can cause abdominal pain, dizziness, and nervous system disorders. (See "applying herbicides", page 161.)	Toxic to some fish. However, moisture causes this chemical to break down rapidly, so it persists in soil and water less than one week.
These products are highly toxic, so must be stored in original container on a high shelf in locked cabinet and handled with gloves and other protective equipment (see page 160). Symptoms resulting from accidental ingestion include nausea and vomiting. Skin contact can also result in redness and swelling.	Can be toxic to fish and birds. Restrict entry of pets and people until the application is dry. Never overapply. Use according to package label. Can persist in groundwater.
These products are highly toxic so must be stored in original container on a high shelf in locked cabinet and handled with gloves and other protective equipment (see page 160). Symptoms resulting from accidental ingestion include gastrointestinal irritation or ulceration. Contact will also irritate skin and eyes, and breathing in vapour may affect respiratory tract.	Low toxicity to insects, birds, and fish. Persists in soil about six weeks, and binds to soil particles so that its leaching potential is very low when used according to package label instructions.
Can cause eye and skin irritation. Accidental ingestion can make people or pets very sick. The most common symptoms of glyphosate poisoning are vomiting and pain in areas of the mouth and throat. Restrict entry to the area until the application is dry.	Low toxicity to insects and birds, and slightly toxic to fish. Usually binds to soil and persists for about four weeks
Unresolved questions about this formula's effects on mammals make it a poor choice in situations where other herbicides can do the job. Ingestion will produce severe nausea and vomiting, as well as pain in the mouth and throat. Prolonged contact with the skin will also result in irritation. Handle with extreme care.	Possible repercussions in every level of the food chain, leading to abnormal reproduction in animals and many other serious consequences.
None.	None. The EPA has exempted corn gluten from being regulated as a pesticide.
Use plastic gloves and eye protection to prevent contact with bleach. Wash hands with mild soap and water after handling.	Desirable plants will not grow in areas treated with chlorine bleach. Use sparingly to avoid run-off problems that could carry these household chemicals into waterways.
None.	None.

Weeds in the lawn

It's the American dream—a sweep of unbroken green blades, trimmed neatly every Saturday, watered and fertilized to its peak of beauty. It's also the American nightmare, as wild garlic crops up even before the first mowing and dandelions break the beauty with their cheeky yellow heads.

Like garden plants, some weeds like soil that's wet, some like it dry, some prefer clay, and others can scratch a living out of gravel. That's why the weeds that plague your lawn are apt to be a different cast of characters than those that snuggle among your perennials or spring up between the bricks.

Preventive measures

- *Mow high* A closely sheared lawn may feel great underfoot but taller grass shades the soil, discouraging germination and inhibiting the growth of weeds. Set the blade to about 2½ to 3 inches instead of 1½ inches and you'll have fewer weed problems.
- *Mow at the right time* When weeds first begin to flower, mow them at a height that slices off the blossoms. No flowers left to mature also means no seeds.
- *Pamper your lawn* Fertilize and water the grass so that it grows vigorously. Quickly reseed or patch any thin or bare spots caused by drought or dogs, so that lurking weed seeds don't get a start.
- *Choose the right lawn grass for your site* Grass is one of the easiest plants to grow, so if your patch is struggling you might have started with the wrong species. Select a lawn grass matched to the conditions of your yard and climate.

COMMON LAWN WEEDS

EASY LAWN CARE Left: A dandelion fork makes light work of levering out stubborn dandelion roots. Right: Make tidying discarded weeds easier by spreading a plastic sheet near where you're working to collect them. When you're finished weeding, pull the sheet together at the corners for the trip to the compost pile.

the soil. Insert the blade deeply, right beside the crown of the weed, then simultaneously grasp the weed with your free hand and use the other to lever the roots out of the soil (see page 158).

- *Three-pronged weeder* Use the curved prongs of this fork to lift the shallow or fibrous roots of chickweed, buttercups, ground ivy, and other spreaders. Once you have the parent plant in hand, carefully continue pulling by hand any tentacles of roots that spread outward; usually they will lift out of the lawn without disturbing the grass. If you're digging bindweed, use a fork after heavy rains (when the roots are less brittle) and make extra sure that you leave no broken roots behind.

GETTING OUT THE BIG GUNS

Your own two hands also make great tools for weeding the lawn, if weeds are scattered here and there. For a severely weedy lawn, you can change your perspective to weed acceptance (even a badly infested lawn looks decent with a fresh haircut), or you might turn to an over-the-counter herbicide. If more than one-third of your lawn is really weeds, commercially formulated weed-control help is probably needed, at least for a season or two:

- *Pre-emergent herbicide* Treat the entire lawn according to package directions with a pre-emergent crabgrass preventer, usually in spring at about the time the forsythias bloom. Corn gluten is an organic over-the-counter alternative (see page 62). Do not use either substance on newly seeded lawns.

- *Post-emergent weedkiller* Apply according to instructions after established grass has begun strong new growth. Check the label to make sure the product is appropriate for your grass species, and follow directions exactly.

- *Spot herbicide* These products kill individual weeds with a spray or dab-on substance absorbed through the leaves to kill the entire plant. If spraying, take steps to protect desirable plants (see "applying herbicides," page 161).

There are some grass-seed blends that contain a wide variety of species, which ensures that one or more types in the blend will thrive in your conditions. It's worth bearing in mind that cheaper varieties are usually less pure and may include dormant weed seeds.

- *Water when you must* If rains are scarce, water your grass deeply and infrequently (about 1 inch every 10 days) instead of giving it a short sprinkle every couple of days. Your turf will develop deeper roots, making it able to better withstand stress.

- *Listen to your lawn* If site-specific weeds such as moisture-loving yellow nutsedge make a frequent appearance, your yard may be telling you something: Problems of compacted soil and drainage are likely, or perhaps you are watering too often. Fix the underlying cause, and you won't have to struggle to grow yourself a beautiful lawn. See page 132 for more details on diagnosing deeper problems through the presence of certain weeds.

Tackling lawn weeds

Hand-held weeding tools are your first line of defense against lawn weeds. Even what seems at first like an overwhelming number can be removed in just one afternoon of not-unpleasant labor. Two tools work best on lawn weeds:

- *Dandelion fork* This inexpensive tool has a long, thin shaft ending in a narrow, forked blade. It's sturdily made, so you can use it like a crowbar to pry deep taproots from

Weeding flower beds and vegetable plots

FLOWER BEDS AND BORDERS

The loose, rich, well-watered soil of a flower bed and the open, sunny space in between rows or plots of vegetables are highly tempting to many weeds, as all gardeners know. Factor in the fertile, well-worked and oft-watered soil, and it's no wonder that these areas of the garden usually take up most of our weeding time.

Learn to recognize the weeds that prefer these conditions; for example, deadly nightshade and a few others look enough like ornamentals in their early stages that it's easy to be fooled. Preventing weeds amid your flowers and vegetables, dealing with them while young using simple steps, and efficiently disposing of them are the best approaches.

FILL YOUR BORDERS Weeds enjoy well-tended soil as much as any other plants, so keeping a border weed-free while it becomes established requires vigilance. Once the border plants are fully grown and overlap each other, weeds will not have space to grow.

Preventive measures

- *Mulch* Your number-one friend in the fight against weeds, mulch prevents thousands of weeds from ever sprouting and smothers young weeds with one scoop of a shovel (for more on mulches, see pages 154-157). Timing the application is a little different in the vegetable patch, though, because many of the seeds and plants need warm soil to flourish. (Cover cold ground with mulch for instance, and your heat-loving cucumbers and corn may never show their faces.) Once the garden season is in full swing, be generous with the mulch and you'll cut weeding chores at least in half.

- *Plant ornamentals closely* Many kinds of weed seeds need sun to sprout, so shaded areas created by overlapping foliage discourage their emergence. Fill your beds with flowers or annual green plants to shade unplanted areas.

- *Keep compost clean* Compost is a superb soil improver, but make sure yours is free of weed seeds that would

contaminate your garden. Trim off flowers and seedheads before depositing weeds in the compost.

- *Watch the birds* Fine natural pest control, birds are also as efficient as Johnny Appleseed when it comes to spreading weed seeds in their droppings. Place your feeders some distance from your flower beds and vegetable patch.
- *Black plastic in the plot* Vegetable gardeners often turn to black plastic to start growing ahead of the season because this economical material collects the sun's warmth to heat up the soil below, allowing earlier planting. It also blocks weeds from emerging, so until you can pile on the mulch, spread out the plastic.
- *Cover crops* Prevent winter weeds from getting a foothold by sowing annual ryegrass, mustard, clover, or other cover crops in bare beds. In spring, turn them under for a nitrogen boost, and be sure to do it before they flower and set seeds.
- *Raised beds* Starting your plants in raised beds filled with purchased, weed-free soil and compost gives them the opportunity to establish themselves without having to compete with any interlopers. To make a frame, use decay-resistant timbers, anchoring the corners with metal supports available from garden centers.

Tackling the weeds

Keeping ahead of flower-garden weeds is much easier if you make weeding a part of every stroll around the yard, instead of saving it up for a long dedicated session. Your best tools

SHRUBS AND TREES The large circle of shade cast by shrubs and trees is usually enough to discourage most weeds from taking up residence. Those that infiltrate can be discouraged by using mulch. Spread a layer about 3 inches thick around the tree or shrub, to a distance of a few inches from the trunk.

COMMON FLOWER-BED WEEDS

baby trees

The winged samaras of maples, the squirrel-planted acorns, the wind-blown seeds of elms and catalpa, the bird bequests of mulberry seeds—all of these progenitors of tree seedlings can crop up in hospitable flower and vegetable beds in surprising numbers. The roots of seedlings go deep, and they hang on with a grip that's hard to believe. Most gardeners reach for a tree seedling and give it a yank as they would a more tender weed, only to end up with a handful of stripped-off leaves and a suddenly sore hand. To uproot a young tree (anything taller than about 6 inches requires shovel work), wrap the tough but flexible stem around your fingers or hand and pull upward with a twisting motion and lots of muscle power. A dandelion fork also works well, or you can try a large pair of pliers. Pliers solve the grip problem, but you still have to put plenty of muscle behind your pull.

are your hands, which are more adept than any tool at wiggling in around plant crowns to lift out a weed. Manual weeding is also a must for vegetable gardens, because you'll be eating the plants you're growing and manufactured weed controls may leave an undesirable residue in the soil or on the plants. Hand tools are an excellent aid to hand power, giving you extra leverage. Look for:

- *Dandelion fork* Use the straight, sturdy shaft and forked cutting edge to pry out dandelions, dock, and other tap-rooted weeds (see page 165).
- *Trowel* Invest a few extra dollars in a cast-aluminum trowel made from a single piece of metal, to prevent the tool from bending at the blade when you use it to pry out stubborn weeds, as you no doubt will. In the friable soil of a flower bed, lifting out chickweed and other fibrous-rooted weeds takes just a few seconds.
- *Claw weeder* Skinny, bent prongs dig down through spreading weeds to grab and lift the roots with a quick twist of your wrist. This tool is also tailor-made for freeing the shallow, spreading roots of ground ivy and other creeping weeds from the soil.
- *Poacher's spade* Also known as a transplanting spade, this tool has a blade about half the width of a typical shovel, which makes it perfect for digging out stubborn weeds between flowers or vegetables without causing undue root disturbance to the desirable plants.
- *Hoe* The long handle makes a hoe comfortable to use when covering a lot of ground. Choose the style that suits your swing and your plantings. A wide blade slices off more weeds with one blow, but is harder to fit between closely planted crops.
- *Rotary tiller* In a large vegetable garden with space between the rows, a weekly to biweekly run-through with a cultivating tiller will turn under any weeds that sprout.

Chemical solutions are a bad idea in areas devoted to edibles. The side effects of ingesting even small amounts of weedkillers can be unpleasant. (For details on the effects of different herbicides, see the table on page 162.) They are also very risky to use in the close quarters of flower beds where a wide variety of plants are being grown. Products containing trifluralin are the best bet, but check the label carefully to make sure all the flowers in your collection can tolerate its use and be sure to follow the guidelines on safe application.

HOW DOES YOUR GARDEN GROW? By far the best way to keep weeds at bay in your vegetable or herb garden is to pull weeds as they start to emerge, on a daily basis. If you wait to do the weeding in one long session, the weeds will be more established. Consider investing in a hand tool (see choices at left) to make working between tight rows easier.

COMMON VEGETABLE-GARDEN WEEDS

BINDWEED *page 44*   BLACK MEDIC *page 78*   BURDOCK *page 28*

CHICKWEED *page 112*   COCKLEBUR *page 128*

CRABGRASS *page 53*   DANDELION *page 116*   DEAD NETTLE *page 73*

DOCK *page 102*   FLEABANE *page 61*   FOXTAIL GRASS *page 106*

GOOSEGRASS *page 66*   JOHNSONGRASS *page 111*

KNAPWEED *page 39*   LAMB'S QUARTERS *page 40*   MALLOW *page 76*

PIGWEED *page 24*   PLANTAIN *page 84*   POKEWEED *page 83*

PURSLANE *page 90*   QUACKGRASS *page 56*

QUEEN ANNE'S LACE *page 52*   RAGWEED *page 26*

SHEPHERD'S PURSE *page 36*   SMARTWEED *page 89*   TEASEL *page 54*

THISTLE *page 42*   WILD LETTUCE *page 72*

WILD MUSTARD *page 34*   YELLOW WOOD SORREL *page 82*

Weeds in paved areas, gravel, and rock gardens

PAVED AREAS

Weeding bricks, flagstones, or other pavers is a task that makes even the most enthusiastic organic gardeners wish for a magic solution. If your paved area hasn't been installed yet, do yourself a favor and include a weed barrier, such as landscaping fabric or heavyweight perforated black plastic beneath the pavers. Even so, weeds have a knack for finding a roothold in the smallest crumbs of soil between bricks or stones. Over-the-counter herbicide products may be the least labor-intensive solution, but there are other options that can make weeding the cracks a less frustrating job.

Preventive measures

- *Sweep paving* Vigorously sweep between the cracks of unmortared paving with a stiff-bristled broom at least once a week to dislodge any weeds that may be beginning to sprout.
- *Plant the cracks* Grow niche-loving plants like creeping thyme or chamomile among your paving stones. They grow fast and thick, preventing weeds from colonizing the space.
- *Herbicides* As long as you protect nearby garden plants from exposure (see pages 160–163), pre-emergent herbicides eliminate weeds without disturbing cracks in masonry, which invites more weeds to sprout.
- *Gravel weed barrier* Cover the ground where you intend to lay your gravel with a weed barrier such as landscape fabric or perforated black plastic before you go ahead and spread. Use edgers sunk into the soil to keep creeping

lawngrasses or lawn weeds from sneaking into a gravel driveway.
- *Hoe or rake* Stir the gravel, which dislodges young seedlings before they develop extensive roots.
- *Keep seeds away from gravel* Mow nearby dandelions and other lawn weeds before they set seed to prevent the seeds from settling in gravel areas.

Tackling the weeds

Pavers, gravel, and rock gardens all require different tactics to send weeds on their way. Mount your attack when weeds are young. If you procrastinate, their root systems grow

CARING FOR YOUR ROCK GARDEN Pulling weeds from between ornamental rocks is an arduous task. When planning a rock garden, aim to fill as many areas as possible with desirable plants to reduce the amount of space left available for weeds.

COMMON WEEDS IN PAVED AREAS

BERMUDAGRASS *page 48* BLACK MEDIC *page 78*

CHICKWEED *page 112* CLOVER *page 118* CRABGRASS *page 53*

DANDELION *page 116* ENGLISH DAISY *page 30* KNAPWEED *page 39*

KNOTWEED, SMARTWEED *page 88* MOSS *page 65* PURSLANE *page 90*

SHEPHERD'S PURSE *page 36* SPURGE *page 62* WILD MUSTARD *page 34*

YELLOW WOOD SORREL *page 82*

COMMON GRAVEL WEEDS

BURDOCK *page 28*   DOCK *page 102*   JIMSONWEED *page 51*

KNAPWEED *page 39*   MULLEIN *page 124*

MULTIFLORA ROSE *page 99*   RAGWEED *page 26*   TEASEL *page 54*

THISTLE *page 42*   WILD LETTUCE *page 72*   WILD MUSTARD *page 34*

bigger and stronger, spreading under the pavers or rocks and perhaps causing damage to pavers when you pry out the weeds. Young children often enjoy this task when they can work side by side with a parent, and their small fingers are adept. Teach them to grasp the weed at its base and pull slowly and steadily to free the root. Hold down the brick, rock, or paver with your hand while you extract the weed.

Mullein, knapweed, and other roadside weed commoners also appreciate the well-drained soil that a gravel driveway or rock-garden slope provide. Beat them at their game by taking preventive measures, and evict them by using the solutions suggested, choosing your method according to the severity of the particular infestation:

- *Knife* A dull butter knife slides quickly into cracks, where you can turn it sideways to lever out the weeds. Choose a knife whose blade and handle are all one piece, for superior strength. You can also buy knife-type hand tools with serrated edges from specialty catalogs or garden

shops; this tool allows you to cover a larger amount of ground in less time.

- *Hand weeding* Hand pulling is the method of choice for rock gardens, because the ornamental plants are too precious to risk accidental herbicide overspray. Using metal tools in stony areas is vexing, but you may be able to wiggle a skinny dandelion fork in among the rocks.
- *Raking gravel* The Japanese rake their gardens for the beauty of the patterned lines, but those metal tines can also efficiently tear up seedling weeds as you rake the gravel. Try this technique if you suddenly are host to a crop of seedling weeds.
- *Spot weedkillers* Kill weeds in gravel and paved areas on contact with spray-on, post-emergent weedkillers that are taken in through the leaves. You'll still have to remove the weed remains after they die over the course of a week or so, but it's less effort than hand pulling live weeds. Use with care, and with extreme caution near desirable plants (see page 160).

WEEDING PAVING AND GRAVEL
Left: Use a slim metal tool such as an old butter knife or a screwdriver to prize weeds from between paving slabs. This can help you to get closer to the roots than hand pulling alone. Right: Brush gravel aside to get a good grip on the base of a root stem before easing it out of the ground. After a weeding session, rake the gravel over the area to ensure good ground cover and to prevent further weeds from taking root.

Weeds in the water garden

Water is home to some truly nefarious weeds, which in the wild have managed to choke waterways so thickly that boat traffic is inhibited. Just imagine what they can do to a garden pool! Other weeds enjoy the moist soil around garden pools, birdbaths, and the outdoor faucet. Get rid of them by hand-weeding those in the soil, and raking out those in the water.

Preventive Measures

Prevention is the best cure for water-loving weeds. Here's what you can do to keep them at bay:

- *Educate yourself about this problem* Contact your USDA extension office for a list of the local aquatic noxious weeds; do not plant any species on the list. Ask garden center staff about potential problems of any plants you're considering for water gardens. When in doubt about a plant's habits, keep it isolated in a plastic gallon pot with slits cut in the side (for access to water) so that it can't colonize your pool.
- *Monitor growth* Water plants sold as ornamentals may be extremely fast spreaders. Keep an eye on your aquatics and don't hesitate to rake out extras to return the population to a reasonable size.
- *Keep garden plants in the pool* Avoid unwittingly introducing a menace to the wild by keeping exotic water plants isolated in self-contained water features. If plants in your water garden can spill over into natural waterways—during spring rains, for instance—restrict your choices to native plants that won't disturb the natural balance of plants in the environment.
- *Plant thickly* Grow a dense planting of appropriate plants around your water garden to crowd out invading weeds.

COMMON WATER-GARDEN WEEDS

DUCKWEED *page 74* YELLOW NUTSEDGE *page 50*

PONDWEED *page 92*

A HAVEN FOR WEEDS A water garden is a wonderful opportunity for all plants to flourish. Many water plants are fast spreaders, so you need to check their growth to ensure that they do not completely cover the water surface.

Tackling the weeds

Use hand tools or hoe to remove offending weeds from wet soils. For aquatic plants, check the catalogs of specialty nurseries or a well-stocked garden center for tools tailored to water-garden needs, or work with basic garden tools already in your shed.

- *Hand weeders* The angled head of hand-held hoes and claw-type diggers is effective for lifting unwanted aquatic weeds from small pools.
- *Short-tined rake* Use a sturdy metal short-tined rake to scoop out weeds from the water.
- *Pool skimmer or minnow net* Catch a bounty of tiny green duckweed plants by skimming the surface with a net. You can also cover a leaf rake with cheesecloth to remove duckweed or algae.

Index

Page numbers in **bold** indicate a main entry which will also include an illustration. Page numbers in *italic* indicate additional illustrations.

Author's Acknowledgments

Writing a book is never a solitary undertaking. The words on these pages are shaped by life and learning, and by all the twists and turns along the way.

As always, my first thank you goes to my mother, Mary Roth, who passed along the love of nature she inherited from her Czech-born father and others who came before.

My husband, Rick Mark, gets the credit for bringing this weed lover out of the closet: When I complained about the weed patch that sprang up in our yard after some construction work, he was astute enough to notice that, for all my griping, I never yanked out a single weed. After listening to me talk about the insects I found among the weeds, and the details I was discovering about the plants themselves, he took to asking, "What's new in the weed observation laboratory today?" That little stamp of science was enough to validate my interest in these fascinating plants, no matter how "unworthy" of a garden they may be.

I'm grateful to the late Bob Brooks of Golden Raintree Books in New Harmony, Indiana, who always had an interesting volume, or two, or ten, to hand over when I came in the door. My beloved collection of old herbals and plant lore expanded greatly, thanks to his finds. Between those hundred-year-old covers, I met many a kindred spirit, and I thank them for passing on their knowledge, too—and their colorful words, some of which enliven these pages.

Thanks to editors Kelly Thompson, Charlotte Beech, and Rachel Aris, who made my enthusiastic ramblings fit these pages, paring and tweaking words with a generous dose of good humor. Experts in pesticides and health concerns looked over my shoulder, too, offering advice to an author who's never used a bottle of pesticide in her life, so my thanks go to Jacintha Cauffield, pharmD., B.C.P.S and Ronald D. Gardner of Cornell University.

A great big thank you to my neighbors present and past, who tolerated my unusual plant choices with good grace and have even been inspired to grow a few weeds of their own.

And finally, to all the weeds I've known and loved, or have muttered imprecations toward, or have yet to discover: Thanks for your determination, your will to survive, and your ability to adapt. You've been an inspiration.

Carroll & Brown Publishers would like to thank:
Production Karol Davies & Nigel Reed
Computer Support Paul Stradling
Freelance Editor Joanna Chisholm
Editorial Assistant Tom Broder
Picture Researcher Sandra Schneider
Illustrator Tony Graham (pages 31, 59, 103, 117, 121 & 123)
Indexer Michele Clarke

Picture credits

Please note that we use two abbreviations in the following text: OSF for Oxford Scientific Films and GPL for Garden Picture Library.

Page 1, 4/5, 6/7 David Murray, **8** Bob Gibbins/OSF, **11** (left & center right) David Murray, (center left) Jules Selmes, **13, 18/19** David Murray, **20** Richard Kolar/Earth Scenes/OSF, **21 & 22/3** Deni Bown/OSF, **24/5** Holt Studios/Nigel Cattlin, **26** Holt Studios/Bob Gibbons, **27** David Boag/OSF, **28** Juliette Wade/GPL, **29** David Fox/OSF, **30** David Murray, **32/3** David Fox/OSF, **33** Bob Gibbons/OSF, **34/5** David Murray, **35** Mike Slater/OSF, **36/7** Deni Bown/OSF, **37** Geoff Kidd/OSF, **38** David Murray, **39** Raymond Blythe/OSF, **40/1** John Miller/GPL, **42/3** David Murray, **43** Jules Selmes, **44/5** G. A. Maclean/OSF, **45** David Murray, **46/7** Terry Heathcote/OSF, **48/9, 49, & 50** Holt Studios/Nigel Cattlin, **51** McOnegal Botanical, **53** Scott Camazine/OSF, **54/5** Brigitte Thomas/GPL, **56/7** McOnegal Botanical, **58** David Murray, **59** G. A. Maclean/OSF, **60 & 61** David Murray, **62** Barrie E. Watts/OSF, **63** Betty Hill Sutherland/OSF, **64, 65, 66, 67 & 68/9** David Murray, **69** Irvine Cushing/OSF, **70/1** Mayer/Le Scanff/GPL, **72** Philippe Bonduel/GPL, **73** McOnegal Botanical, **74 & 75** David Murray, **76/7** Bob Gibbins/OSF, **78/9** G.A. Mclean/OSF, **79** Geoff Kidd/OSF, **80, 81 & 82** David Murray, **83** Deni Bown/OSF, **84/5, & 85** David Murray, **86/7** G. I. Bernard/OSF, **88/9 & 90/1** Deni Bown/OSF, **92/3** Niall Benvie/OSF, **94/5** Stan Osolinski/OSF, **95** McOnegal Botanical, **96** Geoff Kidd/OSF, **97 & 98** David Murray, **99** Deni Bown/OSF, **100/1** David Murray, **101** Michael Howes/GPL, **102/3** David Murray, **104/5** Sunniva Harte/GPL, **105** Philippe Bonduel/GPL, **106/7** Jack Dermid/OSF, **107** Mark Bolton/GPL, **110** Steffen Hauser/OSF, **111** Holt Studios/Nigel Cattlin, **112/3** Bob Gibbins/OSF, **114/5** Bob Challinor/GPL, **116, 118 & 119** David Murray, **120/1** M. Wendler/OSF, **122/3** David Murray, **124/5** McOnegal Botanical, **125** Deni Bown/OSF, **126/7** David Murray, **127** Niall Benvie/OSF, **128/9** Bob Gibbins/OSF, **130/131** David Murray, **132** Doug Allan/OSF, **133** Jojo Maman Bebe **135** (bottom), **139, 150/151, 154 & 159** (top left & center) David Murray, **164** John Glover/GPL, **165, 166 & 167** David Murray, **168** Jerry Harpur, **169** David Murray

Jacket Photography
Front (top and center left, top right), **back & front flap** David Murray